REMEMBERING AND UNDERSTANDING YOUR DREAMS

REMEMBERING AND UNDERSTANDING YOUR DREAMS

Craig Hamilton-Parker

Illustrated by Steinar Lund and Lynne Milton

STERLING PUBLISHING CO. INC., NEW YORK

1 3 5 7 9 10 8 6 4 2

CHRIS SWIRNOFF DESIGN

Published by Sterling Publishing Company, Inc.
387 Park Avenue South, New York, N.Y. 10016
©2000 by Craig Hamilton-Parker
Distributed in Canada by Sterling Publishing
℅ Canadian Manda Group, One Atlantic Avenue, Suite 105
Toronto, Ontario, Canada M6K 3E7
Distributed in Great Britain and Europe by Cassell PLC
Wellington House, 125 Strand, London WC2R 0BB, England
Distributed in Australia by Capricorn Link (Australia) Pty Ltd.
P.O. Box 6651, Baulkham Hills, Business Centre, NSW 2153, Australia
Printed in China
All rights reserved

Sterling ISBN 0-8069-8751-0

Contents

The dream is the small hidden

door in the deepest and most intimate sanctum

of the soul, which opens into the primeval cosmic light...

in dreams we pass into the deeper and more universal truth

and more eternal man, who still stands in the dusk of

original night in which he himself was still the

whole and the whole was in him in bright

undifferentiated pure nature, free

from the shackles of the ego.

CARL JUNG

Part I
REMEMBERING

If you do not remember while you are writing,

it may seem confused to others but actually it is clear

and eventually that clarity will be clear.

GERTRUDE STEIN

Dream Workshop 1

WHAT ARE DREAMS?

To sleep; perchance to dream; aye, there's the rub.

WILLIAM SHAKESPEARE IN *HAMLET*

DREAMS were once considered visions of the highest order. Ancient man was more in touch with his inner self and the workings of the soul than we are today. He went to sleep firmly believing that when he awoke dreams would provide him messages from the gods. For him, dreams may have been easy to recall as they were considered an essential part of life and were highly valued.

In sleep we have the power, in a perfectly normal and natural way, to get valuable instruction and insight. In sleep we can connect with our soul life and discover that part of ourselves that relates to the infinite spirit. The majority of people in the modern world are unaware of this and do not have access to these tools.

Dreams also put us in touch with the dark side of ourselves, the unconscious, unrecognized aspects of our personality. By using dreams to discover this shadowy side, we can become more integrated, self-aware and well-rounded individuals. A great many people are completely unaware of their own shortcomings and faults and will rarely criticize themselves. Instead of looking within to root out the weeds of ignorance they project their own faults onto others or blame circumstances. In particular, they attribute to other people all the evil and inferior qualities that they do not like to recognize in themselves. They criticize and attack these *bêtes noires*, making them the scapegoats, for their own inferior qualities. Everything that is unconscious in themselves is projected onto their neighbors, and they treat them accordingly.

PRIMITIVE AND TRIBAL DREAMERS

Early societies made a similar premise about the environment and people around them. Dreams were considered reality, and people made very little separation between what happened in the world and the psychological processes within. In the same way that many people today project their unconscious hopes and fears onto other people, so early man projected his inner processes onto the world. In short, no distinction was made between the world of dreams and real life.

Many of these beliefs continue in tribal societies today. For example, the Kai tribe of New Guinea and the West African Ashantis believe that if a man dreams of committing adultery, he must be tried and punished. The subject of the dream is also punished. At the trial, the witness is asked to recall his dream in detail. Accepting the reality of the dream, the accused will acknowledge the charge. In such societies, the events that happen in dreams have the same reality and are treated with the same gravity as real-life crimes.

NATIVE AMERICAN DREAMERS

Native American cultures held similar beliefs about the reality of dreams. For example, a Cherokee bitten by a snake in a dream would seek a healer's treatment for snakebite on awakening. Dreams shaped every aspect of traditional Native American life. A dream was the soul's journey to another world, a way to receive spiritual instruction and guidance. Sometimes these visions contained personal content and at other times they pertained to the whole tribe.

Many Native American rituals, dances, songs, and paintings were received in dreams. Medicine men and healers gained their power and inspiration from dreams. Dreams indicated the causes of illness and the individual's power to cure himself. They were also considered the way to maintain good fortune in most aspects of life. A great deal of attention was paid to dreams. Among some Native Americans, the mother customarily asked children in the morning if they had dreamed; dreams were encouraged and acted on.

The dream rituals of the Native Americans and tribal societies encouraged the subconscious to make them remember a dream. (Some modern psychologists call this "pre-sleep planning.") Dances, songs, sand paintings, and rituals were held to encourage dreams of great power that could be used to guide the whole tribe. Sometimes this dream-incubation method involved sleeping in a place of special spiritual significance. The Plains tribes, such as the Blackfoot, Cheyenne, and Crow, believed that the most powerful sacred site was the top of a prominent mountain.

When the Native Americans were expelled from their traditional lands a spiritual crisis occurred in their society. Their visionary quests could not be held in the limited confines of the reservation. For them the land was not just for growing crops; the land had sacred spaces that nurtured the living soul of the tribe.

ABORIGINAL DREAMTIME

Similarly the Aborigines of Australia lived out their dreams in the landscape around them. As with many other tribal societies, dreams were not something separate from waking life. The Aborigines based a large part of their rich culture around a state of consciousness called "Dreamtime." In this strange state of awareness they would wander the outback and be aware of spiritual states. There are stories and songs about these journeys. They have to do with the journeys of the ancestors and the "creation sites," places where different clans and animals were created. Others are about the precise route taken by an ancestor figure. During Dreamtime the past joins the present and future to become one.

According to tradition, Dreamtime originated thousands of years ago when the Aborigines first came to the shores of Australia from Asia. They gradually split into 500 territorially anchored groups and wandered the wilderness in a continual search for waterholes. Today when Aborigines enter this state of consciousness

ABORIGINAL DREAMTIME

they are connecting again to the knowledge and influence of their ancestors.

Aborigines enter this state through lucid dreams or by encouraging a sleeplike state while still awake. They appear detached from everyday existence. Once this hard-to-describe level of consciousness is attained they begin a journey that is both physical and spiritual at the same time. The traveler in Dreamtime goes beyond the world of what is generally accepted as reality and enters a new dimension of consciousness. He or she is able to communicate with the spirits of the ancestors and other spirits including those of nature. Dreamtime signifies continuity of life unlimited by space and time. Only the old men and women have full knowledge of this and are given authority in rituals and matters of social behavior.

Certain "dream elements" in the strange landscape of the Australian outback are important. Waterholes, markings on the landscape, hills, mountains, and the famous Ayres Rock are focal points where these Dreamtime forces are most powerful. The Aborigine will identify with these places of his or her ancestors from the time of creation and merge into this strange surreal world of awareness.

The Native American and Aboriginal dream traditions could be the echoes of far older traditions that stretch back to prehistoric times. Could it be that the megalithic sites such as Stonehenge, Avebury, and Carnac were also places where the worlds of dream and reality met? It is certainly likely that they were used for dream incubation.

My own feeling is that these sacred sites are where adepts of the magical arts would leave their bodies during sleep and travel to stars and other planes of existence. According to Celtic mythology the standing stones at Carnac were the place where the heroes rested on their journey to the Isles of the Blest. Could this perhaps be a symbol of the stepping-off point of the astral journey to the spiritual world that we could once access in dreams? Were Carnac, Stonehenge, and Glastonbury used for ritual reenactments of a cosmic drama where, like the Aborigines, our ancestors could enter Dreamtime?

I believe that our prehistoric ancestors' Dreamtime was intricately linked to the geopathic forces found at the sites of standing stones, sacred wells, and springs. Many people today feel the same eerie feeling when they visit these places. The ancient standing stones awaken something from the innermost depths of the unconscious. You can feel them tugging at the psyche, encouraging us into the ancient world of Dreamtime.

THE MYSTERIOUS TRADITIONS OF THE ANCIENT EGYPTIANS

Many dream traditions similar to those of the early shamans can be found in diverse cultures around the world. For example, the ancient Egyptians believed that certain places were conducive to the recalling of dreams. Theirs was one of the first societies to interpret the meaning of dreams and to develop oneiromancy, or dream divination.

An Egyptian text attributed to King Merikare, the pharaoh who ruled from about 2070 B.C., tells us about the ruler's dreams and what they might foretell. He believed that dreams symbolized their exact opposite. For example, a disastrous dream foretold happiness, and happiness foretold disaster.

This tradition continued for centuries; one of the oldest records of dreams and their interpretations is a papyrus of 1250 B.C., which records some 200 dreams and their meanings. The falcon-headed god Horus sup–posedly penned it.

The Egyptians believed that dreams contained messages from both good and evil spirits. To recall them and stimulate them, the Egyptians used many techniques including ingesting herbal potions, reciting spells, and sleeping in the temple. On awakening, the dreamer would submit his or her dreams to the temple priest for interpretation.

In his book *A Search in Secret Egypt*, mystical writer Dr. Paul Brunton explains how he discovered secret teachings that revealed that the Great Pyramid of Gizeh was once used as a place to dream. In the days before mass tourism he obtained permission from the Department of Antiquities to sleep in the king's chamber.

Brunton had spent many years learning the art of meditation and now slowly sank into a heightened state of awareness between sleep and waking. At first "monstrous elemental creations, evil horrors of the underworld, forms of grotesque, insane, uncouth and fiendish aspect gathered around me with unimaginable repulsion," but these gave way to the figure of a priestly guide who revealed to him the secrets of the pyramid.

Brunton slipped into a "semi-somnolent condition" and was taken out of his body by the figure and into other worlds. The priest told him:

"Know, my son, that in this ancient fane lies the lost record of the early races of man and the Covenant which they made with their Creator through the first if His great prophets. Know, too, that chosen men were brought here of old to be shown this Covenant that they might return to their fellows and keep the great secret alive. Take back with thee the warning that when men forsake their Creator and look on their fellows with hate, as with the princes of Atlantis in whose time this Pyramid was built, they were destroyed by the weight of their own iniquity, even as the people of Atlantis were destroyed."

(Students of American psychic Edgar Cayce, who was often called the "sleeping prophet," will note that Brunton's waking dreams revealed similar information about the link between the Great Pyramid of Gizeh and Atlantis. Indeed Brunton, like Cayce, claims that his dreams reveal the existence of secret chambers containing the lost knowledge from prehistoric civilizations.)

Brunton, like the Egyptians before him, was increasing the likelihood of recalling a dream by sleeping in a sacred place. A psychologist will tell you that these dreams were not stimulated or induced, but instead that the psychological reinforcements of environment encouraged the dreamer to interrupt existing dream patterns. For example, if you tell yourself before going to sleep that you will have a dream, you increase the likelihood of immediately remembering a dream upon awakening. Sleeping in a special place that is said to make you dream will increase the subconscious programming to help you remember a dream when you wake up. The environment reinforces this pre-sleep planning. This technique is called "dream incubation" and will be discussed in detail in later chapters.

Many of the ancient dream rites were an early form of dream incubation. A favorite of the Egyptian priests was to draw a portrait of the god Besa in ink on the left hand. This was then wrapped in a black cloth. The ritual involved silently writing a petition to the god by the light of the setting sun. The ink was made from a magic potion that included the blood of white doves, frankincense, myrrh, cinnabar, rainwater, mulberry juice, and the juice of wormwood. This technique would ensure that the sleeper would remember the dream and that the dream would include a prophecy from the god.

DREAMS OF THE GREEKS AND ROMANS

The ancient Greek civilization was greatly influenced by the Egyptians. The Greeks built more than three hundred temples and shrines that were used for dream incubation. They believed that if you slept in these temples the gods would answer questions or foretell the future with a dream. Dreams were the messages from the gods.

The sleeper would be visited by Hypnos, the god of sleep, who would fan him with the wings on his headdress. Hypnos was the brother of Thanatos, the god of death and the son of Nyx, the god of the night. Hypnos lived in the underworld, in the land of the Cimmerians, or in a cave on the island of Lemnos. Here, in this mysterious, dark and misty chamber ran the waters of the river Lethe, which would wipe away the sleeper's memory of his dream.

Special preparations were made prior to sleep to reinforce a dreamer's desire to remember a dream. The practitioner was expected to abstain from sex and from certain foods, such as broad beans, that were said to prevent dream recall. In addition, practitioners underwent ritual washing and slept on top of the skins of sacrificial animals. Once the dreamer had passed into sleep one of the sons of Hypnos would communicate a dream. Chief among these were Morpheus, who brought dreams of men, Icelus, who brought

dreams of animals, and Phantasus, who brought dreams of intimate things. The messages received were believed to come directly from Zeus, the father of the gods, who passed them to Hypnos and so to his sons.

The most famous place for dream incubation was the temple of Aesculapius, the god of medicine, at Epidaurus. If Aesculapius visited the temple the person sleeping therein was healed. Occasionally formulas for herbal cures would be given to the dreamer by the god. At other times Aesculapius would summon sacred healing snakes to lick the wounds of the afflicted person. To encourage the god, the sleeper would put harmless yellow snakes in his bed. Aesculapius' staff branched at the top and was entwined by a single snake similar to the caduceus, the staff of Hermes, with serpents. To this day, this is the symbol of the physician and the emblem of the U.S. Army Medical Corps.

EXPERIMENT

CREATING A SACRED DREAM SPACE

COULD it be that mankind lost the ability to recall dreams easily when a demarcation line was drawn between the logical world of waking life and the illogical world of dreams? Reason evolved and claimed the throne of consciousness and banished from memory the paradoxical world of dreams. Surely the goal of human thinking now is to integrate the intuitive powers of the past while retaining the discriminative powers of rationality. This symbiosis of reason and intuition will make us better people and more able to understand the great unanswered questions of existence. Dreams are one of the main ways to bring these psychological forces together.

We can apply many dream recall tech-

HYPNOS

niques of the ancients to modern life. It is unlikely that most of us would feel comfortable with sacred practices using fasting, isolation, dance, and even self-inflicted pain to encourage a dream. The idea of sleeping in a sacred space may appeal, but the curators of Stonehenge, Indian sacred sites, or Greek temples probably wouldn't enjoy an influx of visitors carrying sleeping bags. And for most of us it's a long way to travel just to remember a dream!

However, having a special place reserved for receiving special dreams is achievable. If you have a spare room or attic room, it would be fun to fill it with memorabilia connected with dreams. This could include pictures of sacred dream sites, surrealist pictures and sculptures, imaginative picture-forming music, dream catchers, incense, soft lighting, and so on. If you have a particular problem you could retire to your sacred space, use some of the techniques in this book, and encourage your dream recall. This would be popular at residential New Age centers and retreats.

Having a special place reserved for dreaming would certainly show your intention to make dreaming part of your life. The same room could also be used for meditation and other spiritual practices. If a whole room is not available it may still be possible to make part of a room your special spiritual area where you could occasionally sleep on the floor in a sleeping bag.

You may have noticed that you tend to dream more when you sleep at unfamiliar places such as a friend's house, hotels, or when you go camping or on vacation. This may be partly because you have slept more lightly, but mainly it is because you have temporarily broken your habitual sleep pattern. The routines are overturned and you are more likely to interrupt a dream by waking at a time that is unusual for you. It may be as little as half an hour but it is enough to catch a dream.

EXPERIMENT

DISRUPTING YOUR ROUTINE TO RECALL DREAMS

A QUICK and simple way to create an unfamiliar environment to encourage dreams is to sleep at the foot of the bed. Assuming that you sleep alone or that your partner doesn't mind looking at your feet all night, it's an amusing way to encourage a dream. The disorientation you experience when you wake up and see the room from an unfamiliar perspective can act as a stimulus to make you immediately remember a dream before it fades. It may not be quite as romantic a notion as sleeping in a temple but it reinforces your decision to have a dream as you go to sleep and prompts you to remember one when you wake up.

This method can be very helpful when you feel the need to have a dream in order to help solve a problem that's troubling you or if you want to try one of the particular dream experiments later in this book. However, once you begin to get into the habit of routinely remembering your dreams such extreme measures may not be necessary. Nonetheless, this experiment is fun to try.

THE FUNCTION OF DREAMS

The causes and meanings of dreams have been the subject of study by intelligent and learned men and women throughout the ages. Cave paintings and records from the ancient Assyrians, Babylonians, Egyptians, Greeks, Romans, and many others did a great deal to propagate dream lore. Their ideas about the meanings of dreams and their methods of interpretation and recall endured for centuries.

The general belief was that dreams were messages and visions given by the gods. Others believed that they were stories or related to the functions of the body. For example, Plato, writing in the fourth century B.C., believed that the functioning of the liver caused dreams. Similarly, Aristotle argued that dreams had sensory causes.

The Sophist philosopher Artemidorus of Dalis cataloged many of these ancient ideas about dreams in the second century A.D. His set of five dream books were called the *Oneirocritica* and proved so popular, they remained in print for 1,600 years. The first English translation had been reprinted 32 times by the year 1800. Some of the meanings given to dreams by Artemidorus now seem a little strange, but sometimes he came close to modern ideas. For example, he stated that many of the images found in dreams have sexual meanings. Some of his ideas sound surprisingly similar to Freud's. Similarly he recognized that some images represent the masculine and feminine side of a person's nature, a concept that suggests the psychologist Carl Jung's theory of the anima and animus. He even proposed that some dreams are symbols. "Sometimes, there are dreams that cannot possibly happen; as when you dream that you fly, have horns, go down into Hell, and the like: These are allegorical."

Aristotle was one of the first philosophers to come close to a scientific theory for why we dream. He spoke of the soul exercising special clairvoyant powers, in accord with its divine nature, when freed from the body's constraint in sleep. However, he later claimed that the function of sleep and dreams was to dissipate the vapors that rose from the stomach after food. For many centuries it was believed that blood rose to the brain and caused congestion there. Sleep enabled the blood to drain back into the rest of the body.

Although Aristotle and others were clearly wrong about their science, they may have been correct in saying that dreams are a physiological process. Some of the latest theories propose that dreams are the body's way of "rebooting" the brain. Dreams dispose of memories that would otherwise clutter the mind with unnecessary remembered experiences. In particular they enable the emotions to become balanced.

These ideas resemble the first scientific theories from early in the 20th century, which proposed that during sleep and dreams, chemicals such as lactic acid, carbon dioxide, and cholesterol that were collected in the brain during the day were dissipated. Sleep and dreams were thought to be a function of the elimination process of the body.

Today many scientists believe that dreams are the brain's way of cleansing itself and allowing the brain's complex chemistry to stabilize. Dreams also allow the emotions to quiet down. According to this theory, without them we would simply overheat. Recent experiments with "dream withdrawal" suggest that a person deprived of dreams begins to show psychotic tendencies while awake. In the light of this fact some scientists have proposed that the function of dreams is to allow for a time of quiet insanity. It is not sleep that is necessary for well-being, but dreams. According to this theory, we do not dreams. According to this theory, we do not remember dreams because there is no need too; dreams are just psychological junk.

SIGMUND FREUD

Since the time of the ancient Greeks and Romans and the publication of *Oneirocritica* a great deal of research has been done into the reasons we dream. Even with this great body of scientific research nobody knows why. Today there are many psychological theories about dreams, but by far the most important pioneers of modern dream research are the Austrian psychiatrist Sigmund Freud (1856–1939) and his Swiss colleague, Carl Gustav Jung (1857–1961).

Freud believed that the purpose of dreams was to preserve sleep. He accepted the views of his predecessors that dream content consisted initially of the various sensory impressions received by the sleeper during sleep, together with the worries of the previous day and experiences of the recent past. (Aristotle in *Parva naturalia* argued that dreams were in fact fragments of recollections of events of the day.) Freud, however, proposed the radical theory that to this content repressed trends or wishes from the unconscious attached themselves. Dreams were the attempts of these wishes to evade censorship and prevent the sleeper from waking. According to Freud the function and purpose of dreams was to gratify repressed wishes and allow us to sleep. These wishes were primarily sexual.

Freud proposed that the mind consisted of three aspects, which he called the *ego*, the *super-ego*, and the *id*. The id is the unconscious side of ourselves, which he believed consisted of instinctive drives. As the instincts always aim toward pleasure, Freud called the id the "pleasure principle." The primary pleasure principle is the urge towards sexual gratification.

Freud also identified a "moral principle," which he called the super-ego. This roughly corresponds to the conscience. He believed this had a social origin. Living in a sexually restricted age it was natural for him to conclude that the super-ego (conscience) would be in continual conflict with the id (instinctive sexual desires). The super-ego lived in a state of constant tension, trying to control the irrational sexual demands of the id. Between these two opposites sat the conscious self, which acted as a referee between the rival claims of these two unconscious forces. Freud called this the "reality principle" and named it the ego. According to Freud, everyone is to some degree neurotic because the ego will never be able to satisfy the demands of both the id and the super-ego.

When a person sleeps, the ego relaxes and can no longer adjudicate between the conflicting forces of the id and super-ego. At this time the super-ego stands guard over the ego and protects it from the overwhelming instinctive urges of the id. Dreams are the symbolic language by which the id tries to communicate with the ego, but its messages are censored by the super-ego. The result is that the messages from the unconscious come to the ego, only in a disguised or misrepresented way.

Freud believed that the main reason people forget dreams is because they are usually too painful to remember. This is a direct result of the censor, the repressive ego defense mechanism that protects the conscious mind from the overwhelming instincts and desires emerging from the unconscious.

CARL JUNG

Carl Jung was the most enigmatic and controversial disciple of Sigmund Freud. He believed Freud to be wrong in many of his key assumptions about the role of sexuality within the psyche. In particular, he introduced to psychoanalysis important questions about religion and the soul that Freud neglected. Freud had become arrogant and inflexible and refused to change his views in the light of compelling evidence.

Jung realized that the unconscious was not a repository for rejected emotions and desires. He saw that the contents of dreams also showed the way to inner wholeness and healing. According to Jung, the human condition is not a continual conflict between the super-ego and the id. Instead of masking hidden desires, dream symbols *express* what is going on in the unconscious. Dream symbols make an *impression* on the dreamer.

Between 1907 and 1913, Jung fell out with Freud and proposed his own theory of the unconscious. Freud had recognized that the unconscious could retain "daily residues," images from daily life that had been forgotten. But Jung noticed that some of his patients were expressing themselves with imagery from ancient traditions. He wondered if the unconscious could hold ancient or "archaic residues." Jung's patients were using inherited imagery harking back to forgotten mythologies buried in the unconscious.

In 1919 Jung called these images *archetypes*. He proposed a *collective unconscious* formed of instincts and archetypes. The archetypes are inborn forms of intuition that are the necessary determinants of all psychic processes. They manifest as images. They are like primordial ideas and are numinous, electrically charged with a sense of the sacred. Many of the images are archetypal symbols originating in the collective unconscious and are powerful symbols that represent the innermost processes within the psyche.

For Jung it was entirely logical to explore the psychology of religion, astrology, alchemy, the I Ching, the Chinese oracle, and other mystical traditions rejected by science. These traditions provided useful methods for investigating his patients' fantasies, dreams, and psychological problems.

Read about many of Jung's ideas in the pages that follow and realize that remembering your dreams can be a spiritually transforming process enabling you to find inner peace and psychological wholeness.

THE ART OF SLEEP

Oh sleep! it is a gentle thing,
Beloved from pole to pole!
To Mary Queen the praise be given!
She sent the gentle sleep from Heaven,
  that slid into my soul.

SAMUEL TAYLOR COLERIDGE

Getting the right amount of sleep is the first step to better dream recall. If you feel rested and relaxed it will be easier to concentrate on your objective of recalling dreams. Furthermore you won't feel cheated of sleep by taking the time during the night to remember and record your dreams. (You will read about this later.) By getting plenty of sleep your dream periods get longer and closer together as the night proceeds. We all dream every night, about one dream period every 90 minutes. The first dream of the night is the shortest, about 10 minutes in length. After eight hours of sleep, dream periods increase from 45 minutes to an hour. If you can establish a good sleep pattern you will gain great psychological and physiological benefit. Perfect sleep will also help you to awaken feeling refreshed and restored and will increase your energy and alertness throughout the day. In addition, it will put you in harmony with yourself, reduce the risk of nightmares, and improve your ability at dream recall.

Archaic man would rise with the dawn and sleep soon after dusk. It is only recently that this pattern has been disrupted. Today insomnia and sleep disorders are common problems. A great many people now suffer from these conditions caused by uncongenial working hours, stress, worry, and the pressures of modern life. Poor sleep causes drowsiness during the day, which leads to accidents in the workplace, lack of job satisfaction, irritable moods, and arguments. In addition, it affects health, and the heart, brain, and digestive system suffer.

CAUSES AND CURES OF INSOMNIA

Coffee, tea, soft drinks, alcohol, nicotine, and cold and diet medications can contribute to sleeping difficulties. Some people forget that coffee is not the only drink containing caffeine. Tea, chocolate, and cola drinks are also high in caffeine. If you take prescription drugs and are experiencing insomnia, you may want to ask your doctor if they are contributing to your inability to get to

HERBAL INFUSIONS TO AID SLEEP

Hops Tonic

Hops are available from home brewing shops and herbs from herbalists. Mix together equal amounts of hops, pulsatilla, cowslip flowers, and vervain. Weigh out approximately 1 oz. of the mixture and put it into a pan. Pour on about a pint of boiling water, until all the herbs are covered. Leave to stand for 20 minutes. Stir frequently. Strain the liquid. Take one small glass three times a day. This infusion reduces stress and aids restful sleep.

Egg Flip

This was my grandma's favorite (minus the whiskey) to help me sleep as a child. Add 1 teaspoon of sugar to a well-beaten egg. Add warm milk and stir. This drink tastes great with a small dash of whiskey or brandy. Alcohol however is not an aid to sleep. It may get you to sleep quickly but as the effect wears off your body provides extra adrenaline to compensate for the alcohol, overriding the sleep hormones. The result is insomnia.

Valerian Root

Crush a valerian root, which you should be able to buy from an herbalist. Infuse in hot water and sip a maximum of one cup each night before bedtime. Evening primrose oil or crushed evening primrose root made into an infusion also aids restful sleep. Grape juice, lemon juice, or peppermint essence in a cup of warm water is also a traditional herbal sleep remedy.

Onion Delight

Garlic and onion help you sleep. Slice an onion and put it into a jug. Add boiling water and leave to infuse. Strain and drink a cupful of the liquid while it is still warm.

DREAM TEA

sleep. Insomnia is also associated with depression, anxiety, and stress. Clearly if these conditions persist you may want to seek medical advice. However, certain herbs can help combat these conditions and with better sleep you will be more able to overcome these problems.

Traditional herbal remedies include sage, chamomile, valerian, catnip, and hops. Try a cup of hot chamomile, catnip, anise, dill, passiflora, catnip, lemon balm, or fennel tea. All contain natural ingredients that will help you sleep. Most health food stores have special blends of herb tea designed to soothe you and help you get to sleep. Lavender aroma in the bedroom is also soothing and is claimed to aid sleep.

The most common cause of a bad night's sleep is mental overstimulation before bedtime. Avoid demanding, stressful activities for a few hours before you retire. This isn't the time to tackle emotional problems, sort out the bills, or start your tax return. Violent films on TV and even the late news can leave you feeling anxious or stressed. Instead, do something relaxing such as listening to gentle music or reading a not-too-racy book. (You can also try the relaxation techniques discussed later in this section.) If you have a cassette or CD player that will switch itself off, play soft music that will lull you to sleep. Music is available that is designed for this purpose. Similarly, sound recordings of waves rhythmically breaking or the steady pattern of a heartbeat can also do the trick.

The last things you do in the evening and the last feelings and thoughts you have before going to bed will influence your sleep pattern throughout the night. Don't spend this time struggling with conundrums or worrying about problems. An hour spent preparing for sleep or gently winding down will work wonders for the night ahead. For some people anger and resentment are like a "wide-awake pill." In particular domestic tiffs before bedtime can ruin a night's sleep. It is important to manage your anger so it doesn't harm others or ruin your own health. My Indian guru, Sathya Sai Baba, says of it: "When you are agitated by anger or hatred or agony drink cold water; lie down quietly; sing a few Bhajan songs. Or walk some long distance alone, fast, so that the pestering thoughts are driven into silence."

Noise can also interfere with your sleep. Although fresh air helps you sleep, you may want to close the bedroom windows or use earplugs if you are easily awakened by sound. A room temperature between 60 and 65 degrees Fahrenheit will give you the best sleeping conditions. Some people listen to white noise throughout the night. White noise is the hiss when the TV or radio isn't tuned in properly. It has been found that gentle white noise from a radio can help people with sleeping problems.

FOOD TO HELP YOU SNOOZE

Your pattern of eating will also affect the way you sleep. The body has natural biological rhythms that allow it to anticipate large meals by providing enzymes before the food arrives to aid digestion. However, many people are out of step with these natural rhythms and the result is heartburn and gastroesophageal reflux, which occurs when acid escapes from the stomach and travels back into the esophagus or

Foods that contain a substance called tryptophan, which is converted to an amino acid called L-tryptophan, promote sleep. Tryptophan is subject to various changes by enzymes, making the L-tryptophan produce a brain chemical called serotonin. Serotonin is essential for sleep and has been called the "sleep hormone." Here are some tips to encourage your body chemistry to aid sleep:

Eat foods high in tryptophan

Eat these foods during the day to aid restful sleep and to encourage the release of sleep hormones.
• *Foods high in tryptophan include:* Milk, eggs, meat, nuts, beans, fish, and cheese. Cheddar, Gruyere, and Swiss cheese are particularly rich in tryptophan.

Eat to get to sleep

If you have trouble getting to sleep when you first go to bed, eat a high-carbohydrate meal two to four hours before bedtime. You can also include a little food high in fat in the meal as well. This will increase the release of serotonin immediately before going to bed.
• *Foods high in carbohydrates include:* Cereals, milk, cakes, candy, sugar, ice cream, dates, figs, chocolate, cakes, fruit pies, potatoes, spaghetti, honey, and jam.

Eat to stay asleep

Some people get to sleep but then awaken during the night. To overcome this problem the serotonin needs to be released later in the night. Eat a snack of high carbohydrates combined with some fats immediately before going to bed. Banana is a good food to include as it digests more slowly and releases the appropriate chemicals later in the night. Similarly, a warm milky drink at bedtime works very well as milk is high in tryptophan.
• *Foods high in carbohydrates:* See above.
• *Foods high in fats:* Cream, high-fat cheese, meat, saturated margarine, butter, peanut butter, nuts, sausages, milk chocolate, and butter.

mouth. Shift workers are particularly prone to this condition as their natural biological rhythms are perpetually disrupted.

The timing of your meals is important. If you eat too soon before going to bed your metabolic rate and body temperature will increase when they should be decreasing. This makes it harder to get to sleep. It is wise not to eat a large meal within two hours of bedtime. The best routine is to have a large meal during the day and a small meal or snack in the evening. Early afternoon is a good time for a nap; the body temperature is high enough to allow the metabolic rate to slow down and drowsiness to take over. This is also the reason why we often feel sleepy after eating a large lunch.

Experiment with your food intake to determine the optimum size meal to have in the evening. If you fall asleep easily but awaken several hours later, it may be due to low blood sugar. In this instance, try a light bedtime snack of complex carbohydrates such as oatmeal, wholegrain cereal, or a small chicken sandwich. Chicken and complex carbohydrates increase the level of serotonin in the brain. Adequate serotonin levels promote deep, restorative sleep. Also, a glass of warm milk 15 minutes before going to bed will soothe your nervous system. Milk contains calcium, which calms the nerves and helps you relax.

PREPARING TO SLEEP WELL

Getting comfortable is also important if you want a good night's sleep. Some authorities say that it is best to sleep on your back, as this is the best position for relaxing. It allows your internal organs to rest properly. If you prefer to sleep on your side, the right

SIMPLE WAYS TO HELP YOU ZZZZZZZZZ.......

Try these seven simple techniques and soon you'll be in the Land of Nod.

Counting sheep

I'm afraid that this one doesn't work for most people because bouncing sheep are just too interesting. The objective is to slow down an overactive mind, so you need to do a more tedious visualization. Some people succeed by continually repeating a word or a meaningless phrase. For example, you could choose the word "the." As you repeat it over and over again, you gradually bore yourself to sleep. The, the, the, the...zzzzzz. A far more pleasant method is to imagine a beautiful and peaceful place, perhaps with lakes, mountains, and green pastures. You could throw in a few sheep for good measure, but make sure they are asleep.

Remember being sleepy

Think about a time in the past when you were absolutely exhausted. You may want to recall a happy time such as on a holiday or after a festive event. Remember how good it was to sink into bed and drop into one of the best sleeps you've ever had. This is a very simple technique but is very effective.

Don't panic

Don't worry whether you drop off to sleep or not. This will only cause frustration. You can survive on three to five hours and catch up on your missing sleep on the weekend. Many people think they've not slept a wink when in reality they've slept many more hours than they believe.

Face north

In many mystic traditions it is believed sleep is improved if you sleep in the direction of the Earth's magnetic field. Some people believe that negative earth rays can cause a psychological condition called geopathic stress. Similar ideas are found in the Chinese art of Feng Shui. Repositioning the bed can help you identify a more auspicious place to sleep

Wiggle your toes

Another mystic tip. Reflexology maintains that the feet are the place where all of the meridians in the body can be influenced. These are the channels of energy acupuncturists believe connect to all the body organs and regulate health and well-being. If you wiggle your toes while lying in bed this will relax your whole body and aid restful sleep. Gentle wiggling will relax you at night, whereas vigorous wiggling will energize you in the morning.

side is considered best as the left causes your lungs, stomach, and liver to press against the heart. The worst position is to sleep on your stomach as this causes pressure on the internal organs. In particular, the lungs are adversely affected and you can only breathe in a shallow way. This position can also cause a stiff neck and upper back problems.

It has also been shown that exercise in the afternoon may enhance sleep, but exercise in the evening causes restless sleep. People with jobs that require a high degree of mental work and concentration are the most likely to suffer from insomnia and can benefit most from about 15 minutes of exercise during day. Aches, pains, and discomfort can also interfere with sleep. Make sure your bedroom is a comfortable temperature, and put on more blankets rather than leaving the heat on overnight. Also make sure your mattress is comfortable. One of the best ways to combat tension is simply to take a warm bath with Epsom salts before retiring.

LARKS AND OWLS

Different people need different amounts of sleep, depending on their personality and lifestyle. We don't all need the standard eight hours. Research indicates that most people require an average of eight to nine hours of sleep per night. While some people only require six hours of sleep per night, others may require as much as ten hours. Many well-known people such as Napoleon, Churchill, Mozart, and Edison survived on five hours a night. My Indian guru, Sathya Sai Baba, is said never to sleep! Decide how much sleep you need based on your performance during the day. If you feel alert and function well with just a little sleep, you may not need as much sleep as some people.

Nonetheless it is still important to establish a sleep routine.

You cannot train yourself to get by on less sleep. To deprive your body of your genetically required sleep time may result in a sleep debt. If your body requires eight hours of sleep per night and you only sleep five hours, you build a sleep debt of three hours. Every night, as you continue to get less than your normal eight hours, the sleep debt builds. This creates a high "sleep latency quotient," or a tendency to fall asleep. Most people repay their sleep debt on the weekend. Five days are the average time that a sleep debt can be incurred before causing daytime sleepiness or loss of concentration.

A high sleep debt can create periods of inattention or microsleeps, which are unintended sleep onsets. Many fatal errors, accidents, injuries, and deaths are attributed to sleep debt. Notable examples include the space shuttle Challenger disaster, the Exxon Valdez grounding, the Bhopal chemical plant disaster, and the Three Mile Island and Chernobyl nuclear power plant radioactive releases.

If you have an early circadian rhythm you are likely to get up early in the morning and do your best work at this time. Or you may be a night owl and function best during the evening. You should base your routines around your preferred bedtime. A newborn infant may require 16 hours of sleep per day. At age 2, sleep time has dropped to 12 hours. By age 6, the average sleep requirement is 11 hours. And at 18, people sleep an average of 8.5 hours per night. Teenagers tend to have a late circadian rhythm, which means they prefer to go to bed late and get up late. Contrary to popular belief, the need for sleep doesn't decline with age. Older adults still need the same amount of sleep as they did when they were in their 30s and 40s. Sleep doesn't get worse as people age, but the patterns change.

PRANAYAMA BREATHING FOR BETTER SLEEP

Yoga claims that certain breathing exercises bring good health and promote the deep feeling of relaxation necessary for meditation. Correct breathing also aids restful sleep. To a yogi there are two main functions of correct breathing: to bring more oxygen to the blood and brain; and to control the *prana*. (This is the vital life energy or life force that animates matter.) The breathing exercises that follow lead to the control of the mind. Pranayama, the yogic science of breath control, consists of a series of exercises designed to achieve these goals and to keep the body in vibrant health.

When you are angry or scared, your breathing becomes shallow, rapid, and irregular. However, when you are relaxed or deep in thought your breathing becomes slow. Your state of mind reflects the way you breathe, so it follows that by controlling the breath you can learn to control your state of mind. Pranayama thus not only increases your intake of oxygen and *prana* but prepares the mind for meditation or, in this case, restful sleep. It also increases the levels of alpha waves created by the brain, which are produced when we lie in a relaxed, wakeful state just before going to sleep.

If you suffer from insomnia or general anxiety, take up yoga. In particular, study Pranayama in detail. Yoga breathing together with Hatha yoga exercises revitalize the body, steady the emotions, and create greater clarity of mind. Follow its teachings and you will find deep inner peace and will sleep like a baby.

As with any form of exercise, it is important not to use extreme methods to achieve your goal. Yoga is a gentle way to good health. It is particularly important to remember this when doing the Pranayama exercises, or the results will not be beneficial. If at any time you feel discomfort or feel that you want to gasp for air in gulps, stop the exercises and breathe normally. If you experience feelings of extreme heat or cold while doing these exercises, you are pushing yourself too far.

The exercises that follow are simplified versions of traditional yoga techniques. You should find them easy to do and an effective way to calm your mind.

BREATHING EXERCISE 1

SIMPLE RELAXATION USING THE BREATH

THIS is a remarkably simple technique but is very effective. By linking your breath to your relaxation, it is possible to achieve a relaxed body and mind quickly. You can use this method in any tense situation. Try it next time you're in the dentist's chair!

Step 1. Do this exercise sitting down or lying in bed. Relax very deeply and let go of all stress. Feel your body relax completely. As your breathing slows, feel your body become more and more at ease.

Step 2. Now take a slow, deep breath in, and as you do, think to yourself, "I am..."

Step 3. And as you breathe out, think "...relaxed." Let the word "relaxed" feel like a great sigh, and allow your body to sink deeper into perfect relaxation. As you breathe out, let your whole body relax completely.

Step 4. Repeat the process a few times.

Step 4. Repeat the exercise as many times as you like, each time feeling the dark energy being removed and replaced by the soothing warmth of the incoming light. This exercise can be quite mentally stimulating but is effective at removing stress and thereby aiding restful sleep.

❖ **BREATHING EXERCISE 2** ❖

REMOVING SPIRITUAL TOXINS

ANOTHER simple technique to remove stress and promote restful sleep involves the power of the imagination to influence your spiritual state. You can do this exercise sitting in a chair or lying in bed. This simple technique will leave you feeling purified within and help you get rid of negative feelings and influences. It is also a powerful self-healing technique.

Step 1. Let yourself relax very deeply and let go of all stress. Feel your body relax completely. As your breathing slows down, feel your body become more and more at ease.

Step 2. Take a slow deep breath in and as you do, see the air as being made of brilliant white light. Feel it spread from your lungs and fill your whole body. As it does this, you will feel warm and comfortable all over.

Step 3. Now, as you breathe out, see the air you exhale turning into arid black smoke. With it are released all the toxins from your body. Feel also how you let go of all tension, anger, depression, and any other negative feelings you have. Use your breath to remove all this negative energy from your being.

❖ **BREATHING EXERCISE 3** ❖

ALTERNATE NOSTRIL BREATH (ANULOMA VILOMA)

THIS final example is a classic Pranayama exercise that balances the body's energies. It is a little more complicated than the first two and should be done either sitting in the lotus position or in a chair. It is important that the spine, neck, and head be in a straight line to facilitate the movement of the positive living energy called *prana*. This exercise also cleanses the energy channels that run down the spine called the *nadis*. You will be breathing through each nostril separately and thereby balancing the *prana* flow through the body, especially up and down the spine. This exercise also helps to stimulate the spiritual powers and can be used in conjunction with the various esoteric dream techniques that will be discussed later.

In this exercise you inhale through one nostril, retain the breath, and then exhale through the other nostril. The best ratio is 2:8:4, but work at first with whatever you feel most comfortable. Take it gently at whatever pace most suits you. You are not trying to break any records. The objective is to improve your ability to find inner peace by controlling your breath and also controlling your mind.

Step 1. Sit comfortably relaxed, with a straight back, neck, and spine.

Step 2. Tuck the index and middle fingers of your right hand into your palm and raise your hand to your nose. Place the thumb on your right nostril and your ring and little fingers by your left.

Step 3. Breathe in through the left nostril as you close the right with your thumb.

Step 4. Now hold the breath for a few seconds, closing both nostrils with your fingers and thumb.

Step 5. Breath out slowly through your right nostril, keeping the left closed with your ring and little fingers.

Step 6. Now breathe in through the right nostril while continuing to keep the left nostril closed.

Step 7. Again hold the breath as you close both nostrils.

Step 8. Now breathe out through the left nostril, this time keeping the right closed with your thumb.

Step 9. You have now completed one round of Anuloma Viloma breathing. Repeat the exercise. At first you will probably be able to do five rounds. Soon you will feel comfortable doing ten. Build up slowly to 20 rounds.

Breathing in a slow, relaxed way will greatly improve your ability to sleep.

SYSTEMATIC WAYS TO RELAX

Yoga breathing exercises are a positive way to help you relax. Similarly the physical yoga exercises can also aid restful sleep and restore a feeling of harmony throughout the body, mind, and spirit. One of the simplest exercises you can do at any time is simply to raise your hands above your head and stretch your whole body like a cat waking up from a long sleep. When you've finished, allow your whole body to relax.

Stretching helps release the tension within you. This alternate tensing and relaxing is necessary because only by knowing what tension feels like can you be sure you've achieved relaxation. By doing this you achieve a stage of mastery over your body's involuntary processes, because you've sent instruction to your muscles to relax. An adept of yoga can gain incredible mastery over the involuntary muscles of the heart, digestive system, nervous system, body temperature, and so on.

When you are completely relaxed you will have a feeling of expansion, lightness, and warmth. As muscular tension disappears it is replaced by a feeling of gentle euphoria that fills the whole body. Relaxation is a gradual process, and you will feel yourself sinking deeper and deeper into this blissful state of being.

Even a few minutes of deep relaxation will reduce worry and fatigue and will promote restful sleep. The exercise that follows is a powerful visualization technique to help you relax. I use it myself at my spiritual workshops to help people prepare for meditation. (Download an audio file of the following exercise from my website at http://www.psychics.co.uk to have me talk you through this process to music.) This exercise is designed to help you become aware of your body and to teach it to relax very deeply. Some people benefit by stretching and relaxing before beginning the exercise. For example, first stretch your toes and feet and feel them relax. Then stretch just your legs and feel them relax. Systematically stretch your muscles from the toes to the face until your whole body has been prepared for even deeper relaxation.

RELAXATION EXERCISE

Lying comfortably, feel the pressures of the day falling away. Relax very deeply and feel yourself able to let go of all stress. Deeply relax, more and more, and be aware of how good you are starting to feel. You are able to leave your worries behind because this is your time to enjoy your right to deep inner peace.

Notice how your body is becoming more and more at ease. You are probably already feeling that your breath is calming down. So it is easy now to take a deep breath in, and as you breathe out, think to yourself, "Relax." Maybe you want to do this a few times.

How would it feel if you relaxed completely?

You might notice those warm, calming sensations in your toes and feet spreading through your body, easing all tension.

Take your attention to your toes. Wiggle them for a while then let them relax. Be aware of how heavy they feel as they gradually relax more and more. Now move your attention to your feet and notice how they have already relaxed with the toes. Feel them become warm and heavy. Feel the tension that was once there fall away. In your feet are nerves connected to your whole body. As your feet relax, feel your whole body follow suit.

Next, move to your legs. Feel the comfort and peace fill them. All tension is gone. They are completely relaxed. Now become aware that your stomach and hips are relaxed. Letting go of all stress, feel yourself moving toward a soothing cloud of enfolding restfulness.

Your whole torso is now relaxed. Your breathing is restful and your whole body has slowed down. Be aware of how comfortable your hands and arms are feeling. Are you aware how much the shoulders have relaxed? Enjoy the restful feeling in the muscles of your face, especially the muscles around your eyes.

Your whole body is relaxed.

Since you are now totally relaxed, your mind is also quieting down. Notice a growing sense of inner composure and deep peace, an all-prevailing sense of serenity and tranquility. Enjoy this glorious state of physical and spiritual peace. When you feel ready, let yourself go into perfect peace, perfect rest, perfect sleep. You are ready to dream.

HOW TO REMEMBER YOUR DREAMS

It has never been my object to record my dreams, just the determination to realize them.

MAN RAY (1890–1976)

SURREALIST ARTIST AND PHOTOGRAPHER

*N*O-NONSENSE people who proudly boast "I never dream" are fooling themselves. Instead, they should be saying, "I never remember my dreams," for we dream every single night. Psychological tests suggest that non-recallers are often more controlled and conformist than those who can easily remember their dreams. Likewise, people who avoid facing anxieties in daily life may show a reluctance to recall their dreams. The truth is, we all dream and it is easy to remember dreams. All we need is an open mind and a few simple techniques.

Recent research indicates that we dream throughout sleep from the moment we drop off right through the night and to the time we wake up. However, the most vivid dreams occur at regular cycles that can be identified by observing the eyes.

American physiologist Nathaniel Kleitman in 1951 noticed that sometimes the eyes of sleeping infants would move rapidly from side to side behind their closed eyelids. He suggested to Eugene Aserinsky, a graduate student, the study of the relationship of eye movement and sleep. Kleitman and Aserinsky soon discovered that if they woke adults during REM sleep, they would invariably say that they were having a dream. In addition, EEG readings confirmed that during REM sleep there was a recognizable change in the activity of the brain.

These periods of "rapid eye movement" (REM) proved to be extremely useful as they revealed when a dream was taking place. By waking the subject during REM sleep, researchers could guarantee that there would be a dream to study.

It is now known that dreams are not confined only to REM periods but continue throughout the night. Most dream research has been based on waking people during REM sleep, but its now claimed that it is possible to recall a dream at any time during the sleep cycle. Carl Jung claimed that we are dreaming all the time—even while awake—and it is only the distractions of waking life that leave us unaware of our waking dreams.

Nonetheless, the best time to recall a

dream is in the intense period of dream activity found during REM sleep. You are more likely to remember having had a dream if you are awakened at this time. It has also been found that dreams taking place during REM activity have more visual content than those occurring at other stages of sleep. It has been suggested that the brain does not distinguish between the visual imagery of dreams and that of waking life. In effect, the eyes may be watching the events of the dream as if they are taking place in reality.

RECALL METHOD

INTERRUPTING EARLY SLEEP CYCLES

SOMETIMES it may appear that a night's sleep is just a period of unconsciousness. One moment you're dropping off to sleep and the next the alarm clock is ringing and you're getting ready for the day's activities. However, during the hours that have passed, you have experienced a number of changes of brain activity, types of sleep and dreaming. Research has revealed that there appear to be four distinct levels or stages of sleep, each one different and characterized by distinctive brain rhythms and alterations in the bodily condition.

Dr. Nathaniel Kleitman and another of his students, William C. Dement, were the first people to study these sleep patterns scientifically. They found that during the first 15 minutes the sleeper descends through four distinct stages of sleep culminating in the deepest, Stage Four. This period of non-REM sleep lasts about one hour. During this time the body is at its most relaxed, with the brain rhythms at their slowest. Following this is a rapid return to Stage One. It is then

that the first REM episode of the night begins. It lasts about 10 minutes.

If you are married or have a partner, if you ask to be awakened at this time it is likely that you would recall a dream. Your partner should look for a telltale change in body posture and rapid eye movements under the lids. This method is impractical in that it might be difficult to get to sleep knowing that you'll be awakened by a bleary-eyed partner. However, if you're really keen to remember a dream, you could ask to be awakened should your partner awaken spontaneously and see that your eyes show REM activity.

Another somewhat extreme technique is to drink a large glass of water before going to bed. Inevitably, you will wake up in the night. With luck you will interrupt a REM period and recall a dream. I've tried this approach myself but unfortunately always end up dreaming about toilets!

Some herbalists suggest that you drink Dream Recall Tea before bed. The herbs are claimed to encourage dreaming and dream recall. Again, a full bladder will probably wake you up during the night and give you a chance to write down essential points from any dreams you've had.

To make Dream Recall Tea, add $1/4$ cup of dried mugwort to 2 tablespoons of dried rosemary. Add the ingredients to 2 cups of boiling water. Steep for at least 10 minutes before straining. Sweeten with honey if desired.

RECALL METHOD

INTERRUPTING LATE SLEEP CYCLES

THE most vivid dreams usually occur just before awakening, and these are the best ones to interrupt, so it isn't necessary to use bladder-challenging methods. Throughout the night, the process of descent and ascent through the stages of sleep is repeated between four and seven times. This gives you many opportunities to remember a dream. As the night progresses, frequency and rapidity of eye movement increases, as does the period spent dreaming. The final dream period just before awakening can last up to about 40 minutes.

If you set your alarm to ring up to 40 minutes early you are likely to interrupt a dream. Using the techniques described in this book, you will be able to remember it in detail. I suggest setting the alarm at different times each morning for a few days. One morning you may try the adventurous 40-minute-early session, and the next morning rise just 15 minutes early. Dream recall should be enjoyable, so don't overdo it, especially during the work week. Try three mornings in a row, perhaps including the weekend, then let your sleep pattern return to normal. Excessive REM deprivation leads to daytime irritability, fatigue, memory loss, and poor concentration. However, once you get into the routine of remembering your dreams the habit will stick and you'll recall a dream most mornings with no ill effect.

REM sleep is an extraordinary state of awareness: brain activity, adrenaline levels, pulse rate, and oxygen consumption are almost the same as when you are wide-awake. However, muscle tone relaxes and it is very difficult to awaken people at this time. During REM sleep the brain is extremely active, to the point that the body has to be mostly paralyzed to prevent it from thrashing around and acting out dreams. This com-

bination of an active brain and an immobile body so mystified the early sleep researchers, they called this state "active sleep" or "paradoxical sleep." It is considered by some psychologists to be a third basic form of human existence. This corresponds to the ancient Hindu tradition that consciousness consists of three separate states: waking, dreamless sleeping, and dreaming. We will consider these ideas in detail later in the book.

RECALL METHOD

STIMULATING THE BACK OF THE BRAIN

HAVE you ever dreamed about being unable to run, attempting in vain to scream, or being stuck in mud or quicksand? This type of dream may be caused by the physiological changes that happen to the body and brain during REM sleep and in particular the areas of the brain that keep the body immobile during sleep. Irrespective of the dream content, during REM sleep the heart rate and breathing often become erratic, the gastric acid in the stomach increases considerably, and there is an increased tendency to cardiac arrest. In addition, limb twitches, middle-ear muscle twitches, and sudden respiratory changes occur. Men tend to have a penile erection. Yet despite all this physiological and psychological activity, the body remains immobile and sleep is preserved.

So what is it that stops people from thrashing around in sleep? Animal studies have identified the locus ceruleus in the pons section of the brain as the probable source of this inhibition. (The pons is in the brain stem at the bottom of the brain, directly above the medulla oblongata; the

RAPID EYE MOVEMENT

locus ceruleus borders on the brain cavity known as the fourth ventricle.) Animal experiments have shown that when this part of the brain is surgically destroyed, animals periodically engage in active, apparently goal-directed behavior during REM sleep. They appear to be acting out the content of their dreams.

Mysticism also considers this area at the bottom and back of the brain to be important for dreaming. Patanjali, the author of the *Yoga Sutras* (4 B.C.), tells us that meditation upon this area of the brain will put us in touch with celestial beings. Similarly, in Tibetan mysticism it is taught that this is the part of the brain responsible for out-of-body travel as it is linked to the throat chakra (center of spiritual energy). And in my own work as a Spiritualist medium, I have noticed that meditating on this area of my brain before a demonstration appears to improve the accuracy of my mediumship.

As far as I am aware, no scientific research has been done into these metaphysical claims, and much of the evidence remains anecdotal. However, you can test these claims for yourself. Workshop 4 will show some mystical techniques that use this part of the brain for out-of-body travel and communication with spiritual guides. Prior to Workshop 4, you may want to practice with this part of the brain to increase dream activity.

EXPERIMENT

THROAT CHAKRA

Objective: To stimulate the back of the brain to increase dream activity.

Step 1. Lying flat on your back, allow yourself to relax deeply as you did in Workshop 1 in the relaxation exercise on page 29.

Step 2. Visualize a brilliant blue light unfolding at the top of the throat chakra. This is located at the top of the throat and is a center of spiritual energy called the *Visuddha* in India. Its element is ether and it traditionally represents communication and self-expression through thought, writing, speech, dance, and art.

Step 3. *Chakra* is a Sanskrit word meaning "wheel." You may now see this center spinning with brilliant blue light. Feel how the light brightens as this spiritual center floods with radiant light. The light expands and unfolds like a blue lotus flower of light. Notice how the energy here increases as you see the glittering light flood this area of your body.

Step 4. As this lotus unfolds, be aware of how the blue light now floods the back of the head. Bathe the back of your head in this beautiful, soothing radiance. Enjoy the way it brings you inner peace and calmness. Bask in the light that radiates from your throat.

Step 5. Retain the light in the back of your head but see the throat center close. It fades to darkness as the lotus closes its petals. Now go to sleep as normal.

Result: You may find that by doing this technique before bedtime you will increase the vividness of your dreams. Nobody yet knows how or why these ancient techniques work, but it is claimed that they do more than plant a suggestion in the subconscious. They unlock your spiritual energies and can make dreaming part of your spiritual work.

This mystical technique may help you increase the likelihood of remembering a dream. Just thinking about dreams before going to sleep can also help you encourage dream recall. Read this book in bed to encourage you to remember a dream in the morning or to awaken just after you've had a dream.

Another important aspect of dream recall is to eliminate the barriers that stop you from remembering. To do this, you need to approach your dream in the right way.

DEVELOPING THE RIGHT ATTITUDE

Sometimes dream memories may elude you because you are unconsciously blocking your ability to recall them. You may have hidden fears about what your dreams reveal about your personality, attitudes, urges, and desires. Part of you doesn't want to know the truth about yourself.

Freud believed that the main reason people forget dreams is because the dreams are too painful to remember. This is a direct result of what he called the *censor*, a repressive ego defense mechanism protecting the conscious mind from the overwhelming instincts and desires emerging from the unconscious. According to Freud, the primary purpose of dreams is to prevent us from waking.

Similar ideas are postulated by psychodynamic dream theory, which says that the reason for lack of dream recall is that dreams contain things we just don't want to remember. This is material the waking self just can't cope with or that would cause too much distress if remembered. This dream material is referred to as "ego toxic."

This agrees with Freud's theory that dreams are mediating desires that are seeking expression and counter forces keeping those thoughts and impulses from disturbing the sleeper. The content is disguised before reaching consciousness, but some gets kept away from the waking ego altogether. Hence the memory loss.

Many clinicians believe that the theory is useful and that the process can be observed over time. For example, new patients recall fewer dreams, but as patients begin to show other signs of less resistance to the material that the dream content is displaying, more of this dream content shows up. The greater the degree of repression, the lower the dream content.

The question posed by Freud remains unanswered. We still do not know whether a dream's function is to preserve sleep or whether we sleep so that we can dream. Freud's views are still a subject of debate, but nonetheless it is clear that most people create barriers between the conscious mind and the world of dreams. Here are a few simple tips to help you change your attitude and make dream recall easier:

1. Enjoy your dreams.

If you look forward to having a dream when you go to bed, you are more likely to recall a dream when you wake up. The more you want to dream, the easier it becomes to remember dreams.

2. Give yourself permission to dream.

Dreams may contain material that you've repressed or pushed out of your awareness. Look forward to the reconciliation of your hidden fears. Soon you will be able to leave these fears behind you and take the first steps toward discovering your true identity.

3. See your dreams as valuable.

Dreams are not a load of old nonsense. They are the key to self-discovery and personal growth. Perhaps you could repeat an affirmation to help hammer this message home. Repeat "Dreams are important to me" a number of times at regular intervals. This will encourage you, on a subliminal level, to automatically recall your dreams. A physical "trigger" along with the verbal suggestion often helps, i.e., pressing your thumb against each finger as you say each word of the suggestion.

4. Feel and accept the emotional content of dreams.

Some people find sexual dreams disturbing or are frightened to uncover the truth about themselves. Accept whatever occurs in a dream and use the material to gain insight into yourself. After all, what is there to be afraid of? Everything in dreams is a part you.

5. Let dreams solve your problems.

The messages from your unconscious deserve to be heard. Consider dreams to be a best friend who will help you identify your faults and capitalize on your strengths. Dreams seek to reveal the truth about you. Armed with this knowledge you can learn to change your behavior and attitude in positive ways. Also, hidden within your dreams may be simple solutions to difficult problems. Once you start drawing upon this inner wisdom, you will discover the benefits of your dream memories.

6. Be creative.

The Japanese filmmaker Akira Kurosawa said, "Man is a genius when he is dreaming." Many great novels, inventions, music, paintings, and scientific breakthroughs have been directly attributed to dream insights.

The more you allow your dreams to be recalled, the more creative material you will have at your disposal.

7. Examine your motives.

Dreams originate from the core of your being. They reveal your true motives and desires. From a spiritual standpoint, motive is everything. If the motive is correct, good karma is generated and happiness is guaranteed. A remembered dream can put you in touch with the hidden motivations and spiritual prompting that can direct your life toward true happiness.

RECALL METHOD

THE BASICS OF DREAM RECALL

IF YOU don't know the right techniques it can be very frustrating trying to recall dreams. Not only do most people never remember most dreams, the ones they remember can easily slip away and evaporate. However, with a little guidance and effort, you will soon remember more dreams than you know what to do with. The techniques will be explained in detail later; first consider the basic steps that will empower you to remember your dreams.

These simple recall methods will be discussed in detail soon:

1. Be prepared.

Before you go to sleep, make sure you have a pen and paper within easy reach by your bed. When you awake, whether in the night or in the morning, jot something down. Even writing "I don't remember anything this morning" will do, but a more positive statement such as "I will remember my dream at the next opportunity" is much

THROAT CHAKRA

better. The important thing is to establish a habit of dream recall and to train yourself to remember your dreams. Your intention to have a dream and make an effort to remember it in itself will help you to recall dreams.

2. *Contemplate your day.*

When you go to bed, relax your body and think about the day's events in reverse order. This is a technique that will teach you how to reflect and can itself be very relaxing. It will also help you remember your dreams. For example, ask yourself questions such as: "How did I get ready for bed?" "What was I doing just before going to bed?" "What did I watch on TV this evening?" "What was it like coming home from work?" "What did I do at work?" The events of the day will start to unfold naturally and you may feel like you are watching a videotape recording. Finally, you will reach the point where you woke up in the morning. Can you go back just that little bit further and remember what you were dreaming?

3. *Program your unconscious.*

As you get close to falling asleep, repeat, "When I wake up, I will remember my dream." The unconscious and the memory are influenced by repetition. You may think you sound stupid, but actually saying the words aloud reinforces this inner command. Some authorities say that a physical "trigger" along with the verbal suggestion often helps. Again, try pressing your thumb against each finger as you say each word of the suggestion.

4. *Don't jump straight out of bed.*

When you wake up in the morning, lie still. Relax your body and let your mind drift. With practice, you can easily hover between waking and dreaming without falling back to sleep. Remind yourself that you want to remember your dream. You may prefer to keep your eyes closed or look at something bland such as the sheets close to your face. Whatever you do, don't start running through lists of what you have to do during the day. If you do, your dream will evaporate immediately.

5. *Write, write,...write.*

Most dreams are forgotten within 10 minutes, so start scribbling as soon as you remember the first snippet of a dream. Write down whatever you remember immediately so you're not trying to remember that material while trying to recall new material. Do it as it comes to you or you will forget what came a few seconds earlier. Don't give yourself a chance to forget. If you prefer, review the parts of your dream in your mind once or twice before recording them on paper. Work whichever way best suits you, but act quickly.

6. *Tell someone.*

It is surprising how many extra details surface if you talk about your dream. Someone you can trust may even be able to help you with the interpretation. In most tribal societies it was a tradition to share dreams with other members of the tribe.

❖ **KEY RECALL METHOD** ❖

THE SIMPLE DREAM DIARY

THE simplest and easiest way to remember your dreams is to write them down. At first, you may be content to write them onto scraps of paper or a notebook. However, if you are serious about learning dream recall, I suggest you make yourself a proper dream diary. This will give you a permanent record that can be used to cross-reference dreams over many years. Furthermore, you can identify recurrent themes and have a record of any dreams that prove to be prophetic. A dream diary is not only useful but can be a very creative and enjoyable exercise.

Start by creating a basic dream diary. Later you'll learn a more comprehensive method and may also want to introduce techniques and layouts of your own. But begin with a very simple and easy-to-use dream diary:

First, buy a large sketchbook. You will need the space later on, when you introduce sections for sketches, mind-maps, future dreams, past-life logs, and so on. Some people prefer a large loose-leaf ring binder, but a properly bound book will last for years. Some specialty art and stationery shops have them. I opted for a large corporate desk diary with one day per page. I ignore the dates.

There are also a few well-designed dream diaries on the market, but they may limit you to the techniques favored by the designers. The truth is that everyone thinks differently. What works for one person may not work for you. Later, as you learn various techniques, you will choose the methods that suit you best so your dream diary will become uniquely your own. There are no hard and fast rules. You must use whatever technique helps you the most.

In the front of my dream diary, I have written a quote by Oscar Wilde: "I never travel without my diary. One should always have something sensational to read on the train." It reminds me that creating a dream diary is fun. The absurdity of the quote also encourages me not to take myself too seriously. When you start working with the unconscious, it is important to be cheerful yet honest with yourself. In this way, you will get to know yourself better and acknowledge those parts of you that until now you have ignored. So your first step may be to find a quote or make something up that expresses the way you feel about your dream. This is not essential but it sets a creative precedent.

Always keep your dream diary beside your bed. Make sure you put it where you can see it, such as on the bedside table. If it's the first thing you see when you wake up, this will help jog your memory that you have had a dream. The first moments of waking consciousness are the critical point at which a dream is remembered or lost.

Step 1. Before Going to Sleep: Write the next morning's date at the top of the page. Doing this the night before will help convince your unconscious to reveal a dream. As well as being an act of faith, it also frees you to get straight on with the process of scribbling down your dream immediately when you wake up. Use the relaxation techniques from the first chapter and get in the mood for a dream. Do this as you drift off to sleep, repeating: "Tonight I will have some wonderfully vivid dreams." You may also like to read about dreams before going to sleep or read dreams you recorded from previous mornings. This may be a good time to work out an in-depth interpretation of the last dream you had from the previous morning.

Step 2. Waking Up: Remind yourself you want to remember your dream. Shutting your eyes may help. Lie still and think about your dream. Take your time coming round; you only need a few minutes and will not be late for work. At first stay in the same position and let the dream unfold. When you have exhausted the recall in that position, move slowly to another position that feels natural. See if your can remember anything else. If so, write it down.

Step 3. *Write a Title:* Give your dream a title right away or leave a space for one so you can put it in later. It should express something succinctly about the content so you can easily refer to it later. A title can also help in cataloging and locating dreams. Also, the title itself may be influenced by your unconscious and may give clues to an interpretation.

Step 4. *Record Names First:* Quickly write down anything you heard in the dream, because auditory information is the first thing to be forgotten. Include any names of streets, people, countries, and so on. In particular make a note of anything anyone said.

Step 5. *Don't Worry about Sequence:* Dreams can sometimes have confusing plots that jump back and forth between times and locations. The important thing is to get as much information on the page as quickly as possible. You are not trying to write a masterpiece or your novel. Write down everything that comes to mind, even the embarrassing bits.

Step 6. *Forget Spelling and Grammar:* Concentrate on the dream. It doesn't matter if you make grammar or spelling mistakes. When something is hard to describe in words, draw a quick sketch.

Step 7. *Write in the Present Tense:* Write the dream as if you were experiencing it as you write. This will help keep it fresh in your mind and keep your attention focused. It also allows you to experience more closely the feelings you were having when you had the dream. Here's a simple example of writing a dream in the present tense: "I am walking toward a big building. I can see that it is old and decayed. There is a smell of dampness in the air. I hear a call: 'Hey, you! What are you doing here?' It is the woman from my dream of last week. I can see that she has a flower in her hand."

Step 8. *Include Everything:* List everything that happens, no matter how trivial. For example, the weather in your dream may represent something about the way you are feeling; colors have special symbolic significance, as do shapes and numbers. Everything you think, see, feel, smell, and hear in your dream is there for a reason and says something about you. Nothing is insignificant.

Step 9. *Dig Deeper:* Once you think you have everything, go back over the first things you can remember about the dream. How did the dream start? You may find a whole sequence of dream events you completely forgot about. Once you remember a small part, it unlocks the door to another dream entirely. Make notes about this dream also. When you can't remember any new material, review whatever you have written. Sometimes that will trigger forgotten parts. Ask yourself questions about it. For example: "Who else was in the dream? What color was it? How many were there? How do I feel about that? How far away was it? Were there any noises or smells?

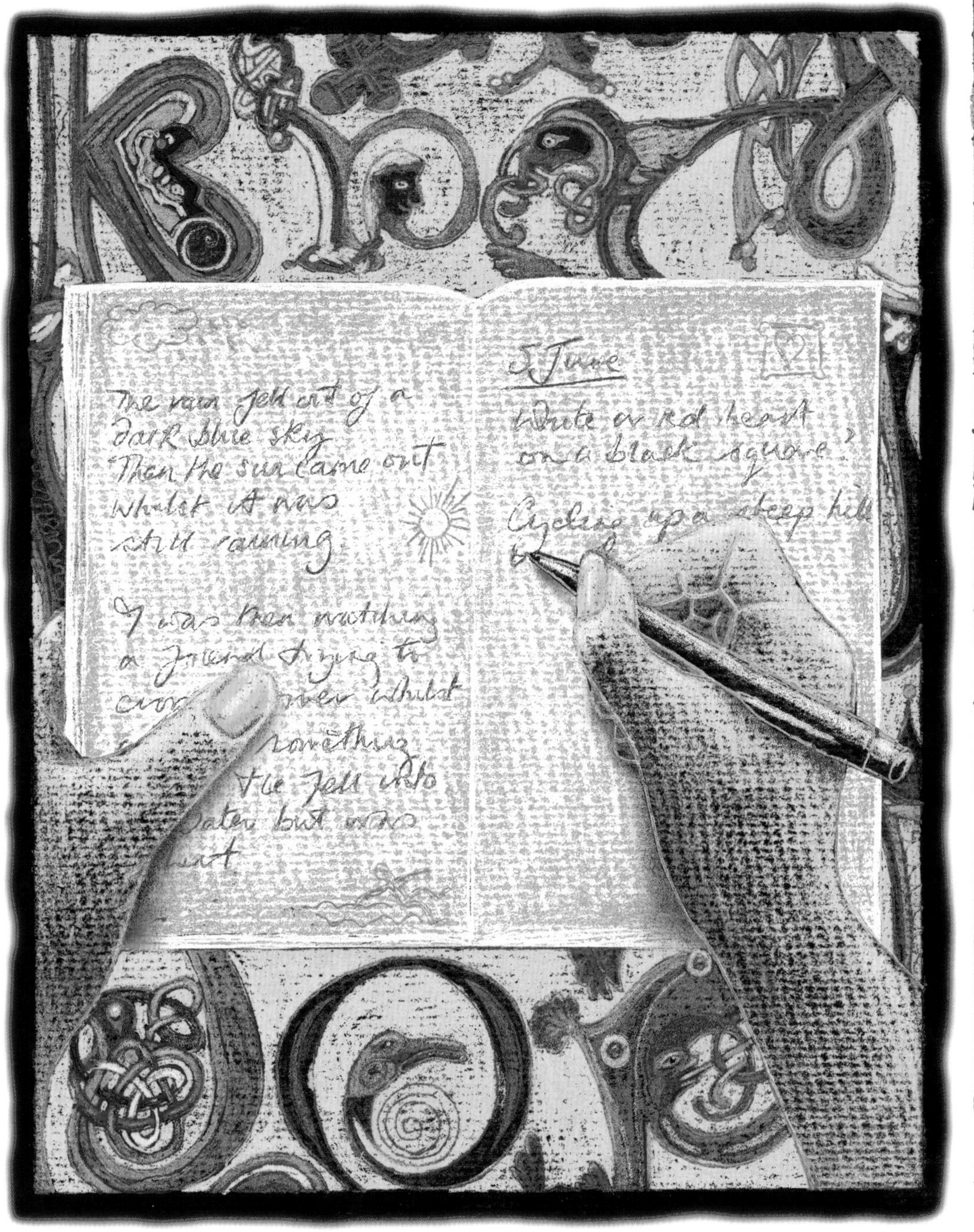

KEEPING A DREAM DIARY

What was on my left and right? What was I wearing? What time of day was it?"

Step 10. If All Else Fails: If you cannot remember having had a dream, write down whatever you are thinking about. Your thoughts may be mundane or banal or about something completely removed from dreams, but write them down anyway. If you are unable to recall any images, just experience your feelings. Each morning when you wake up, you feel a little bit different. Express that feeling. The first feelings you have on awakening may be caused by your dreams. Writing down your thoughts and feelings will also get you into the habit of recording your inner world first thing in the morning. A particularly good technique is to write down a short made-up fantasy about what you would have liked to have dreamed about. Eventually, the action of writing will be the catalyst for a dream memory. Finally, put the title as "I will remember my dream at the next opportunity." Sometimes a dream will come back to you if you just it let go. Intentionally let the dream go, telling yourself that it will return to you within a few minutes and you will soon catch it.

Step 11. Finishing: Leave enough space below the dream for a quick interpretation now and space for a more detailed one later. At the bottom of the page, make a few notes about what is going on in your life at the moment. This will help you with your interpretation and, at a later date, to see patterns.

Step 12. Add the Date: This will help you later when you want to make connections between your dreams and the events in your life.

REMEMBERING SIGHTS, SOUNDS, AND SENSATIONS

As far as we know, everybody thinks in different ways. Do you think in pictures (seeing), words (hearing), or feelings (sensing)? You probably do a mixture of all three, but one of these senses is likely to dominate. For example, if you respond to someone by saying, "I see where you're coming from," or "I get the picture," or "Let's get things in perspective," you're more likely to be a person who thinks visually.

If you were to say, "I hear what you're saying," or "That rings a bell," or "You're speaking my language," you're most likely to be a person who thinks in sound. However, if you respond with "I can handle this," or "I get your drift," or "I feel the same," you're most likely to be a person who thinks with feelings.

If you listen very carefully to a person talking you will soon notice that the person mainly use one of these senses. Once you've recognized the way the person speaks you can respond in the same way. So if you want to flatter a visual thinker, use phrases such as "You've really brightened up my day," or "We look good together," or "You make me shine."

In the same way, you can influence a verbal thinker by saying things like "We're on the same wavelength," or "You're really chirpy," or "We seem to click."

■ Most people use a combination of visual, auditory, and sensory thinking during their everyday life. The list below will help you identify your own predominant characteristics. Also observe people you know. Become aware of their language, eyes, and body posture to reveal their hidden self.

The Visual Thinker

You speak quickly, miss details, and often speak in a higher-pitched voice. You will use words that refer to seeing, imagination, and color. You tend to look upward when thinking, keep an erect posture, and can have jerky movements.

The Verbal Thinker

Your smooth language flows like music. You use words that refer to hearing, speaking, and listening. Your eyes move from side to side when you are thinking. You keep your head square, have flowing gestures, and keep an upright posture.

The Touch Thinker

You speak quietly and slowly with long pauses. You use words that refer to touching, such as "feel," "touch," "hold," "heavy." You look down when you are thinking, like to make physical contact, and slouch slightly.

With the sensory person, use words about touching, such as "You're really warm," or "I like your pushiness," or "I'm glad we made contact."

These are techniques used by highly trained and motivated salespeople. Many of these persuasive techniques are also used in advertising, television, and newspaper advertising slogans. It's possible to exert a powerful influence on people by using these techniques because the person believes that you think in exactly the same way as they do. They find themselves responding to you but don't quite know why.

Dreams are primarily visual in their content. However, if you tend to be verbal or sensory during you day-to-day life, sounds and sensations may be an important part of your dreams. It is therefore very important to note these things in your dream diary to help with your dream recall.

In addition to the visual content of the dream, here are other qualities you may be aware of:

Sounds

What words were spoken in the dream?

Always make a note of these before you write down anything else, as words and sounds are invariably the first thing forgotten.

Did you hear sounds in the background?

Traffic noise, birds singing, bells ringing, the distant sound of a ship's foghorn—all these seemingly irrelevant sounds may have important symbolic meanings. Loud sounds and explosions may represent something your unconscious is telling you about that requires your urgent attention. Quiet or distant sounds can represent things you are only just beginning to become aware of or that have become less important to you. For example, the sound of distant thunder may show that you are aware that problems are ahead and that you should prepare. It could also show something you've put behind you. If you think mainly in words and sounds, noting these things first may help trigger recall of the rest of the dream.

Are their any puns in the dream?

If you think in words your dreams may use visual puns to represent words. For example, you dream of drinking out of a mug. Perhaps the dream is saying that you're being taken for a "mug." A similar sentiment could be expressed if you dream of a baby octopus. It could bring to mind the saying of Phineas T. Barnum (1810–1891), "There's a sucker born every minute." Dreams twist words and phrases in innumerable ways. A pun depends on a similarity of sound but a difference in meaning. Other examples include dreaming of the sole of the foot as a symbol of the soul, or going to Hyde Park in London to representing something you have to hide or are hiding from. Freud believed that the unconscious used puns to disguise secret fears and desires.

Sensations

Did you touch anything in your dream?

The sensations you experience may indicate the way you feel about yourself or an issue that's bothering you. Something with a rough, unpleasant texture may reflect the way you feel. It could mean you are treating people in a rough way or feel you are being treated roughly. It could also indicate coarseness in behavior. Your dream

may be using sensation to express hidden feelings. Things may be going "smoothly," or you may dream of finding yourself in a "sticky" situation. If you think in a sensory way, these aspects of the dream should be recorded first.

Did you smell anything in your dream?

Most of us neglect the sense of smell, but it can have significance in dreams. We talk of "smelling a rat" or the "sweet smell of success" or of "a stinking argument." As part of the discipline of dream recall, make a careful note of smells in dreams. Smells are symbols for feelings being revealed by the unconscious and conditions we are just becoming aware of. Smells can often remind us of childhood or events from long ago.

What feelings and emotions did your dream reveal?

If you cannot remember the content of your dream, try to relive the emotions and feelings you had when you woke up. For example, if you woke up feeling angry it was probably connected in some way with your last dream. Reexperiencing this emotion will help you remember the dream scenarios that gave rise to this feeling. Feelings and emotions are not symbols but they reveal a great deal about your attitude toward the issues that are the subject of the dream.

Did you feel pain in your dream?

Sensory thinkers may use physical pain to express emotional pain. However, dreams can also reveal ailments and illnesses. Often they exaggerate the condition in order to make us aware of it. The first doctors of ancient Greece believed that dreams could reveal the causes and cures of illness. Perhaps your dream is urging you to see your doctor? Make a note of the actual or imaginary pain you experienced on waking and keep a careful check on your health. Future dreams may talk about the same issues in a symbolic way.

Conclusion

It is useful to include everything you experience in your dream diary. Some people make subheadings at the bottom of the page saying WORDS: PUNS: SOUNDS: SENSATIONS: FEELINGS & EMOTIONS: SMELLS:. These simple reminders that encourage you to recall sounds and sensations encourage better dream recall and may be more akin to your personality type and the way you think. Of course you will need to prepare a few pages of your dream diary layout in advance in order not to interrupt the smooth flow of your writing in the morning.

ENCOURAGE YOURSELF TO DREAM

THE act of putting a dream diary beside your bed may in itself encourage you to remember a dream. Writing something in it before you go to sleep then writing again as soon as you wake up reinforces the fact that the diary will help you to remember. Other bedtime rituals can also make stronger this affirmation to remember. For example, many people hang a Native American dream catcher by their bedside. This is a hoop that has a crisscross of patterned lines running over it with hanging beads. It is said to capture the spirit of the dreams that leave the sleeper's body. By hanging one near the bed, dreams are cap-

tured and remembered upon awakening.

This may sound like hocus-pocus, but dream catchers work. They help program the subconscious before going to sleep to remember a dream and jog the memory immediately upon awakening.

Simple rituals before bedtime can help with dream recall. In "Message from Forever" author Marlo Morgan talks of a traditional Aboriginal dream-recall technique:

> Mapiyal used the same procedure as the others. Taking a seashell container of water, she swallowed half and made her request for information about the object in the sky. The other half of the fluid would be consumed upon awakening to connect her conscious mind to the memory of the dream. She could then have better recall for finding meaning and direction.

You could try a simplified version of this by drinking half a glass of water before you sleep and the other half immediately upon awakening.

In Europe an old superstition says you can influence your dream by writing a note to the fairies of sleep and putting it under your pillow. In the morning look at the slip of paper and you will remember a dream. In addition it will give you the answer to the question you asked. Again this technique helps you to connect your conscious mind to the memory of the dream.

Sometimes the simplest triggers will help you remember your dreams. Have you ever been talking to someone then suddenly been reminded of a dream? It could be a simple word or the mention of a person or place that sets off the recall. Once you have one image, a whole series of remembered dream events comes flooding back to you. Once you get the link, the rest follows. The key is remembering this first snippet of information. Keep your dream in the back of your mind during the day. Does something remind you of your dream? Ponder any images that you remember. Doing this will help you remain connected to your dream. If, during the day, you find yourself thinking of your dream, try to remember other parts of the dream starting at that point. Also, try a little synchronicity. During the day you may encounter some element of your dream. These chance encounters can often act as triggers to help you recall other parts of your dream.

Daytime Routines

It is unlikely that you will be able to dedicate the first part of every morning to writing in your dream diary. Sometimes you may forget, and there are likely to be many times when you simply oversleep and it's a choice between your dream diary and being late for work. It's easy to lose the habitual routine of dream recall. That's why it's important to find ways of remembering dreams later in the day.

One of the most effective methods is to carry a notebook with you. When a dream comes to mind, stop what you're doing and write down whatever you can remember immediately. It's important that you don't put it off, as your memory of the dream will fade just as easily as when you first awaken. The information you write in your notebook can be added to your dream diary when you get home. Collecting dreams can be fun and very satisfying. I get a slight feeling of triumph when I remember a dream. Think of the feeling of frustration when you can't remember someone's name—when the name is on the tip of your tongue but you

just can't bring it to mind—and finally it comes to you. It seems to have been so obvious. And it's such a relief to remember it at last.

The simplest triggers can help you remember a dream. Put a few prompts in your environment to help stimulate your ability to remember. You could perhaps write notes to yourself to help you remember. Put them in places where you are likely to be doing jobs that don't require a great deal of concentration and where you are likely to be in a contemplative state of mind. Above the kitchen sink is a good place to start, on the mirror in the bathroom or near the bath, or on the dashboard of the car. My favorite place in on my key ring. It catches my attention when I least expect to be thinking about dreams.

The note need say nothing more that

USING IMAGERY TO HELP YOU REMEMBER

■ Treasure whatever you recall. It is part of you that was once lost. Also understand that your dream images are perfect! With practice, you will develop your ability to recognize their perfection. You could construct an image of yourself recalling your dreams or use an imaginary scenario to help with your recall. For example, if trying to remember dream scenes feels like fishing, then see yourself fishing when you are recalling dreams. Other images may feel more suitable. Every time you remember, see it as scoring at golf or your favorite sport. You could imagine yourself opening a container to see if anything is inside. Or you could be on a TV game show answering questions about your dreams. Perhaps it's like watching a movie that's slowly playing backward. The best image will be the one you make up for yourself.

"What did you dream?" You can choose from the list of suggestions in the section "Dream Notices." If visitors ask why these notes are all over the house and all but tattooed across your forehead, tell them about your methods of dream recall. One of the best ways to remember your dreams is to tell people about them. Do this as often as you can. Most people won't find you a bore so long as you let them describe their dreams as well. It is much more interesting to talk about what you dreamed than what you watched on TV. In some cases it is much more exciting material. Most people enjoy talking about dreams. The more you talk about them, the easier they are to recall. Perhaps you and a friend could agree to call each other in the morning or meet every lunchtime to talk about and interpret each other's dreams. It could turn into a very therapeutic friendship!

⬖ ROUTINES FOR RECALL ⬗

DREAM NOTICES

WHEN you place notes to yourself around the house, use positive commands that encourage your subconscious to recall a dream. You should make up your own statements as well. Write the following statements on bright yellow stickers and post them in strategic places around the house, office, and car.

"I want to remember my dream because…"

"Remember your dream NOW!"

"Did you dream last night?"

"Let events remind you of your dream."

"Realize your dream."

"I can remember my dreams."

"Did you dream this?"

"Remembering my dreams is easy."

"Nothing is ever forgotten. Every minute of your dream is there to recall now."

"I want to remember my dreams."

"It is enjoyable to remember dreams."

⬖ RECALL METHOD ⬗

STREAMS OF CONSCIOUSNESS

YOU will notice that often you unexpectedly remember your dreams during the day. They come to you when you are off guard. This may be because the rational mind likes to keep control during waking life and so the unconscious content has trouble getting your attention. You can get around this problem by occasionally allowing yourself to enter a fluid state of mind in which you relax and let the rational mind take the back seat for a while. Not only is the next experiment an excellent way to remember dreams, it is also a first-rate way to recharge yourself and release stress.

The objective of this experiment is to deliberately induce a state of consciousness that psychologists call hypnagogic/hypnopompic dreaming. These dreamlike states are experienced as a person falls asleep and on awakening, respectively. In this state there can be an incredible flow of visual imagery before the mind's eye. It could be called a visionary experience. Sometimes the pictures and images are so vivid, the dreamer believes he is actually wide-awake and having hallucinations. They may be visual (such as seeing scenes or figures) or auditory (such as hearing your name called). A frequently occurring hypnagogic hallucination is the sensation of loss of balance, often accompanied by a "dream" of falling. This is sometimes followed immediately by a jerking reflex recovery movement (the myoclonic jerk) that may jolt the sleeper back into full wakefulness.

In the next experiment you are going to use the hypnagogic state of mind to help you connect with your dreams. You will enter a light hypnagogic state of mind while remaining fully alert and in control. You will not experience hallucinations or waking dreams but should witness a wonderful flow of incredible imagery in the mind's eye.

These amazing visions are sometimes experienced in the deeper levels of meditation. For example, the mystical writer P.D. Ouspensky, who was a pupil of the guru Gurdjieff, believed that his initial spiritual preparation to receive instruction came as a child, when he would spontaneously experience this high state of consciousness. He discovered that it was possible to remain in a semi-waking state in which dreams continued and could be observed. The philosophy that he and Gurdjieff later taught was that human beings are basically asleep even when we believe ourselves to be awake.

The following experiment can be spiritually significant and a helpful way to connect with your dreams. It is also a step toward lucid dreaming, which you will read about in later chapters.

Step 1. As with many other experiments, first relax completely. Set aside a special time to work with your dreams and choose somewhere where you will not be disturbed or distracted by noise. As part of your ritual you may want to light a candle and some incense to set a contemplative mood. Also, choose a comfortable chair or sit on the floor propped up by cushions. Get yourself as comfortable as possible.

Step 2. Now let the feeling of relaxation spread through your whole body. Feel a warm sensation in your toes and feet spreading upward, relieving all stress. Notice how your shoulders become relaxed and how all the pressures of the day fall away. Let the tension fall away, especially around the eyes.

Step 3. Once you are completely relaxed you will notice how your mind slows down and becomes at ease. Let go of all worries and notice your imagination beginning to activate. You may see pictures and images arising in your mind's eye. Allow the moving images to come and go. They may move from the left or right of your peripheral vision. Don't try to hold or follow the images. Let them rise and fall. When thoughts come to mind observe them, then let them go. If emotions well up, observe them and then let them go.

Step 4. Now draw the images toward you and let them become exceptionally vivid. You may fix on one and look at it in detail. Look at it from above or become aware of its shape, texture, and color. Let the image become super-real, then let it drop away as you move on to the next spontaneous vision. Let your consciousness flow. Try not to fall asleep but remain in this state between waking and sleeping. You may see frightening or unpleasant images, but treat them with the same detached attitude as you did the beautiful visions. Let thought rise and fall like a gentle sea. The more you relax, the more vivid the images become. It's like dreaming, but you are wide-awake.

Step 5. At first the images will be a complete muddle of strange landscapes, faces, and pictures. They may seem to have very little bearing upon you or your life. This type of conscious dreaming does not have the complicated story lines of the dreams you normally experience during sleep. However, this level of awareness gives you an insight into the creative mental processes that stir in the depths of the unconscious. Practicing this technique will help you get in tune with these inner forces.

Step 6. You will probably feel extremely relaxed when you finally switch into this state of mind. Sometimes playing gentle music such as New Age, ambient, quiet classical, or Baroque can help you hold this state. In particular ambient music is subtle enough to give you a means of holding the attention but not intrusive enough to break the flow of your consciousness. The temptation will be to fall asleep, but try to resist and stay awake.

Step 7. Stay in this state for as long as you

wish. Afterward think about the images that came to you. They will fade very quickly, probably too quickly to be able to write much down. However, this experience will help you spontaneously recall dreams you have had just recently. It is likely that many fragments will have been given you as you did the experiment. Sometimes you will emerge from a session feeling relaxed and clear-headed, but on other occasions you will have a head full of dream memories that can be written down and worked with. Some

of these will be snippets from recent dreams, some will be from long ago, and some will be completely new ones.

The state of mind you have experienced is hard to describe and for many people hard to trigger. However, with practice you will be able to enter it at will. The trick is to let go of thoughts yet remain fully conscious. It is tempting to follow them or be drawn in by their strange beauty. Deep relaxation, the type where the body feels heavy and distant, can also aid this state of mind.

Some authorities believe that visionary hypnagogic states are a product of the ego's attempt to regain control over thought processes after the rapid change in consciousness caused by the loss of contact with waking reality. My own observation of this state is close to what can be experienced in deep meditation. It is like the blissful state that can occur when you finally let go of thoughts and just observe them rather than being drawn along by them. Similarly in this state you are free of worry and overexcited emotions. Instead of thoughts and feelings' controlling you, you can now control them. It is clearly a step toward self-mastery.

An additional benefit is that this state of consciousness can be tremendously relaxing and within 10 minutes can completely refresh you. This state of mind can draw you away from the pressures and stress of waking life and promote personal growth and development. This dreamlike state does not have the narrative and emotional complexity of ordinary dreams and can give you the opportunity to observe your unconscious as if you were seeing it on a TV screen. It can open up your spiritual insight and creative talent. Later you will learn how to use a similar technique to gain insight into the future.

THE INKBLOT TECHNIQUE

Sometimes when a person awakens from a hypnagogic or hypnopompic dream the imagery in the person's mind is projected onto the environment. The bedroom walls can turn into a cinema screen with incredible pictures unfolding like a film. You may have awakened from a dream and seen a sinister figure or face in the folds of the curtain or in a pile of crumpled clothes. The mind will often project pictures into random shapes. For example, as a child you may have allowed your imagination to create fantastic scenes, strange faces, and weird mythical beings in the puffy white shapes of cumulus clouds against a blue sky.

These changing images come from the unconscious and are projected by the mind onto the random shapes. The pictures formed reveal the hidden processes from deep within you and the thoughts being generated by your innermost self. The pictures are keys to your dreams.

If you gaze at any random pattern, you are soon likely to start seeing faces and pictures in its haphazard form. Many people claim they can see a face in the shadows of Mars or in the patterns on the moon's surface. Similarly, you may notice that when you look at the coals of a fire, the patterns in sand, a rock formation, or the gnarled bark of a tree, pictures are revealed in its shape. Psychics use random shapes such as tea leaves, hot coals, smoke patterns, or the flaws in a crystal ball to project the images from their intuition.

While working with adolescents in a Swiss psychiatric hospital, Hermann Rorschach noticed that certain children gave characteristically different answers to a popular game known as Blotto (*Klecksographie*). The game involved looking at inkblots to see who could see the most interesting pictures in the random shapes. It struck Rorschach that what the children were seeing revealed a great deal about their psychological condition. From this simple game, he devised the Rorschach Test, which today is considered one of the best psychodiagnostic procedures and an indispensable tool of psychiatry. In 1921, Rorschach published his ideas in his book *Psychodiagnostik*.

The modern Rorschach inkblot tests involve complicated procedures to study the personality and the unconscious. They use specific cards with specific interpretations for each area and clearly define interpretations of the possible responses to the printed inkblot shapes. However, inkblots can be used outside the psychiatrist's room as a means of accessing the unconscious and are an excellent way to help you remember your dreams.

In this next experiment you will use the shapes you see in a random inkblot to trigger dream recall.

❖ **INKBLOT EXPERIMENT** ❖

MAKING YOUR INKBLOT

Step 1. It is simple to make a suitable inkblot. You will need India ink, watercolor paper, a paintbrush, and water.

Step 2. Flick ink from your brush onto the paper. Now flick about the same amount of water onto the page. You will probably need to try this a few times until you get the right proportions of ink and water.

Step 3. Fold the paper in half and press it together on a flat surface. Using a thick book, press it flat. Now unfold the sheet and allow the symmetrical inkblot to dry.

The inkblot may look a little like a butterfly or an insect. Try also just flicking ink close to the edges of the page but leaving the center blank. In this way you get other strange shapes that will suggest less obvious images. The objective is to get plenty of gray tones and contrasting areas of black and white shapes.

USING THE INKBLOT TO RECALL DREAMS

Step 1. Put the inkblot inside your dream diary beside your bed. Use one of the techniques in this book to help you remember a dream. For example, as you get ready to go to sleep, say to yourself, "Tonight I will remember my dreams."

Step 2. If you wake up and remember a dream, log it in your dream diary in the normal way. If you cannot remember a dream, then lie in the same position for a while and allow yourself to drift between sleeping and wakefulness. Continue to relax and allow your mind to float. This will give your intuition a chance to draw a dream to your attention. Allow yourself time for a dream to form in your mind. Do not start planning your day.

Step 3. Continue to keep your attention on remembering your dreams, and remain in a state as close to sleep as possible. Now look at the inkblot and allow the pictures to form. You'll notice that the pictures appear in the inkblot more easily when you are in a sleepy state. Don't try too hard. Let your mind drift and allow the pictures to form spontaneously. Look at the shapes made by the ink but also observe the negative shapes made by the white paper. Turn the page upside down or sideways and see what other shapes are formed. Look also at the images you see in the smallest details of the inkblot. It may help to gaze at the page and watch what appears as your eyes go out of focus.

Step 4. As the pictures form you will be reminded of similar pictures that were in your dream. The inkblot will act as a sounding board and the images revealed will be very close to those found in your last dream. The more you allow your imagination to work with the shapes, the more of the dream you will remember.

You can also use an inkblot to help you recall a dream during your normal waking day. In fact any random shape can be used to encourage recall. For example, the pictures you see in a coal fire, clouds, and random patterns of tea leaves or coffee grounds can all form pictures. The images you see are projected from your unconscious mind. They tell you something about yourself. Just as dreams do.

TALKING TO INVISIBLE DREAM FRIENDS

The inkblot method works well because it enables you to give expression to your dreams in a concrete way. It externalizes your dreams. This process can bring previously unconscious material to the conscious mind and can help dream recall.

Children who have suffered physical and sexual abuse are usually encouraged to talk to dolls and teddy bears about their ordeal. This method provides a way of expressing what happened without fear of interrogation or adult reprisal. Children will tell their dolls things that would be very hard to confess to an adult therapist. A similar technique can be applied to dream recall.

Again, by externalizing the dream you can bring unconscious memories to the surface.

"AS IF" EXPERIMENT

EXTERNALIZING YOUR DREAM

Step 1. Sit in a comfortable armchair with another chair within view of you. Imagine that sitting in the chair opposite is someone who is a personification of your dream.

Step 2. The person you imagine could be someone whom you remember dreaming about or someone who represents the dream in general. Act as if a real person were in front of you. If you can recall any snippets of your dream, include these in the personification. For example, I recently had a vague recollection that my dream was set in Israel, but I couldn't remember anything else. I therefore chose my fantasy character to be Woody Allen dressed as a rabbi whom I then cross-examined about the dream. (Choosing a fun character makes this technique more vivid and helps you not be too serious about yourself.)

Step 3. Ask the imaginary person about your dream. To continue the example of the Woody Allen rabbi, I then asked him: "Why can't I remember my dream?" He replied:

"My boy, you got up too quickly. Already you missed an important dream about the Holy Land. The dream is about your spiritual path." My fantasy wouldn't win an Oscar but it worked, and important dream information was given to me very quickly. You just ask the question, then let your imaginary figure give an answer. You can speak out loud if you prefer, although I've found that it's quite adequate to do this whole exercise with the imagination.

Step 4. Ask a variety of questions. You may for example ask about how the dream influences your feelings and ask about the details of the dream. My own dream about Israel reminded me of the happy days I spent working on a kibbutz and the freedom I felt. Spirituality should be like this—free and happy. My dream figure pointed out to me that I was becoming too serious and ponderous about my spiritual work. Everywhere should be a Holy Land.

Step 5. Ask the fantasy character to bring forward other people from the dream. In my own case, the rabbi example showed me other characters from my dream I could

QUESTIONS TO ASK YOUR INVISIBLE FRIEND

"Who are you and why are you in my dream?"

"What part of me do you represent?"

"Who else is in my dream? Can you introduce me to them?"

"What does the dream mean?"

"What should I be learning from this dream?"

then cross-examine as well. Now I could play "as if" with a whole cast of characters.

Step 6. Ask your dream characters to interpret your dream for you. You could ask them what they represent about your own personality or circumstances. Ask them why they appear in your dream and what they are trying to tell you about yourself. You could ask: "Who are you and what is your reason for being in this dream?" Once you get into the swing of this internal dialogue you will find that it a very effective way not only to recall your dreams but to understand them as well.

Step 7. If you find it hard to imagine a fantasy figure, try out the technique by talking to a doll, to yourself in the mirror, or to a photograph of someone you admire. For example, I find it helpful to talk to a photograph of my spiritual guru, Sathya Sai Baba. Sometimes answers are given to me via my inner voice that contain the solutions to problems that have dogged me for years.

DRAWING DREAM DOODLES, MANDALAS, AND MIND MAPS

Drawing and painting are excellent ways to get in touch with your inner self and are often used in therapy to help subjects express themselves. Many famous men and women have used art as therapy. Sir Winston Churchill was an accomplished painter, for example, as was Adolph Hitler. Recent famous amateur painters include Prince Charles, John Lennon, David Bowie, Jade Jagger, Jayne Seymour, and Sylvester Stallone.

Art can be a direct route to the unconscious, particularly if you allow yourself to be influenced by whatever your imagination sends you. Art that is spontaneous rather than meticulously planned is often influenced by the unconscious. Sometimes unconscious symbolism creeps into a work without your conscious realization it has happened. For example, art critics observe that the paintings of Van Gogh express his psychological state of mind. The dark crows that cower above a swirling sea of wheat, a spiraling night sky, and a solitary white iris all express his inner turmoil and loneliness. However, Van Gogh may have been completely unaware of the subtle symbolism that he was including in his paintings. These moving symbols may have arisen spontaneously as Van Gogh immersed himself in the creative process.

Mysterious unconscious imagery appears in the work of many of the world's great painters. The works of Hieronymous Bosch, Titian, El Greco, William Blake, Henri Rousseau, Holman Hunt, Paul Klee, Willem de Kooning, and thousands of others all have subtle symbolism I'm sure did not arise by conscious choice. (The main exceptions are the surrealist artists such as Salvador Dali, Max Ernst, and others who were consciously influenced by the works of Freud and other psychologists.) Art is like dreaming. It brings to light the unconscious workings of the soul.

You may not be able to draw or paint like the Old Masters, but everyone can doodle and sketch simple drawings. These drawings, which come when you are not thinking about what you are doing, can be a doorway to the hidden you. Doodling enables you to access your unconscious and is an excellent method to help you recall your dreams.

Simple doodles and scribbles reveal the way you feel. When you are thinking about something else, on the telephone for instance, you may tend to doodle. The doodle reveals your unguarded personality traits. The subconscious flows onto the paper and only needs to be read. By interpreting your doodles you can learn a great deal about yourself and the home truths that they conceal.

The boxed-off section gives you a few interpretations for some of the more common doodles people scribble. Interpret your doodles as messages from your unconscious. What do the shapes and images represent about the way you are feeling? Perhaps they remind you of something you were dreaming about. Just like dreams, these simple pictures are messages to the

SOME COMMON DOODLES AND THEIR MEANINGS

Crosses

This may reveal that you feel angry about an issue or person. You want to remove something from your life.

Check Marks

This shows your approval. It may also show your desire to do things in an orderly way.

Spirals

A spiral moves inward and shows your introspective side.

Continuous Loops

You may feel that your life is repetitive and monotonous.

Circles

This illustrates your agreement. You are in harmony. It can illustrate your desire to conclude a matter. It may also show that you feel that you are running around in circles!

Squares

This could show that you are searching for stability.

Triangles or Arrows

Upward pointing may reveal your ambitions, downward may show your disap-

pointments. Arrows may show similar qualities.

Animals

The animals you draw may express your feelings. For example, a bird may show your desire to escape (perhaps from a boring meeting); a bull may express anger; a snake or snakelike squiggle may reveal sexual feelings or mistrust; a cat may symbolize intuition, and a fox, cunning.

People

Matchstick drawings of people may show that you are thinking about or concerned about social issues. If the people are fighting, you may be itching for a battle with someone. If you mutilate them, this may show that you harbor a hidden resentment toward someone. The scenario that surrounds your matchstick figure reflects the way you feel about your own life and the people you know.

Buildings

People often draw simple houses similar to those we drew as children. Buildings can represent the self and also the human body. A large house may show self confidence, even egotism. A small house may show that you feel insecure or just want to go home!

conscious self from the unconscious mind. Sometimes the pictures you create can be a direct reference to a dream you recently had.

It's best to doodle when you're distracted and not consciously thinking about what you're doing. Try it while you're on the telephone or at a dull corporate meeting. Scribble while watching TV or waiting on line. Don't think too much about what you're doing. Some people find that doodling brings interesting results if they use the other hand and not the one they normally use. If you're right-handed, try doodling with your left hand. The nerves that use the left hand are connected to the side of the brain that is holistic and intuitive. Consequently the images you draw are spontaneous and come directly from the unconscious side of yourself.

Mandalas

Psychologist Carl Jung encouraged his patients to draw. He discovered that as their therapy progressed the images would also evolve like a visual story. Often this method would trigger a series of dreams changing and evolving parallel to the progress of the art. Jung found that art therapy helped his patients understand their dreams and encouraged new dreams to emerge.

Carl Jung was intrigued by the fact that many of his patients, without any prompting, drew mandalas. *Mandala* is a Sanskrit word for "magic circle." Mandalas are used in Eastern art as a means of meditation and are characterized by a circle and a square that radiate from a central point. Some of the examples found in countries such as Tibet are magnificent works of art that are considered very sacred.

Mandalas appear spontaneously all over the world. For example, the great rose window in Notre Dame Cathedral in Paris is a perfect sacred mandala. Carl Jung interpreted mandalas as an archetypal expression of the self and wholeness. Mandala images often emerge spontaneously in dreams. With a mandala everything returns to a single central point. Jung believed that this symbolized that the goal of psychological development is the "path to the center." The circular structure of the mandala represents the self, which is the totality of the individual. It includes both the conscious and unconscious sides of the psyche and gives the individual a sense of meaning and purpose as the seeker moves toward it.

Jung spent a great deal of time sketching mandalas of his own. In his autobiography, *Memories, Dreams, Reflections*, he says: "My mandalas were cryptograms concerning the state of the self which were presented to me each day. In them I saw myself—that is, my whole being—actively at work....The self, I thought, was like the monad which I am, and which is my world. The mandala represents this monad, and corresponds to the microcosmic nature of the psyche."

In 1927 Jung had a dream that confirmed the symbolic importance of the mandala. He dreamed he was in Liverpool. The various quarters of the city were arranged around a square. In the center was a round pool, and in the middle of it, a small island. The air was murky but the central island blazed with sunlight. In the very center stood a beautiful magnolia tree.

The name Liverpool, Jung understood to mean "the pool of life" (the "liver," according to an old view, is the seat of life, that which "makes to live"). Jung continues:

"The dream brought with it a sense of finality. I saw that here the goal had been revealed. One could not go beyond the center. The center is the goal, and everything is directed to the center." (Jung wrote at length about mandalas in *Psychology and Alchemy* and *The Archetypes of the Collective* and also in his foreword to a Chinese alchemy book called *The Secret of the Golden Flower*.)

Mandalas are a good way to get in touch with the unconscious because they are symbols. By sketching them during your free time they will help reveal the images that are trying to emerge from the unconscious, the same images that are occurring in your dreams.

EXPERIMENT

DRAWING A MANDALA

MANDALAS can occur as spontaneous psychic events at times when you are attempting to integrate discordant elements within your personality and when disintegration is threatened. They help you find harmony within yourself. Using their structure as a framework for doodling and sketches encourages you to recognize the images that occur as being part of you.

Step 1. You can simply sketch your ideas with pen or pencil directly into your dream journal. If you get really inspired you may want to buy paint, paper, or canvas and turn your inspiration into something special. Many of the mandalas produced by Jung's patients are very beautiful. You may also enjoy looking at pictures of sand paintings by Native Americans or the incredibly intricate designs of the Tibetans. Your mandalas can be simple doodles or works of art.

Step 2. Think about your layout. Traditional designs are usually based around a circle divided into four or multiples of four. Tibetan mandalas often contain three concentric circles painted as a rim in black or dark blue. They are meant to shut out the outside and hold the inside together. Often these enclose a square-walled courtyard with four gates. In Tibetan mysticism this signifies sacred seclusion and concentration. These enclose the colors red, green, white, and yellow, which represent the four directions. The center is usually marked off by another magic circle symbolizing the objective or goal of contemplation.

Step 3. Your mandala can be whatever shape you like. All you need to do is lightly map out a simple framework and your unconscious will give you ideas to fill in the rest. You could start with a squared circle divided into four quarters across the center of the circle.

Step 4. Once you've planned your basic layout, fill the spaces with any shapes or images that come to you. These can be abstract, such as lotus flowers, squares, circles, repeating patterns, and so on. You may include pictures of animals, faces, figures, or any images that pop into your head. At this stage, don't worry whether the images relate to dreams you've had, just enjoy jotting down whatever pictures come to mind.

Step 5. When you've finished, sit comfortably and prop your drawing in front of you. Consider each of the shapes or images and let your mind make associations with each one. For example, you may have drawn a tree within the shape of the mandala. It is there for a reason. Your uncon-

MANDALA

scious has given you this idea because it is connected with an inner message. Think about what things you associate with the tree. What sort of tree is it? Does it bear fruit? Is it old or young? Does it remind you of any events in your life? Does it represent something about the way you feel? In this example a tree may symbolize spiritual growth, strength, or stability. Perhaps you associate mythical stories with the image you have drawn. You can interpret the images in your drawing in the same way you would a symbol from a dream.

Step 6. Ask yourself whether anything in the picture reminds you of a dream you've had recently or in the past. Any parts that remind you of a part of your dream can be contemplated to help you recover these lost memories. If you are reminded of a past dream, consider whether it also reminds you of more recent dreams. Are you experiencing today similar emotional conditions you did when you had the past dream?

Step 7. Finally, note your observations in your dream journal. Give your entry a title and date, and log the information in the same way you would a normal dream. You may want to make a note to say that this is a "recovered dream using a mandala."

Dream Maps

The architecture of the brain is incredible. It is estimated that we each have about one million million (1,000,000,000,000) brain cells (neurons). Every one of these is connected to others by thousands of threadlike tentacles called dendrites and axons. It has been calculated that the number of possible combinations/permutations in the brain, if written out, would be 1 followed by 10.5 million kilometers of zeroes.

It appears that the brain works by connecting everything together like the mycelium of a mushroom. Thought cuts through this jungle of connections, and a biochemical electromagnetic pathway is formed. Every time you have a similar thought the pathway is reinforced as the connections between the cells becomes greater. This theory explains why repetition is the best way to remember things or establish a behavior pattern. Whether you learn your multiplication tables by rote, practice a sport, or repeat a spiritual mantra, you are establishing patterns of thought. Repetition of mental events increases the probability of further repetition.

Dreams, like conscious thoughts, leave traces in the brain. It may be that they fade quickly because of their surreal unusualness. For example, I once dreamed of traveling by bicycle to the star Sirius. This clearly has never happened to me so it is not a memory that has been established by habit. Bizarre dreams may not leave deep memory pathways through the forest of the dendrites and axons. They are not going to be easy to access because the pathways made by unfamiliar experiences leave faint traces that are hard to find.

However, if you can remember one small fragment of your dream it can provide you with a link that connects you to the other parts of the dream. To continue the analogy of the path: it's like finding one part of a trail then systematically looking for clues to retrace your steps. This next method works well because it functions in a similar way to the brain itself. Just as the brain cells are connected together, so too are the memories of a dream. Once you find a marker you can follow it back from one dream event to another.

So get out your old Davy Crockett hats to sniff out the hidden pathways of dreamland.

CREATING DREAM MAPS

Step 1. You need a snippet of a remembered dream to work with in this experiment. For example, you may only remember that your dream was set in Switzerland and that you were eating something. Write this snippet in the center of a blank page of your dream diary: "Dream of being in Switzerland eating something." Now draw an oval around it.

Step 2. Now draw two separate branch lines to two new ovals. Put one above your original oval and one below. Write "Switzerland" in one and "eating" in the other. If you remember more than a couple of snippets of the dream you can add more ovals connected by lines to the central oval. Break what you remember into as many components as possible.

Step 3. Now draw new branch lines and ovals from each oval with associated words in them. Ideally, from these associations you will recognize something from your dream. To get started, write down anything that comes to you. For example, from the oval "eating something" you may link things like cheese, chocolate, fondue, or any of the foods you may associate with Switzerland. You can continue by writing down other foods that spring to mind— pizza, chewing gum, pastrami, and so on. You can also ask yourself where you were

eating and what time of day it was. Note also your feelings associated with the dream snippet. Put each into an oval from the "eating" oval. You can of course go on forever, so limit yourself to about 12 associations.

Step 4. Now do the same for the word "Switzerland." First write some obvious associations such as William Tell, cuckoo clocks, bank accounts, mountains, yodeling, and so on. Next add any unusual associations that spring to mind. You may remember a holiday in Italy or France near the Swiss border. Or you may think of a Swiss friend you once knew. If anything incongruous comes to you, add it as well, even if it isn't directly connected logically to the subject of your free association of ideas.

Step 5. Pause and think about any subjects you wrote in the ovals. Do any of them remind you of something from your dream? If none do, continue adding more ovals until one does. The act of trying to remember your dream may trigger new material that comes spontaneously. It might not be anything to do with Switzerland or with eating. It could be a completely new snippet. Put this in a new oval linked from the main one and add associations to it as you did with Switzerland and food.

Step 6. If you find that one of the things you've written down does remind you of something from your dream, continue to build more links from it. For example, you remember that it was cheese you were eat-

ing. Start making links around the word cheese. This could include names of cheeses, or your personal associations with cheese; you may even think of things like the moon, cheesy (smelly) socks, and so on. Again, one or two of your associations may bring to mind more details about the dream.

Step 7. You can continue making associations with each part of the dream for as long as you like. Your branches and notes in the ovals will gradually spread out from each other until they fill the page. Dreams are naturally very fragmented, so this technique also helps you bring together the parts of dream story lines that run in different directions.

Step 8. Finally, write a summary of the dream that you have recalled. Date it and give it a title as you would for a normal journal entry.

Using Dream Maps to Recall Other Dreams

The dream-map technique can also be useful with dreams that have been clearly recalled. Once you've logged your dream in your journal, write the title of the dream in the center of a page and draw an oval round it.

This time draw branches from it to ovals that contain other dreams that you can associate with this current dream. For example, you have the classic dream of being chased by a shadowy figure. It may remind you of dreams from childhood, perhaps from a time when you were going through a difficulty such as being bullied at school. Give the past dream a title and draw new branches and ovals with as many details as you can remember.

You may find that dozens of dreams from the past come to mind. Some may be fairly recent and others may reach back to early childhood. You will begin to see that patterns emerge in your dreams. Dreams also have a strange way of picking up on the thread of a story that they left a long time earlier. Sometimes you have to wait many years for the next episode!

DREAM DICTIONARY

By working with dreams over many years and recalling dreams from a long time ago you may come to realize that you have another life that lives in tandem with your present waking life. This inner life has its own stories, high points, tragedies, and episodes just like your outer life. Most people associate their lives with the world outside themselves—career, family, status, possessions, and so on. A rich dream life reveals another you that is not dependent on these things. Your dream journal is the history of this inner you.

If you recall dream sequences from your past, you will notice that many themes and images return time after time. Certain symbols, metaphors, and allegories will recur that have a meaning that is uniquely yours. If you keep good records you can identify common symbols from your dreams and make them into a personal dream dictionary. This could be made as a separate book, or you can use the back section of your dream journal.

Keeping a Dream Dictionary

Step 1. As you did with the dream maps, you must break your dream down into its components. For example, suppose you dream about a blue tree being washed by the sea. In this dream are three possible entries to your dictionary section: tree, sea, and the color blue. Once you have understood the dream you can write your interpretation for the meaning of each of the symbols. Dedicate the last 26 pages of your dream diary to your dictionary; give at least one page to each letter of the alphabet. If you use a loose-leaf binder you can add new pages as your dictionary grows.

Step 2. Read through the dreams in your journal and identify any symbols you may find. Remember that every entry may reveal many symbols, such as color, imagery, places, and people. In addition you may want to list actions and scenarios such as being chased, falling, teeth falling out, or being in your childhood home.

Step 3. Make a reference to the dream titles and dates so that you can quickly cross-reference your entries.

Step 4. Give your interpretation of the meaning and include some of your personal associations with the symbols. For example, you may dream of falling. You may notice that this dream always happens when you are "falling" asleep. A drop in blood pressure may cause the dream. Alternatively, you may also notice that you dream of falling when you feel insecure or have difficult problems to sort out. The date entries you make will help you identify some of the sit-

uations in real life that trigger this common dream. The dream may also bring to mind memories of a fall you had as a child. Note everything that feels important in association with this dream metaphor. Next time you have a similar dream, half the work of the interpretation will already have been done when you analyze it.

Step 5. Leave a little space below each entry so you can add more detail the next time you have a similar dream. You will discover that your dream symbols can change their meaning as you work with them. Dreams use symbols similar to the way we use words. We string words together to create sentences that convey meaning; so, too, is a dream like a sentence of symbols. Just as words mean different things depending on their context, so do dream symbols. As has been mentioned already, we dream in symbols because that may be the way the subconscious mind talks to the conscious, or waking, mind.

Step 6. You may never really know the exact meanings of the symbols or why they come into your dreams. They are elusive and change and evolve as you work with them. However, it will help you understand them better if you also study the traditional meanings of symbols while considering your own interpretations. A symbol dictionary can give you ideas to explain things that appear in your dreams. It will show you the psychological way to understand dream symbolism as well as show you some of the strange superstitions associated with each dream symbol.

DREAM DICTIONARY TIP

■ Near each dream entered in your dictionary, record the date of the dream. Check if anything reminds you of things happening in your waking life. Include this under the dream dictionary entry. Use a different color pen for the notes about your waking life to make it easier to differentiate them.

THE *I CHING* AND DREAM RECALL

The *I Ching*, or the *Book of Changes*, is an ancient oracle that originated in China and has been used throughout the Far East for thousands of years. It is principally a work of guidance to help anyone seeking help and enlightenment on any subject. It has also been used to augur how to find good fortune and avoid adversity. In China it was so influential, matters of state were often decided by it and it was one of the few books not obliterated during the Cultural Revolution. Even in Japan it was and still is used extensively. For example, the decision to make the sudden attack on Pearl Harbor in December 1941 was made only after experts had consulted the *I Ching*.

It has today caught the imagination of many Westerners and is used throughout the world.

The wisdom of the *I Ching* is older than Christianity and has been passed down through the generations since the fourth millennium B.C. It is much more than a means of prediction. It is a book that offers advice on how to cope with your fortune.

The central feature of the *I Ching* is the hexagram, a pattern of six horizontal lines that are read from the bottom upward. The random division of yarrow sticks, wands, and coins determines these. According to the Chinese sages who wrote the book, the resulting hexagram is not a product of chance but is the touchstone that will answer the questioner's predicament. (The ancient Chinese believed that the spirits [*sh'n*] of the ancestors were communicating with them through the medium of chance.) Once the hexagram has been determined, it can be looked up in the text of the *I Ching* and the answer interpreted in the light of the question asked.

The philosophy of the *I Ching* is based on ancient Taoism and is also profoundly influenced by the teachings of the philosopher Confucius and by the religion of Buddhism. Taoism proposes that in all pairs of opposites in nature, such as male and female, light and dark, and black and white, each contains the seed of the other. They continually transform into each other, thus creating perpetual change and order within chaos. The Chinese called these two forces *yin* and *yang*. This polarity theory underlies most of the great religions of Asia.

Material reality is yin. Yin covers all things tangible, things that can be held. Yin is a feminine force and represents earth or matter. It is symbolized by a square, is black, and is associated with night, stillness, downward motion, introversion, winter, and the north. Yang is the intangible aspect of creation represented by heaven. Its symbol is a circle, and it is considered a masculine principle. It is white and is associated with daytime, activity, upward motion, outward expression, summer, and the south. Yin and yang are fundamental to Chinese philosophy. They are not seen as opposite forces but as complementary, altering, and moving each other in an eternal process of change. The interaction of these two principles gives rise to all things.

In the early 1920s, analytical psychologist Carl Jung met Richard Wilhelm, who had translated the *I Ching* into German. In 1923, Jung invited Wilhelm to lecture in Zurich, where he spoke on the *I Ching* at the Psychology Club. Jung was deeply impressed by what Wilhelm had to say and began an intensive study of the oracle. In *Memories, Reflections, Dreams*, Jung wrote: "I would sit for hours on the ground beneath the hundred-year-old pear tree, the *I Ching* beside me, practicing the technique by

I CHING

referring the resultant oracles to one another in an interplay of questions and answers. All sorts of undeniably remarkable results emerged—meaningful connections with my own thought processes which I could not explain to myself."

Jung realized that the *I Ching* was a means by which he could access the unconscious mind. The paranormal chance phenomena of the *I Ching* appeared to be "meaningful coincidences." In 1930, he first used the term "synchronicity" to describe an "a-causal connection between psychic states and objective events." His initial theories were influenced by a classical idea of astrology called the "objective moment." This is the basis of most fortune-telling systems and proposes that certain quality exists in a given moment of time itself. For example, whatever is done at this moment of time, has the quality of this moment of time. In other words, random events such as the dealing of Tarot cards, the position of the stars at your birth, and the fall of dice or coins are influenced by the conditions of the present moment. Oracles that use these methods reflect the underlying conditions and can reveal the potential for the future.

Carl Jung understood that the *I Ching* was a means by which he could look into the underlying influences that were creating current psychological conditions. He found that the *I Ching* could be used to interpret dreams. It could also identify underlying psychological conditions and reveal what was denied or hidden. Furthermore, it was a useful tool to restore psychological equilibrium and integration.

The *I Ching* gave Jung an insight into what was happening in the unconscious of himself and his patients. In his foreword to the *I Ching*, Jung wrote: "The method of the *I Ching* does indeed take into account the hidden individual quality in things and men, and in one's own unconscious self as well."

Clearly the *I Ching* can be used to help interpret dreams, but it can also be used to help you get in touch with your inner self so that forgotten dreams can be remembered.

EXPERIMENT

USING THE *I CHING* FOR DREAM RECALL

IT is customary to consult the *I Ching* for its permission and comments before writing about it. Jung did a similar exercise when he prepared the original foreword. In Jung's case the *I Ching* had compared itself to a cauldron (*ting*)—a ritual vessel containing cooked food. Here the food is understood to be spiritual nourishment. This is clearly an apt metaphor for the *I Ching*, which provides spiritual nourishment and wisdom to many people.

I asked for its opinion how it should be used as a means of recalling dreams and was given hexagram 37, The Family (*Chia J'n*). At first this made no sense to me, then partway through my second reading I remembered my dream from the previous night. The *I Ching* was demonstrating dream recall by example.

That morning I had overslept and had no time to write my dreams in my diary. I knew I had had a dream but I could only recall a few snippets. As soon as I got up I rushed straight into my home office to make a few important telephone calls. In my haste I had completely forgotten my dream.

Later that day when I cast the hexagram of The Family it brought the dream memory back. I had dreamt about being in a graveyard surrounded by family crypts. One was of famous people, one was of rich people, and the last, which I had to clear weeds to find, was titled "ordinary folk." I had a bunch of flowers and decided to lay them on the family crypt of "ordinary folk."

This strange dream made sense. It symbolized my work as a spiritualist medium. I have given consultations to the rich and famous but it is the consultations for "ordinary folk" that are spiritually the most important. These are the readings that unite parents with their departed children, husbands with wives, and bring together loved ones and family across the veil of death. Correct mediumship proves that families are forever and that love is eternal and will never die.

Clearly, the *I Ching* had helped me remember an important dream about families that highlighted the values that need to be remembered with my spiritual work.

❖ EXPERIMENT ❖

I CHING EXPERIMENT

THE *I Ching* does not always give you the answer you expect. It has been said of the *I Ching* that it has a personality of its own and even a sense of humor. Jung advised that the *I Ching* be approached with the reverence due a wise sage.

Step 1. The *I Ching* will answer your question in accordance with the way the question is phrased and its text must be regarded as though the book were the speaking person. You may ask it "Help me remember the dream I had last night" and you will get clues and prompts to help you recover lost dream memories.

Step 2. Cast the hexagram and read the text. To do this you will of course need a copy of the *I Ching*. There is not space here to describe how to cast the *I Ching* or to reproduce the 64 hexagrams with their many moving lines.

Step 3. Read the text through without trying to relate it to your life or to the dreams you've had. This relaxed state of mind will allow the imagery of the *I Ching* to sink into your unconscious and draw information to you. You may find that the title of the hexagram, the qualities of the trigrams, and the characters, scenarios, and images from the text act as direct clues that trigger spontaneous recall. Don't worry too much about what the text means; be concerned about the images that it provokes.

Step 4. If a dream memory is not triggered with the first reading, read the text again but this time think about the psychological qualities that the hexagram describes. For example, hexagram 28, The Preponderance of the Great, can show someone who is under pressure. Was your dream about being under pressure? Hexagram 5, Waiting, talks about nourishment. Perhaps your dream contained images of food or involved a situation where you were waiting for something? Hexagram 14, Possession of Great Measure, may refer to dreams about finding treasure, and hexagram 27, The Corners of the Mouth, may refer to the common dream of teeth falling out. Hexagram 29, The Abysmal, could trigger the recall of a dream about falling, and hexagram 15, Modesty, may indicate Freud's favorite dream: being naked in public!

Step 5. The hexagrams of the *I Ching* contain many archetypal images and potent symbols that arise from the unconscious. The mythical and magical qualities of the *I Ching* are conducive to dream recall. However, there are no set rules about which hexagram relates to which dream. The symbols within the book are flexible. They are a mirror to your unconscious mind.

Step 6. If you recall a dream, write it in your dream diary. Also include the hexagram and the main images that prompted the recall. If you get the same hexagram again when you next do this technique, you may find that the oracle is pointing to a recurring dream or an ongoing sequence of dreams. Your records will help you with dream recall in the future.

Step 7. If you fail to remember a dream using this technique, note the hexagram in your dream diary anyway. The hexagram will reveal information about your inner life, which is one of the main functions of dreams. Later, you can return to the hexagrams you cast to reevaluate your original interpretation. If you cannot discover any immediate relevance in a given response, you may be limited by your expectations. Later the hexagram may make sense in the light of future events and future dreams.

Step 8. If you recall a dream using this technique, try casting another hexagram to interpret the dream. The *I Ching* can give remarkable insight into the psychological influences that are responsible for the inception of your dream.

For some people the spirit of the *I Ching* is clear and for others it may convey nothing. Jung found that the Western mind tends to shut out intuitive prompts because reason and the intellect rule most of us. However, an open-minded attitude toward oracles

such as the *I Ching* can reestablish a rapport with the intuitive self and can bring great benefit to the personality. Recognizing your intuitive side as well as your intellectual side can help you become a more stable and well-rounded individual.

TAROT CARDS AND OTHER ORACLES

Most oracles can be used to access the unconscious and help you recall dreams. Tarot cards are particularly rich in the archetypal symbolism that emerges from the world of dreams. Even if you have no idea of the traditional meanings of the cards they can reveal a great deal about what's happening in your unconscious. For example, if you randomly draw a card while asking about your dream, the picture on the card can act as a trigger to help you access this knowledge.

Traditional oracles are rich in dream symbolism. Just as you use the *I Ching*, so too could you easily adapt oracles such as runes, dice, cards, sand reading, and so on. Instead of asking questions about your life, ask instead about your dreams. They will help you recall forgotten dreams as well as help you with the task of interpreting the dreams you do recall.

Long before science took an interest in the study of dreams, mystics were using dreams to foretell the future, diagnose illness, and give counseling and guidance. In particular, dreams have been revered by seers and prophets as messages from God. Psychics and spiritualists have seen them as ways to access the past, the future, and the spheres of the spirits and angels. Dreams have been remembered and interpreted since the dawn of consciousness, but perhaps the man who did most to secure mystical dreams a place in the modern age was the American prophet Edgar Cayce.

EDGAR CAYCE

Edgar Cayce was born in Kentucky in 1877. He was a humble man with a Presbyterian background who ran a small photography business for most of his life. What singled him out from ordinary individuals was what happened when he went to sleep. He was known as "the sleeping prophet." While asleep (it was actually a trancelike state) he would make predictions and give medical treatments. When he awoke he had no recollection—or even understanding—of what he had said.

During his life Cayce gave over 14,000 "readings," as he called them. These included herbal cures, correct diagnoses and treatments for patients who were not even present at the consultation, and many predictions about the future of mankind. For example, in April 1929, a stockbroker consulted him about a dream, and the sleeping Cayce declared that there would be panic on Wall Street and around the world. He said that prices would fluctuate over a period of six months and then collapse. On Friday, October 29, 1929, Wall Street crashed, bringing chaos in its wake and the Great Depression.

In June 1931, Cayce spoke about the coming of the Second World War. He also foresaw the end of communism in Russia, which would result in an alliance between Russia and the U.S. that would be the "hope of the world." He further predicted the Christianization of Red China, massive earthquakes, the sliding of much of Japan into the sea, the destruction of most of Los Angeles, San Francisco, and New York, and the tilting of the earth's rotational axis with a drastic reversal of global climates.

Perhaps it would have been better if Cayce's dreams had remained forgotten!

Cayce's theories about dreams were very different from those of Freud and Jung. Cayce believed dreaming to be the body's way of "self-edification," a term he used to describe the building up of the mental, spiritual, and physical well-being of the individual.

Dreams are a form of spiritual growth that speed the dreamer toward his/her human potential. A good night's sleep results in a better person who has more mature values and creative thinking. A good night's sleep develops in a person proper conduct and thinking.

According to Cayce, dreams have five different levels: the body level, subconscious level, level of consciousness, level of superconsciousness, and level of the soul. Dreams can help to bring health and insight into each of these parts. For example, they could present messages about the body and call for aid during illness.

Cayce believed that in order to interpret dreams correctly it was first necessary to study oneself thoroughly. The primary purpose of dreams is either to solve problems and adapt to external affairs or to alert the dreamer to new potential. The first step is to determine whether the dream is about problems or potential.

The next step is to take an inventory. It is important to know your conscious and subconscious hopes and fears. You must also be aware of your future plans, goals, interests, opinions, and decisions. Similarly, you must be honest with yourself about your hidden fears, longings, dependencies, and denials. Know too the cycles, needs, habits, and stresses of the body. Only when you are aware of all these things can you interpret your dreams satisfactorily.

Dreams function on all five levels. If you know yourself, you can more easily make the decisions that help you better yourself physically, subconsciously, consciously, super-consciously, and at the level of the soul.

Cayce's Dream Recall Methods

Cayce believed that all normal people—people without severe brain damage—dream but have problems remembering their dreams. He coached many "non-dreamers" how to recall their dreams without difficulty. However, he always advised that they first be prepared to confront whatever their dreams revealed. Furthermore, they had to be willing to apply the dream revelations to their lives.

People who wanted to recall their dreams had to be ready to make changes to their life and to themselves. Cayce considered this the key to dream recall.

Practical methods included dream incubation, such as telling oneself, just before dropping to sleep, to remember a dream. Some people were encouraged to stimulate dreams by reading and talking about them, others were instructed to pray for dream guidance. Different methods of dream recall suit people of differing temperaments and inclinations.

Cayce also believed that the body had a role in remembering dreams, that retaining the same position on awakening and allowing oneself to drift in and out of sleep could help a dream be revealed. He stressed the importance of getting enough rest. He also encouraged his students to talk about and record their dreams. He spoke of the need for an "inquiring mind." He explained that even a fragment of a dream could be the key that unlocked the whole dream. If a fragment could be recalled, Cayce would sometimes give a prompt using clairvoyance to remind the sitter of the missing memories.

Cayce also spoke about what happened to dreams that were not recalled. According to him, many dreams exist to advance the dreamer's spiritual growth but others are just worries, dreams about food or bodily processes, or dreams to help the dreamer continue sleeping. Some dreams are clearly not that important. Cayce also said that dreams of the sick or damaged body are not worth recalling and interpreting. However, he insisted that dreams were a natural aid by which the personality and body regulate themselves and improve the dreamer's situation. Significant dreams will repeat and appear in different forms and continue to convey the same message until the dreamer remembers them.

For Cayce, dreams were not something odd and removed from everyday life. Just as dreams can reveal the future, so can a waking hunch. Dreams give important insights into and highlight weaknesses, but this same information can be discovered through introspection. Perhaps the most important thing Cayce had to say about dreams, and something he constantly emphasized, was that dreams are recalled so they can be used. It is important to act on the dreams you recall. If you do this you will increase your self-knowledge and enhance the quality of your daily living.

WORKING WITH YOUR DREAMS

Learn from your dreams what you lack.

W. H. AUDEN (1907–1973)

I F you've used the techniques already shown, you should now have many dreams to work with. In fact, you may have too many! Once you get the knack of dream recall you remember so many dreams, you may feel swamped. You must decide which ones are the most important ones you have remembered. In this section, you'll work with your most important dreams to discover what they are trying to tell you about yourself.

You may have noticed that certain themes recur in your dreams. For example, I occasionally dream about missing the train, running out of paper for my computer printer, or being unprepared for an important talk. These are common anxiety dreams that can arise when I feel under pressure. This type of dream contains metaphors, allegories, and symbols that express my feelings of being unprepared. I often have them if I am struggling to meet a publisher's deadline!

Identify the dreams you have had that

share a common theme. Dreams sometimes expand on themes from the previous night's dreams and present similar material in a different way. In the example I cited of my own dreams, all the dreams have the same theme presented in different ways. They all highlight my feelings about being unprepared and my anxiety about not being able to complete the job I have to do. Similar dreams could include rushing to get the bus but missing it or taking an examination and realizing that you do not know the subject matter.

Similar emotional themes can be presented in many different ways. Once you recognize the emotional theme of the dream, it is important to make changes in your life and to act on what your unconscious is telling you. Put the dream's advice into practice. In my case, I took a day off and ignored the panic deadline. When I returned to the job at hand, I felt refreshed and able to cope. The result was that I could complete the job with twice the efficiency I would have had if I had continued to be anxious. The dream pointed out the problem and I acted upon it.

PREPARATION

Go through your dream diary and decide which types of dreams have been occurring the most. They may be sexual dreams, anxiety dreams, dreams about childhood, and so on. Perhaps you have been dreaming about a specific person or place. Recurring dreams are important because they show inner conflicts or difficulties that you have not resolved. They may point to problems you are experiencing now or to unresolved problems from long ago. Many recurring dreams and nightmares deal with the issues you refuse to face.

When working with your dreams, it is important to get in the right frame of mind. It is best to be cheerful, open-minded, and prepared to accept what you discover about yourself. It is wise to be resolved that you will act on what you discover. If you recognize a fault in yourself, you may want to

EARLY DREAM INTERPRETERS

■ In the fifth century B.C., the Greek philosopher Heraclitus suggested that a person's dreams were created by his own mind. This may seem obvious but at the time this was a revolutionary idea. Other philosophers believed that outside forces were responsible for dreams. They were given to men by the gods, angels, or spirits. Aristotle took the idea a stage further and in *Parva Naturalia* suggested that dreams were in fact a recollection of the day's events. He attributed dreams to sensory impressions from "external objects... pauses within the body... eddies... of sensory movement often remaining like they were when they first started, but often too broken into other forms by collision with obstacles." Aristotle also proposed that dreams could reflect a person's health and warn of the onset of illness or give remedies and cures.

The first comprehensive book on the interpretation of dreams was the *Oneirocritica* by the Roman writer Artemidorus (A.D. 150). This five-volume work proposed that dreams were unique to the dreamer. Artemidorus argued that the person's occupation, social status, and health would influence the dream. The dream would represent these aspects of the person's life by means of symbols.

A second version of the book was written by Astrampsychus, another Roman writer. Unfortunately, instead of helping the dreamer to see the true psychological meaning of the symbols, this *Oneirocritica* version gave specific meanings to each category of dream. Some of the interpretations were ridiculous. For example, it stated, "To wear a purple robe threatens a long disease," and "To hold or eat eggs symbolizes vexation."

Although the ancients may not have understood the causes or psychological significance of dreams, they nevertheless knew that dreams were important. As messages from the gods, they could be used to guide our lives and give answers to problems that worried us. Many ancient texts are full of references to dreams. The Egyptians, Greeks, Romans, Jews, and Christians were all fascinated by dreams and based many of their personal, religious, and political decisions upon what their symbols revealed. Dream interpretation was a skilled and revered art.

correct it. Interpreting your dreams will require you to make changes in your life and in your attitude toward others. And most importantly, you will feel the urge to make changes in yourself.

Inevitably, you will be dealing with some of your most sensitive points and may unearth things about yourself you would prefer not to know. Sometimes working with dreams can be difficult. We all have petty thoughts and infantile attitudes hidden behind the mask we show the world. None of us are the people we would like to think we are. Nobody is faultless. Some of your thoughts and motives may not be wholesome. We all harbor hidden resentments, jealousies, insecurities, and so on. Bringing them to the light of day unmasks hidden fears and loosens the grip they have at an unconscious level. They will then no longer be terrifying. Finally, by resolving inner strife and integrating the dark side, it is possible to become much happier and more peaceful within.

DREAM SYMBOLS

Many of the dream guide books and dictionaries that you buy today are based on old superstitions. The specific interpretations for each dream are all but useless and say very little about the true meanings of dreams. Dream dictionaries written from a psychological standpoint can be a useful guide to help you unravel symbols you find difficult. However, dictionaries that say things such as "To dream of being scratched by a black cat signifies that an enemy will steal your business" are utter nonsense. Wacky things are fun but not much use as a tool to help you interpret dreams.

You need to know the psychological meaning of a dream and not base your interpretation on the nonsensical arbitrary interpretations of superstition. But most important are your own personal associations and feelings connected with the symbols of the dream. For example, if you are a cat lover, a cat may represent companionship, perhaps with a wild streak of independence. For another person a cat may be associated with witches or the incarnations of the Egyptian souls of the dead. Common interpretations for cats are treachery and deceit.

Every dream you have is unique to you. Dreams describe your innermost self. They reveal the truth about you. Carl Jung put it succinctly when he said that a dream "shows inner truth and reality...as it really is: not as I conjecture it to be, and not as the dreamer would like it to be, but as it is."

Symbolism is a living thing that changes and develops within society and for the individual. Many of the superstitions found in dream dictionaries are thousands of years old. Their meanings may no longer be relevant to modern times and they may mean something completely different. If you feel that the meaning in a dream book is wrong for you—even in dream books by me!—examine exactly what the dream object means for your life and go with that interpretation. There are no "oven-ready" answers to the meanings of dreams. The best way to understand them is simply to trust your instincts.

Many psychological interpretations of dreams are also dubious. For example, few people today believe that Freud was right in presuming that so much of the symbolism of dreams is sexual. Clearly some of it is,

ANGEL ARCHTYPE

and Freud made some tremendously important observations about the forces that are at work below the surface of consciousness. However, Freudian theories, like all psychology and psychological theories, are just that: theories. Theories come in and out of fashion. We still have no clear picture what dreams do or what they mean, if anything at all. The truth is, only you can decide what the real meaning of your dream is. After all, your dreams, like your thoughts, are yours.

COMMON DREAMS

Many dream images are personal: the figure of a friend, an object you once owned with particular associations, the recollection of a holiday, or a house where you once lived. To understand the meaning of most dreams you need to decipher the complex associations that you have with the many symbols that occur. However, there are also many dream symbols and themes that most people have in common. For example, have you ever dreamed of being chased? This is a metaphor for insecurity. You may feel that circumstances are closing in on you and you are at the mercy of feelings that are out of control. This type of common dream is urging you to stop running away from your problems and to face up to something. You may be attempting to escape from something about yourself you don't like. Perhaps you've done something and you want to escape the feelings of guilt or shame. Alternatively, you may be running from something that worries you in your life. For example, children who have this dream may be worried about being bullied at school.

There are many such common dreams. Flying is a common dream and usually denotes a release of tension. You may dream of being nude in public, showing that you may have sexual inhibitions or a fear of having something about you or your life exposed. You may dream of finding treasure, or dream of sex, accidents, snakes, or strange buildings. You will find that a great many people have had the same or similar dreams. Most dreams are metaphors and symbols for your emotional states of mind.

Dreams often contain archetypal images that are found in religious and mythical symbolism all over the world. Dreams use these collective symbols as artists use color. However, your dream paints pictures based on your unique experience.

DREAM INTERPRETATION

It is generally agreed that dreams are the voice of the unconscious talking to you in the language of metaphor, allegory, and symbolism. They are rarely what they seem to be and may sometimes appear to have nothing to do with your life now. However, once you observe the emotions, moods, and symbolism of your dream you will find that they are expressing things about you and your situation that are relevant to your life at the moment. They are there to help you.

EXPERIMENT

INTERPRETING A DREAM

Objective: In this experiment, you will interpret one of the dreams you have entered in your dream diary.

Step 1. Choose a dream. Choose one that is recent and that follows a similar theme as other dreams you've been having. In your dream diary, you will have written this dream on the left. You will now write your interpretation in the right-hand column.

Step 2: Examine Your Feelings. At the top of the right-hand side of the page write down the feelings the dream invokes. For example, is it a happy or sad dream? Perhaps the dream makes you feel frightened, worried, or joyous and exhilarated. If the dream contains a mixture of emotions, write all of them down. Clearly identifying the emotions the dream contains helps you see the part of your life the dream is talking about.

When did you last feel the same feelings in your waking life? If you felt fear, think about what things have frightened you lately. It may not necessarily be something tangible. You may be frightened by the implication of what someone has said to you or you may have hidden fears about a potential situation. Similarly, if you have good feelings think about the time you last felt these feelings. Perhaps they represent the way you wish you were feeling now? Often dreams will compensate for emotions that cannot be expressed in general life. Most people do not spontaneously express extreme emotions like anger or respond actively to every sexual urge. In life we have to control ourselves, but in dreams the emotions run free.

Write down the emotions in your diary and also the part of your life you feel they express. For example, you may write:

"Anger? Fear? Relationship worries? Injustice at work?" As soon as you link the feelings from your dream with something recognizable in your life, the dream may spontaneously make sense. All of a sudden, it will click. "Aha! So that's what it's talking about," you say.

If you feel sufficiently relaxed about working with your dreams, you may find that the meaning will become clear as soon as you start writing. If it does, just go with the flow and write down whatever meaning becomes immediately apparent. Usually your first thoughts about a dream's meaning are the right ones.

Step 3: Establish an Overview of the Content. Dreams describe your problems in story form. They say things such as: "My frustration with this situation feels just like walking through a muddy field," or "I feel that if my emotions get out of control it will be just like having a car accident," or "I feel so unprepared for my presentation it's like turning up for a public meeting without my notes." Ask yourself if your dream is an allegory that represents something that has been happening to you in real life. Write down your observations in your dream diary. At this stage, take an overview rather than getting tied down with specific details.

In the following steps you should make detailed notes in the column on the right and highlight any areas of the original dream that you feel are especially significant. You may also wish to make sketches, draw mind maps, or use various colored pencils to help you come to your conclusions.

Step 4: Consider the Dreamscape. The landscape you see in your dream can also express your innermost thoughts. For

SUN & MOON

example, mountains can represent the lofty planes of consciousness. It is the realm of the higher self, the part of you that has higher, transcendent knowledge. Dreaming of being at the top of a mountain may show how you now feel that you have risen above the common routines of life and achieved something with spiritual meaning. On a more mundane level, climbing a mountain may symbolize your sense of achievement and the arduous effort needed for a long-term undertaking. You are on the slippery slope of success and have the self-determination to reach the summit.

Similarly, a plain may symbolize feelings of loneliness or an easy pathway ahead. A valley may show that your choices are limited. A journey through a valley sometimes symbolizes the transition from one set of circumstances to another.

Look to see if you noted in your dream diary anything about the environment you saw in the dream. Interpret this as a symbol of the way you feel or as an expression of what you feel about the course of your life at the moment.

Buildings and houses will also express aspects of yourself. The upstairs can represent your conscious mind and the lower floors and cellar, your hidden self. The cramped feeling of the cellar can indicate frustration and a need to expand your activities or thinking. Decayed or crumbling buildings may indicate that your self-image has suffered. Different parts of a house may symbolize different times. For example, modern rooms may represent the conscious mind whereas the oldest areas may repre-

sent the ancient mind, the unconscious. Also, the condition of the building may express how you feel about yourself. Sometimes decayed buildings are the prelude to the onset of an illness.

Your moods and feelings may also be described by the weather that occurs in your dream. For example, stormy skies may show arguments and anger; sunshine may show happiness, rain may show release from tension, and snow may indicate that your emotions are frozen.

Step 5: Observe Colors and Feelings. What do the colors in your dream tell you about your feelings? Color can evoke strong emotional responses, and the colors in dreams can reveal a great deal about your emotional state. Psychologists use color tests to judge the emotional condition of their patients. However, color meanings can vary from individual to individual, and you may have your own personal associations with a particular color. Red represents passion and sexuality. It can also represent anger or blood, the color of the life force. Yellow is often associated with artistic inspiration. Yellow is sometimes considered the color of the coward. Green is the color of nature and brings new life and hope. Its negative association is with jealousy. Blue is the spiritual color. It is claimed to be the color that healers have in their auric field. Blue brings harmony and, like the sky, implies freedom. And of course, it can sometimes represent depression, when we get "the blues." Black is usually a color associated with depression. Time to get rid of those black thoughts. It may also indicate unconsciousness, whereas white is usually a symbol of purity.

Step 6: Who Is in Your Dream? If you dream of people you know, it may be your unconscious making you aware of qualities and feelings you desire. The feelings that your interaction with them gives you will be those you are becoming aware of in real life. If you dream of people you do not know, this may be a way of confronting aspects of yourself. Ask yourself what the dream says about the hidden aspects of you. Do you like the person in the dream? What does this person mean to you? Often the people and characters who appear in dreams represent aspects of you or your life.

Most of the people we dream about represent aspects of ourselves. Supposing you perceive your mother as bossy and you dream about her, your dream may be saying you're getting too bossy, just like your mother.

Step 7: What's What? The people, animals, and objects that occur in your dreams are symbols that usually comment on your feelings. For example, suppose you dream about wiping your muddy boots on a doormat. Such a dream may indicate how you treat other people. You walk all over them and rub in the dirt! The dream could also represent the way you feel others mistreat you. You could be the doormat who is being walked over. It is important to understand that you have to work your way around every symbol to come to a meaningful interpretation. Carl Jung wrote: "Even if one has great experience in these matters, one is again obliged, before each dream, to admit one's ignorance and, renouncing all preconceived

ideas, to prepare for something entirely unexpected."

You may also find that some of your dreams contain animals. Animals signify the primal, instinctive, and sometimes base desires. Your dream may be drawing your attention to an aspect of your nature that you undervalue or part of yourself that you repress. Try to get in touch with the "natural" you. Be more spontaneous and less rational. Within everyone is a deep instinctive energy that has a transforming power. Animals may also express certain qualities: for example, a dog may represent devotion, a cat may represent intuition, a tiger may represent fear, and a pig may symbolize gluttony and bad behavior. Sometimes animals can represent other people, i.e., we often describe people with animal images: "sly as a fox," "slippery as a fish," "a lying snake," "strong as an ox," etc.

Step 8: Look at the Specific Details. Once you have established a general meaning for your dream you can look at the specific details to see if they can reveal more information about the meaning of the dream. For example, dreams often contain puns. I once dreamed of using a pencil, and when I unraveled the dream I realized that it was about my friend Mark. Most of the things found in dreams are symbols specifically for you. Your dream will be drawing comparisons and will remind you of many things from your own life. It may be saying that you feel happy just like the day you got married, or you need a break just like your holiday in Florida, or the pressure you feel is just like the day you took your exams at school.

Step 9: Look Back. By considering the above aspects of your dream you will gradually unravel its mystery and come to a clearer understanding of what your dream is saying about you and your life. Having kept scrupulous dream records you also have many other dreams you can work with. You may want to note the main symbols of your dream in the back of your dream diary to form a simple dream dictionary. This will also help you identify other dreams that have a similar theme or have the same symbols. Once you have enjoyed deciphering your initial dreams you will soon be looking forward to the sequels.

INTERPRETING DREAMS FROM A LONG TIME AGO

You may find it useful to practice your interpretation skills by working with memorable dreams from the past. Try recalling your worst nightmare. Note the details in your dream diary and give an approximate date or year when it occurred. What is it that frightened you? Can you now relate these fears to problems you were experiencing at that time?

Analyze the dream using the techniques you've learned so far and try to discover what it was that was troubling you. In retrospect, it is easier to see through worries you had then now that you're free of them. If the nightmare still recurs, you will need to work with the dream to discover what it is that still calls for your attention. There may be things about yourself or your life that you don't want to know and have pushed into the unconscious. The nightmare is telling you that you need to pay attention to what the unconscious has to say. It wants to help you establish inner harmony and well-being.

Similarly, work with the best dreams you remember. Again, write down in your dream diary what you can recall about these dreams. Collect dreams the way people collect butterflies. Use your interpretation techniques to find out what your dream was telling you about your feelings at that time. Pleasurable dreams may be showing you your hopes and ambitions. Have you fulfilled these yet, or are there still hopes and wishes you have not achieved? Dreams are an important way to get to know what you really want out of life.

PUTTING YOUR DREAMS TO GOOD USE

Imagine what it would be like if you could harness the power of dreams and use dreams to solve your creative and intellectual problems. Dreams are a powerful creative tool. They reflect your emotions, feelings, anxieties, and problems but also offer solutions how to solve them. Dreams are a creative experience providing solutions to problems and occasionally giving brilliant ideas that might never occur in waking life.

Many creative people have been helped by dreams. For example, the story of *Alice in Wonderland* came to author Lewis Carroll in a dream that occurred during a period of sickness. Similarly, the English poet Samuel Taylor Coleridge claimed that he had written the poem "Kubla Khan" as the result of a dream. He fell asleep after reading about the Mongol conqueror. When he awoke, he remembered and wrote a fully developed poem which he had composed while dreaming. Also, novelist Robert Louis Stevenson said that "little people" in his dreams developed much of his writing. He specifically cited the story of *Dr. Jekyll and Mr. Hyde*, claiming it was inspired by a

SNAKE FORMING CIRCLE

dream. Likewise Jules Verne and Charles Dickens were inspired by dreams, and the characters in *Jane Eyre* were spun from the dreams of Charlotte Brontë.

Remarkable scientific discoveries have also been made because of dreams. The German chemist A. Kekulé von Stradonitz attributed his interpretation of the ring structure of the benzene molecule to his dream of a snake with its tail in its mouth, a discovery that launched the German synthetic-dye industry. Similarly, German physiologist Otto Loewi attributed to a dream inspiration for an experiment with a frog's nerve that helped him win the Nobel Prize.

In many cases, solutions given by dreams come after considerable time spent thinking about a problem. Dreams take over where the conscious mind leaves off. Dreams can sometimes cut to the heart of an issue and offer simple answers to complex problems. There are times when a dream presents a solution to a problem when you don't have all the facts at hand. It could be that some dreams access information by paranormal means. For example, naturalist Louis Agassiz dreamed of the complete form of a fossil fish that was mostly hidden within a stone slab. Stumped by the faint traces on the surface, Agassiz dreamed of and forgot the shape for two nights running. His third dream gave him the answer: he drew the dream fish while half awake. The fossil he chiseled from the stone slab the following day matched his drawing exactly.

As was observed in the first section of this book, the ancient Greeks slept in temples so the gods would give them solutions to problems in dreams. And while you might not

expect a visitation from the gods, you can still use similar techniques to ask your unconscious to provide answers to questions.

USING DREAMS TO SOLVE PROBLEMS

Objective: To program your inner computer to solve your emotional, creative, or intellectual problems.

Step 1. Clarify the problem. You need to be clear in your mind the exact nature of the problem you want to solve. You may have many troubles—work, money, exams—or may just be stumped for a creative idea. Just before you go to sleep, write your question at the top of a page in your dream diary. Keep it clear and simple, i.e., "Should I change my job?" "What is the best way to patch up my relationship?" "How should I go about refurbishing the living room?" The act of writing the question will encourage the subconscious mind to go to work on your problem.

Step 2. As you go to sleep, run through the problem in your mind. Don't just think about the question in words, use pictures as well. For example, if you are worried about your job, picture yourself at work. Imagine talking about your problems with your colleagues. Imagine the sounds and smells of the office. And most important, be positive. Avoid gloomy thoughts; you don't want to go to sleep feeling depressed.

Step 3. Once you know that the information has seeped into your unconscious, let go of the problem. Forget about it. Reassure yourself that you are doing the best you can to solve it. The subconscious is going to give you a dream that will wipe away all your troubles. Believe in what you are doing. Have faith in the power of your dreams.

Step 4. Your dreams will now do the rest. By thinking about the problem in an unattached way, you have given it to the subconscious. As you relax and enjoy a good night's sleep, your subconscious will be busy at work solving your problems. This is what it does anyway, but in this instance you are taking conscious control and using your sleep more efficiently. Normally the subconscious presents answers in a hit-or-miss way. This time you will be prepared to catch what it throws at you.

Step 5. In the morning write your dream in your dream diary. Telling yourself that you are going to dream will increase the likelihood that you will. Now interpret your dream as you did in the last experiment. What does the symbolism reveal about your situation?

Remember that dreams do not always give obvious answers. Sometimes they address a problem in an oblique way. For example, suppose you asked a question about work and then dreamed that you arrived at a business function dressed only in your underwear. Clearly, this is not something you should do (although the idea could be fun to imagine). The dream may be showing you that you feel vulnerable, exposed, and intimidated. The dream has pointed out that you are perhaps not self-assured enough to take on the corporate monster. Maybe you should wait until you feel more confident and prepared. Perhaps someone will expose a flaw in your strategy.

Use your dreams to help improve yourself. If you dream of something negative, take the opposite attitude in real life. For example, suppose you ask about a relationship and you then dream about being beaten up by the school bully. The dream may illustrate that you feel dominated in your relationship. Clearly, you feel the need to develop a more assertive attitude. Make a point of behaving in the opposite way. Throughout the day, focus on being more assertive. Write yourself a note and carry it with you: "Be assertive." Practice the dream's advice all day. If you do this, you will open new doors to self-confidence.

LUCID DREAMING FOR TOTAL RECALL

I can never decide whether my dreams are the result of my thoughts,
or my thoughts the result of my dreams.

D. H. LAWRENCE (1885–1930)

For most people dreams are a vaguely remembered experience. They are something that happened during sleep but are forgotten within moments of awakening. Most people don't realize they've been dreaming until after they have awakened and the dream has come to an end. Dreams are muddled, fuzzy, and infuriatingly hard to recall. But what if it you were able to experience dreams with the same lucidity as in normal waking consciousness? What if dreaming could be just like being wide-awake? Suppose you could wake up in a dream and experience and remember it in the same way you experience daytime events?

You may already have had one such dream. Perhaps you have "awakened" in a dream and realized you were dreaming. When it first happened to me, I dreamed of waking up, getting out of bed, and starting my usual morning routine. As I brushed my teeth, I realized I was dreaming. At that point I panicked because reality was somehow wrong. I then actually woke up. For a long time I lay in bed, unsure whether to get up or not. The dream had been so real, it was hard to know whether I was now dreaming or not.

Have you ever been dreaming, then, partway through, realized it was only a dream? Perhaps you interrupted a nightmare and realized you could stop being frightened. Dreams in which you "wake up" while the dream is taking place can become extraordinarily vivid and are believed by many societies to be especially significant. Some Native North American tribes believe it's possible to overcome many problems by using these special dreams.

Many people have the recurring dream of being chased by a shadowy figure or vicious animal. If you "wake up" in a dream such as this, according to the Native Americans, turn around to your attacker and wrestle him to the ground. In this way you will overcome your greatest fears and can become a great warrior. Similarly, if you learn to "wake up" in your dreams, you can overcome the fears that pursue you in modern life. Once challenged, such forces lose their power. There is nothing to fear, for the dreamer realizes he is dreaming and has chosen to confront his inner fears. Facing these inner demons lessens the terror they are able to exert on you. In addition, this technique creates positive psychological energy that helps you to take control of your situation and state of mind.

LUCID DREAMS

In 1913, the Dutchman van Eeden called these dreams "lucid dreams" and recognized that they were not only extraordinarily vivid but could be controlled. It has been reported that 73 percent of the population have had at least one lucid dream, and lucid dreaming comes naturally to between 5 and 10 percent.

Lucid dreams can be remembered with remarkable accuracy because they are similar to normal awareness. They are close to normal waking experience and are usually free of the irrationality and disjointed narrative of ordinary dreams. The dreamer is as conscious as in normal life and can think and remember as if wide-awake. It may appear that there is no difference between being awake and being asleep.

Awareness that the experience that seems so real is in fact a "lucid dream" occurs abruptly when the dreamer notices something unusual, inaccurate, or illogical that is happening in the dream. Something about the scenery, people, or events alerts you to the fact that you are dreaming. With this realization comes a surge of excitement and a strange feeling of higher consciousness.

Sometimes the initial reaction is frightening, because you are in such an unfamiliar state of awareness. Don't panic. Relax and go with the flow. You will soon learn to enjoy it. The inner world can appear more real than reality, with impossibly vivid colors and intricate patterns and forms. This experience may be very similar to the mescaline-induced states described by Aldous Huxley in *The Doors of Perception*: "The typical mescaline or lysergic acid experience begins with perceptions of colored, moving, living geometrical forms. In time, pure geometry becomes concrete, and the visionary perceives, not patterns, but patterned things, such as carpets, carvings, mosaics. These give place to vast and complicated buildings, in the midst of landscapes, which change continuously, passing from richness to more intensity colored richness, from grandeur to deepening grandeur."

Perhaps the most remarkable thing about lucid dreams is the dreamer's ability to control dream events like a director directing a film. The dreamer can decide where to go and what to do and can change his dream at will. Despite this, the dreamer never has complete control over the dream state. Uncontrolled events still take place and lucidity can slip in and out of ordinary dreaming. If you succeed at having a lucid dream after following the instructions later, be prepared for some surprises.

Lucid dreams have been described for centuries but are only recently being taken seriously by today's dream researchers. Freud, Adler, and Jung, although aware of them, virtually ignored them in their theories. Yet references to lucid dreaming are found in the writings of Aristotle. Saint Augustine records a lucid dream of his friend Gennadius, and Saint Thomas Aquinas also writes about them.

One of the first systematic studies of lucid dreams was made by the ancient yogis of Tibet, who were well known for their extraordinary psychic, physical, and mental abilities. According to the esteemed Oxford scholar Evans-Wentz, who edited "Tibetan Yoga and Secret Doctrines," the Tibetan adepts mastered the lucid dream state. "The yogin learns by actual experience, resulting from psychic experimentation, that the character of any dream can be changed or transformed by willing that it shall be."

DREAM DOPPELGANGERS

Many esoteric traditions claim that seizing the initiative in dreams allows the dreamer to perform seemingly impossible things. For example, Hindu mystics claim it is possible to use dreams to bilocate. In other words, they can appear in two places as the same time. This is an ancient tradition that many advanced yogis and holy men and women still practice today. Once they achieve a state of lucid dreaming they visualize a location or person to visit, then by the power of dream control can appear visible to others, not just as a hazy phantom, but solid and real. Examples of this are found in the stories of the guru Yogananda as well as in the books about the secret teachings of Tibet by authors such as Alexandra David-Neel.

My own guru, Sathya Sai Baba, first called my wife Jane and me to India through lucid dreams. He appeared to both of us in dreams and also to our daughter Danielle, then seven years old, who claims she saw him standing in the hallway at the top of the stairs beside her room. She is adamant that he was physically present!

One dream I had about Sai Baba saw me talking to him in my home office where I write my books. It was a wonderful feeling. He hugged me and we both laughed. Partway through the dream, I said, "My God, this is not a dream. This is completely real!" What I was experiencing was as real as waking consciousness. I was completely aware. It was a remarkable experience.

Sai Baba continued by telling me all about my life and what I should be doing with it. Suddenly everything seemed so simple. As I looked at him, I could see the center of his forehead open up and "thoughts" stream from him like waves of multicolored lights. Now we were talking without language. Realizing the importance of what I was experiencing and how far removed it was from my ordinary life, I said "Oh, no, I will never remember any of this! It is all a dream and dreams fade away."

Sai Baba looked at me and said: "Yes it will fade, but you will remember a little of this dream whenever you need to." With that, I saw Sai Baba turn into a television camera. "I see everything. You need only ask." When I awoke I was amazed that any dream could be so real. I could recall a great deal of the dream but knew that parts were to be remembered in the future. (Much of it was very personal.) I continued to have many vivid dreams about Sai Baba and so did my wife, Jane. They were so compelling, so real, and so mysterious that they were to lead us on a wonderful spiritual adventure to India. When we got to Sai Baba's ashram in India, we met many other people who were called via lucid dream, including some who claimed Sai Baba had appeared before them in his physical form. Some seekers have been fortunate enough to talk about their dreams with Sai Baba, who was able to tell them every detail of their dreams and the exact words they dreamed he'd said to them.

In his book *My Baba and I*, Dr. John Hislop gives a fascinating example of this ability to bilocate. Victoria, Hislop's wife, began to ask Sai Baba about an experience she'd had when she was one year old, when her mother was teaching her to walk. In the corner of the room, she remembered seeing a man and she called out to him, "Dada," and took a few steps forward. However, this puzzled her for she had just left her father in the room:

> At this point in the story, Baba interrupted and said, "Yes, yes, I was there. I was standing against the wall like this." Swamiji then stretched out his legs, crossing one over the other. Then he continued, "I had a cloth around my head like this." He illustrated by moving his hand around his head. "And I had a cloth around my waist." And, indeed that was what Victoria had seen.

The spiritually advanced teachers from India remind us that both the waking and dreaming states exist in the mind. Even what we call reality is in fact an illusion, a dream from which we will one day awaken. Men and women who have seen through the illusion realize that reality is a dream. Or, as they say in Tibet: "As images seen in a dream, thus should one see all things."

The adept who has truly awakened gains mastery not only over dreams but also over matter itself. Enlightened beings have the power to materialize items at will or to be in many places at the same time. The student who succeeds in understanding that his life is a dream that he himself supplies with pleasant or terrifying scenes can ensure that the dream does not become a nightmare. By controlling your dreams you begin to control your destiny.

According to many Eastern teachings, many yogis use lucid dreams to attain higher consciousness. Tibetan Buddhism tells that adepts of the meditative arts retain consciousness throughout dreaming and dreamless sleep. In other words, all their dreams are lucid. Tibetan teachings also advise the dreamer that, although lucid dreams can be very pleasurable, ultimately the dreamer must go beyond the phantasmagoria they watch and play a part in. This only increases the desire to remain spiritually asleep. Enlightenment—awakening—is the goal.

Today many scientists are studying lucid dreams and believe that they can be therapeutic. The ability to control the events in dreams increases the dreamer's ability to take control of his own life and face up to difficulties and challenges. Using these dreams the dreamer can reach into the unconscious, have deeper levels of self-knowledge, and unlock creative potential.

For those who have acquired the knack of lucidity, the benefits can be enormous: lucid dreaming gives you the chance to experience amazing inner adventures rarely surpassed elsewhere in life. These experiences can increase creativity and promote personal growth and self-confidence. In addition, scientific studies have shown that there is a strong connection between dreams and the biological functioning of the body. Lucid dreaming may be able to improve both your mental and physical health. In short, lucid dreaming is good for you.

Scientists have now developed lucid dream techniques aimed at help ordinary dreamers "turn" lucid:

TRIGGERING AND RECALLING LUCID DREAMS

THERE are now many techniques available to help you trigger and recall lucid dreams, but the simplest, and in my opinion the most effective, is to ask yourself many times during the day whether you are dreaming.

Objective: To trigger a lucid dream.

Step 1. Stop yourself during your daily tasks and ask yourself, "Am I dreaming?" Of course, you are not dreaming, but each time you ask this question, look for evidence proving you are not dreaming. For example, the most reliable test is to read something, look away for a moment, and then read it again. If what you read is the same twice then it is unlikely that you are dreaming. (By doing this, you are helping to establish a habit of questioning reality and will continue this habit when asleep.)

Step 2. Once you have proved to yourself that you are not presently dreaming, imagine yourself doing something you really love doing. (This time you are associating a controlled fantasy with the act of noticing that you are lucid.) Now tell yourself, "In

the same way I will remember and control my dreams." If the situation permits, say this aloud. It will reinforce the habit of questioning reality and of taking control.

Step 3. Continue to practice this technique as many times as you can over the coming weeks. You are trying to remember to wake up in your dream. It's a bit like picking up milk on the way home after reminding yourself to do so an hour before.

Step 4. Before you fall asleep say to yourself, "Tonight I will wake up in my dream." Again, you are reinforcing your inner programming to encourage a lucid dream. At first, triggering a lucid dream takes a lot of effort, but it gets easier once lucid-dream habits are established.

Step 5. Most people have their first lucid dream when they experience unusual or bizarre occurrences in their dream. You may dream of doing something that is normally impossible such as flying, levitating, or breathing underwater. In these dreams, you wake up in the dream as it is taking place. You recognize that what's happening to you is impossible and thereby realize that you are dreaming.

Step 6. Your initial reaction to "waking up" in a dream is likely to be to actually wake up, and you may not be able to retain your lucid dream state for very long. If you do, it is helpful to return to the dream immediately. In this instance, you can break your usual rule of always logging your dreams in your dream diary immediately on awakening. Go back to "sleep" but try to continue with the same dream.

■ During lucid dreams you will become completely aware that you are dreaming as the dream is taking place. However, it is still easy to forget that you are dreaming and slip back into an ordinary dream. The following simple methods will help you attain and maintain consciousness during your lucid dream. All the methods are designed to encourage you to question the reality of your dream and help you realize that you are dreaming. There are many methods you can try and you may enjoy making up your own. Here are some of the most widely used lucid dream techniques:

Look at Your Hands

Most people find this the simplest way to take control of a dream. By looking for your hands in a dream you use the power of your will to control the dream. This technique was suggested in the books of Carlos Castenada in which he allegedly meets a Yaqi Indian sorcerer who instructs him in the art of dreaming. His teacher Don Juan Matus tells him to look for his hands while dreaming. This establishes a link between the waking lives and the dreaming lives. Looking at the hands is a cue to lucidity. (In fact any object could act as your lucid dream trigger. For example, you could decide that every time you see a tree in your dream it will act as your inner prompt that you're about to go lucid.)

Dream Jumping and Flying

Only in dreams can you fly or make superhuman jumps into the air. When you start to become conscious during a dream, try this simple reality test: jump into the air and try to prolong your stay up in the air. Even if you stay up for a split second longer than you would in waking life it will prove to you that this is not waking reality. You are dreaming. You can try doing other impossible things such as walking through walls or growing wings. All these illogical events will reinforce the realization that you are dreaming.

Dream Illiteracy

In an ordinary dream it is often difficult to read. Words often appear nonsensical. If you find yourself reading in a dream, prove to yourself that you are dreaming by reading the same thing again. It is most likely that the information you already read will have changed.

Dream Memory

When you are awake it is easy to remember what you have been doing over the last few hours. Try doing this in a dream. You will discover that you either have no past at all or a very strange one. This method will help you recognize that you are dreaming, as this is clearly not normal reality.

Change Reality

In normal waking life only people like Uri Geller can influence the material world with the power of the mind. However, in a dream anything is possible. Pick up an object from your dream and see if you can bend it with the power of your mind. If the object bends to your mental command you are obviously dreaming.

Step 7. As you return to the dream, you will discover that you have some control over the way it progresses. Try gently to steer its course. You may want to change it slightly by adding another character or event that wasn't in the first dream. By doing this you gradually learn to influence and change dreams. Also, remind yourself: "I am dreaming, I want to remember to recognize that I am dreaming." At first, it may be difficult to retain your lucidity for very long and you will fall back into ordinary dreaming. With practice, you will extend your period of control.

Step 8. In the morning, enter the lucid dream into your dream diary. (Write "Lucid Dream" beside it so you can compare it with other lucid dreams you will have in the future.) What was the dream content that first helped it turn lucid? Perhaps next time you dream about this same thing it will again trigger lucid dreaming.

Step 9. Once you've ingrained the question "Is this a dream?" into your consciousness, you can expand the range of questions. You could ask, "How do I know that I am not dreaming?" or "What would be different about this situation if I were dreaming right now?" Again you will need to continually repeat these questions to yourself until you spontaneously ask them in your sleep.

Once you have mastered lucid dreaming, your dreams will never be the same again. The problem of recall will diminish because your dreams will be so vivid that it will be hard not to remember them. Your dreams can become almost as clear as normal waking consciousness.

However, not every night should be spent in dream aerobics. Too much of a good thing may interfere with your sleep patterns. I've certainly found in my own experience that a series of nights spent lucid dreaming can leave me tired and moody. It is of course exciting to start having lucid dreams, and the temptation is to keep on trying for better and better results. Understand that lucid dreams are most readily achieved with an attitude that is concentrated, persistent, and at the same time playful. You should consider it an enjoyable, creative experience. It is not an act of will but a gentle art.

IMPROVING LUCID RECALL

According to many Eastern religions, all life is a dream. To start remembering to awaken from a dream is to begin lifting the veil of illusion. The Hindus call this *Maya*. Maya is the dream we dream while awake, the illusion that this is all there is. Realizing the illusory nature of dreams you have in sleep may help you see through the illusion of what you believe to be reality. Lucid dreams may be a useful tool to help you attain spiritual realization and enlightenment.

In dreaming, the brain relies on its own internal stimulation rather than external stimulation to create the dream situations, characters, and dreamscapes. It is a complete inner world but is as much part of reality as is perception of the outer world. Both worlds are constructed by the workings of the brain. This book that you now hold in your hands and read is actually a picture, with sensations of touch, that is formed in your head by information given to the brain by your perceptions. It is a picture reconstructed by the chemistry and electrical conditions of your brain.

You cannot prove what reality is. Many mystics believe that realities exist outside normal awareness but can be accessed through dreams. Once you master lucid dreaming, anything is possible.

By following the exercises and techniques in this book you are probably now able to recall more than one dream per night. You have developed a rapport with your unconscious, realize that dreams are important and useful, and are more likely to be able to move into the lucid dream state. Increasing your ability to recall was your first and most difficult step. And most importantly, you have created within yourself the desire to master the art of dreaming. Without intent, dream recall is difficult. Just as the desire to have a dream increased the likelihood that you would have one, so too will your desire to have a lucid dream increase the likelihood you will have one.

Lucid dreaming is a form of dream recall in which you remember the dream as it is taking place. Lucid dreams are easier to remember than ordinary dreams, but you should continue to note them in your dream diary and continue to use the recall methods that you mastered earlier in this book.

USING REM CYCLES TO IMPROVE LUCID DREAMING

One of the first ways suggested for remembering a dream is to set the alarm to ring earlier than usual to interrupt a REM period (when your eyes rapidly move beneath the lids as you dream). There are products on the market that can detect eye movement and turn a light on, causing you to become aware that you are dreaming without waking up. These are very good products. It is also possible to interrupt a REM cycle without having to wear this special sleep mask.

Objective: The object of the next experiment is to wake up before you have finished sleeping and then return from an ordinary dream state to a lucid dream state. Try this over the weekend, when you have no work obligations.

Step 1. Sleep cycles last from about 90 to 120 minutes. Set your alarm to go off 100 minutes before you ordinarily wake up so you interrupt the start of your next dream cycle.

Step 2. When the alarm wakes you, remain awake for the whole cycle before returning to sleep (100 minutes).

Step 3. When the time has elapsed, go back to sleep.

Step 4. Within about five minutes you will begin to have vivid dreams. By waking up early, and staying awake for a full REM cycle, you have deprived yourself of essential dream time. You have created a temporary REM deficit, which leads into extended REM once you return to sleep. Your dreams are likely to become intense very quickly.

Step 5. Use this opportunity of intense dreaming to seize control of the dream.

GETTING UP TOO EARLY

A REM deficit occurs if you get up too early. When you are deprived of this essential period of dreaming, your mind will compensate at the earliest opportunity. If you take a catnap in the afternoon, you are likely

ALARM CLOCK

to go straight into a dream cycle immediately because of the REM deficit from the morning. You will increase the likelihood of turning these dreams into lucid dreams if you can hold yourself on the brink between waking and sleeping.

Some of the most vivid dreams of my life occurred when I worked on a kibbutz in Israel. We would get up at 3:00 a.m. and work in the fields until 11:00 a.m. After breakfast we would take a siesta. These catnaps were extraordinary experiences as I was thrown into an immediate lucid dream state. In one of these "dreams" I saw the city of Haifa being destroyed by an earthquake. At the next day's work session in the banana groves I started to tell a friend about my vivid dream. Within seconds, the ground beneath us started to shake.

It was only a minor earth tremor and not the cataclysmic disaster I saw in my lucid dream, but the experience demonstrated to me in a startling way that lucid dreams can give us access to information through clairvoyance.

TIBETAN LUCID DREAM CONTROL

Once you have mastered becoming conscious while a dream is taking place, the next step is to take control of the dream. This all sounds very dramatic but is a very old art and is accessible to anyone who is prepared to work with dreams. Dream control is an integral part of the mystical teachings of Tibetan yoga and of many shamanic traditions. Tibetan Buddhists believe that controlling dreams gives control in the realms after death.

One of the most important Tibetan Buddhist texts is the *Bardo Thodol*, better known as *The Tibetan Book of the Dead*, which explains how to travel in the worlds beyond death and also gives guidance about controlling the dream state. *Bardo* means "intermediate state" and denotes the period that lies between a person's death and his rebirth. *Thodol*, pronounced *"thos grol,"* means "liberation through understanding." The *Bardo Thodol* is a "treasure text," which means it is attributed to Shakyamuni Buddha himself.

According to the *Bardo Thodol*, we can divide our existence into four interlinked realities: life, dying and death, after death, and rebirth. These are called the four *bardos*: the natural *bardo* of this earthly life, the painful *bardo* of dying, the luminous *bardo* of *dharmata*, and the karmic *bardo* of becoming. (*Bardo* is a Tibetan word that translates as "transition." *Bar* means "in between" and *do* means "suspended.") These texts are read to the dying and are believed to help them either enter the light of pure consciousness or attain a better rebirth. Many lamas occupy themselves with the writings of the *Bardo Thodol* throughout their lives and not just at the time of death.

Bardos have been likened to a gap, or a period in which the possibility of awakening to higher consciousness is present. These opportunities can happen at times of great uncertainty, particularly when dying, but also, to a lesser extent, at times of crisis. To the Tibetan Buddhist, the turbulent uncertainty that prevails in modern life provides plenty of opportunity to experience the *bardos* without having to die to do it!

Bardos are opportunities but at the same time they are the inner incentive that drives you to seize the opportunity they offer.

They can represent different states of reality as well as different states of consciousness. Tibetan Buddhists believe that lucid dreams are a doorway into these sought-after states of consciousness.

TIBETAN CLOUD-WALKING

According to the Tibetans, going to sleep is similar to the *bardo* of dying. In deep sleep the elements and thought processes dissolve and open into the experience of "ground luminosity" (described as the dawning nature of the mind). Also, there is a *bardo* to be found between the period after falling asleep and the period before dreams begin. This is called the *bardo dharmata* and is said to be the "radiance of the nature of the mind," also known as the "clear light."

Dreaming is akin to the karmic *bardo* of becoming, which to the dying person is the intermediate state that lasts right up to the moment of taking a new birth. In this state the dreamer has a clairvoyant and highly mobile "dream body" (also translated as the "mental body").

The dream body is similar to the duplicate etheric body described by mediums and by spiritualists, and is called the "spirit body." Similarly, the Hindus describe it as the "subtle body," which carries the *Jiva*, or personal self, into the afterlife or to the next incarnation. It is a body made of life energy and appears as light. It is a spiritual duplicate of the physical body.

While in the dream body you feel extremely light, lucid, and mobile. The Tibetans tell us that its awareness is seven times clearer than in life. In this form you are endowed with clairvoyance and, in particular, have the power of telepathy, the ability to read minds or communicate by thought. The dream body can pass through walls and go wherever it wishes unobstructed. If you think of a place or person, you are instantly transported there by the power of thought. In this *bardo* world, you can meet many other travelers and converse with the spirits of people who have died.

The Tibetan Book of the Dead says that it is very difficult to retain awareness while in the dream body while still alive. The experience of these states at death is of course far more powerful than anything experienced in sleep. The Tibetan masters also teach that remaining conscious during the dream state can prepare a person for death because, as in ordinary dreams, the spirit can lose awareness in the after-death state. Also, say the Tibetans, the state of your mind in the sleep state and dream states indicates how your mind will be in the corresponding *bardo* states after death. According to the Tibetans, the way you react to dreams and nightmares shows how you might react when you die.

Tibetans therefore consider lucid dreaming to be a high form of spiritual yoga and as important as meditation. Meditation is the yoga of the day and lucid dreaming is the yoga of the night.

LEARNING TO FLY

Many lucid dreamers claim they dream of being able to fly. It is a thrilling means of travel. Many dream flyers claim it is a real experience that transcends the illusory dream state. Some find deliberate dream flying a useful tool that has helped them return from the nightmare of an endless

THE DREAM BODY

fall. Dream flying usually brings with it a feeling of safety, exhilaration, and pleasure.

Objective: In this first flying lesson, you will fly using lucid dreaming techniques. By practicing these methods, you will gain greater mastery over dreams. It is one more step toward complete recall, as you retain your waking consciousness during sleep.

Dreaming of flying is a form of dream control that is easy to master. It is great fun, gives you a wonderful sense of freedom, and is the perfect means of travel in the dream world.

Step 1. Whatever you focus your attention on grows in strength. Over the next few weeks, pay particular attention to dreams that hint at dream flight. Note any symbols of flight, such as dreams about birds, air-planes, and so on. You may spontaneously dream about flying or falling. Many people dream of falling as they "fall" to sleep. This can be caused by a drop in blood pressure or the movement of the fluid in the middle ear. Turn your fall into a flight.

Step 2. Whenever you become aware that you are dreaming, try to turn all movements into flight. Fly rather than walk. You can reinforce this during your waking life by imagining what it would be like if you could fly to your destination. Every time you take a stroll, think about flying. This will help you to condition yourself to fly in dreams.

Step 3. Before you go to sleep, use dream incubation to encourage a dream about flying. In bed, repeat these words: "Tonight I fly." As you say them, imagine yourself flying. Think about all the different landscapes you could fly over and remember the times you have flown in an airplane.

Step 4. If you find yourself flying, you are of course dreaming. Once you realize that you are dreaming you will be reminded of your desire to fly. As you continue flying, say to yourself: "This is a dream." This will increase your lucidity and help you remain conscious throughout the dream.

LINDBERGH'S ASTRAL FLIGHT

■ Charles Lindbergh was the U.S. aviator who made the first solo non-stop flight across the Atlantic Ocean from New York to Paris in 1927. In the 22nd hour into his flight aboard his monoplane Spirit of St. Louis, he was enveloped in a dense fog. He battled to keep in control, on course, and awake.

Fifty years later he recalled: "I existed independently of time and matter. I felt myself departing from my body as I imagine a spirit would depart—emanating into the cockpit, extending through the fuselage as though no frame of fabric walls were there, angling upward, outward, until I reformed in an awareness far distant from the human form I left in a fast-flying transatlantic plane. But I remained connected to my body through a long-extended strand, a strand so tenuous that it could have been severed by a breath."

He denied that his experience was a hallucination brought on by extreme fatigue. In his autobiography he wrote: "My visions are easily explained away through reason, but the longer I live, the more limited I believe rationality to be."

Step 5. As you become comfortable with this unusual state, you may want to try a few experiments. You can try jumping off cliffs, leaping high into the air, or running at high speed, taking huge steps before you take off. Win your cosmic pilot's wings by continually practicing your flying skills.

Of course you cannot hurt yourself, but take it easy at first just in case so you don't get scared. Don't try this awake.

Step 6. If you become skilled at "waking up" during flying dreams, you may want to try experiments to test the limits of this state. For example, can you fly to the moon or Mars? How high can you fly? Can you fly through brick walls? How fast can you go? This dream fantasy will bring you hours of fun!

OUT-OF-BODY DREAMS

In the last experiment, your flying dream was fantasy. It is a useful method to help you recall dreams by intensifying your lucidity. But what if it were actually possible to fly? Suppose there were a way to have a real flying experience. Suppose you could step out of your physical body and fly over the Earth and through strange new worlds.

Many philosophies and religions believe that the spirit and the body exist separately and that the spirit body survives after death. Many people also believe that it is possible for the spiritual body to journey outside the physical body during deep meditation, at a time of extreme shock or critical illness, or during dreams.

In this next experiment, you will learn to leave your physical body. Once you perfect this technique you will be able to access the planes of existence that contain the collective storehouse of human knowledge and memory that mystics call the "akashic record."

EXPERIMENT

HOW TO TRAVEL IN THE DREAM BODY

DR. Eugene E. Barnard has estimated that one out of every 100 people experiences out-of-body travel at some time. It is certainly not a new phenomenon and descriptions can be found in many ancient texts. For example, the ancient Egyptians thought of the astral body, or *ba*, as a birdlike spirit with a human head. In the Old Testament, the prophet Elisha is described as moving through the air into the bedroom of the hostile Syrian king. Here he overheard the king's military plans and was able to warn the Israelites of the forthcoming Syrian attack. Mystics have given this spiritual body many different names including the "astral body," the "body of light," the "duplicate body," the "etheric body," and the "dream body."

In modern times, Theosophy and Spiritualism took a great interest in OBE phenomena. The British physicist and vocal Spiritualist Sir Oliver Lodge undertook a great deal of research into OBEs. He was also a member of the Society for Psychical Research, which in 1886 published a collaborative work by its leading members called *Phantasms of the Living*. This massive two-volume book by SPR members Edmund Gurney, Frederic Myers, and Frank Podmore took three years to compile and was hugely influential. It cataloged 702 cases of "crisis apparitions," or appearances of the dead at or immediately after the moment of death. It also cited many instances where the apparitions were of living people who had temporarily left their mortal frame. Some instances told of cases where people claimed to have purposely willed their discarnate selves to appear in the view of others.

One of the most famous contemporary out-of-body travelers was businessman Robert Monroe. He had his first OBE in 1958 and initially thought he might be hallucinating or going insane. He was at first shocked and distressed at what was happening to him. However, soon he began to enjoy his out-of-body journeys and delighted in his amazing discoveries.

Monroe began to log his explorations into the non-corporeal worlds in a dream journal. He kept meticulous records and participated in laboratory experiments to find out more about the phenomenon. In 1971, he published *Journeys Out of the Body*. This first-person account of his multi-dimensional journeys became a bestseller. Eventually Monroe gave up his business and concentrated full time on his OBE experiments. Today The Monroe Institute is dedicated to the research and understanding of OBE phenomena.

This next experiment is based loosely on Monroe's recommendations:

Objective: To travel in the dream body.

Step 1. Lie on your bed in a dark room and in a comfortable position. If possible, lie with your head pointing north. The Earth's magnetic field will help your release. (Some modern mystics think that the special alignments of places such as Stonehenge and the Pyramids were designed to enable people in the ancient world to have OBEs. In one OBE of my own, these places had an irresistible pull. My own feeling is that they are sign-posts to the astral realm. They point the way or act as reference points by using the powers of the Earth's energies. You become conscious of these energies when moving in the astral body.)

Step 2. Let yourself relax completely. Close your eyes and become aware of how your breathing slows. It becomes more rhythmical as you sink deeper into total relaxation. You may want to reread the relaxation experiments in the first part of this book in order to ensure that you relax as completely as possible. This is a very important.

Step 3. As you drift toward sleep, focus on a single image. Once you are in a state that is neither sleep nor wakefulness, deepen your relaxation by concentrating on the blackness beyond your eyelids.

Step 4. Now focus on a point about 12 inches (30 cm) from your forehead. Gradually extend the point of focus to a distance of about six feet (1.8 m). Some people find it easier to focus on a tangible object such as a light fixture or a mark on the ceiling. Keep your eyes closed but imagine that you are drawing it toward you. When an OBE takes place, you will realize that it is not being drawn toward you. You are being drawn toward it! This is one way also to move around the astral world. Imagine drawing objects toward yourself. This will help you move in the astral form. If you think movement, it becomes a fact.

Step 5. Imagine that there is a line parallel to your body. Focus on this plane and imagine that vibrations are running down it and toward you and into your head. Monroe claims that awareness of vibrations is a sign that you are close to an OBE. In my own experiments I usually become aware of a deep purple light at this stage and am aware that I can see the room even though my eyes are closed.

Step 6. Once this feeling of vibration becomes clear, then you are ready to leave your body. You may find it easier to imagine the vibration as a pulsing light that fills you. Alternatively, perhaps you are better working with sound vibrations. For example, inwardly chanting the Hindu "om" mantra can increase your awareness. Use the imagination to trigger the sensations that accompany an OBE.

Step 7. To leave the body, concentrate on how pleasant it would be to float upward. You may imagine that the physical body is heavy like clay whereas you are as light as a feather. You are a wisp of fine smoke. You may prefer a more dynamic image. You can imagine that you are in an elevator or aboard a rocket. If sound appeals to you, you may imagine that the mantra is rising in pitch. You could think words such as "up," "flying," "lightness," "feathers," "clouds," and so on. You may be aware of physical sensations as you leave your body. For example, you may alternate your awareness between the heavy sensation of the physical body and the lightness of your spirit.

Step 8. These techniques will become easier with practice. Try them every time you go to bed. Eventually you will have the sensation of floating upward and leaving your physical body.

Step 9. Returning to the physical body is much easier, and there is no danger that you will be "locked out." Simply think about the physical body and the two entities will re-engage.

When I was a teenager, I had my first out-of-body experience. I was so shocked to see my body lying on the bed, I panicked. The result was that I reentered my body like a whiplash. I heard a loud bang like a gun firing, and there was a brilliant flash of white light. I awakened drenched in sweat.

This need not happen to you. At the time, I had never heard about astral traveling so my immediate assumption was that I was dead. The shock triggered a very fast return to the physical body, which resulted in the uncomfortable sensations I experienced. Remain calm and your OBEs will be pleasant experiences.

THIRD EYE

Out-of-body travel can be further improved if you learn to open your spiritual center called the "third eye." This is one of the vital chakras, which are wheels of spiritual energy found at various focal points in the body.

The first chakra is found at the base of the spine at the coccyx, the second is just below the navel, the third is at the solar plexus just below the rib cage, the fourth approximates the level of the heart, the fifth comes at the level of the throat, and the sixth is at the eyebrow level. This sixth chakra is nick-

DREAM BODY SENSATIONS AND PERCEPTIONS

Paralysis

As you come close to an OBE, you will have the feeling that the body is rigid. You may feel that you cannot manipulate your own limbs.

Weightlessness

When you separate from the physical body, you will experience a feeling of weightlessness. This can be a very enjoyable feeling that brings with it a feeling of freedom.

Attachment

Some claim to see a silver umbilical cord that joins the astral and physical bodies. It attaches from the astral body to the head of the physical body. As the two bodies move farther apart the cord becomes thinner but will not break.

Perceptions

You will experience colors as being preternaturally sharp and vivid. You will have a heightened awareness of sound.

Vitality

The physical body will appear dull and lifeless, whereas your astral self will feel vital, energetic, and alive.

Movement

You will travel at the speed of thought. Think of a place and you will go there immediately. You can slow down or increase your movements by focusing on the physical objects around you. Draw them to you very slowly and you will add grace to your astral movements.

named the "third eye," and above it, at the top of the head, is the seventh chakra, called the "crown chakra." As the spiritual energies rise through these centers, the person becomes more spiritually aware and can develop psychic and paranormal powers.

For centuries, the sixth chakra at the third eye has been considered the point where the spirit and body meet. As long ago as the fourth century B.C., Herophilus described it as the organ that regulated the flow of thought. (He compared it to the sphincter!) Its position at the center of the forehead and just above the eyebrows is directly even with the pineal gland, which is located in the center of the brain. This tiny but important gland controls the production of hormones that influence consciousness. When you meditate or concentrate on the center of the forehead, you influence this gland. Melatonin is manufactured by the pineal gland through the action of a hormone upon serotonin, a chemical messenger that transmits nerve impulses across synapses. It is thought that these chemicals are somehow connected to the higher functions in people. This appears to confirm the mystical significance of this area of the brain.

During out-of-body travel, energy emanating from near the third eye links the spiritual self to the body.

Earlier you learned how to open the throat chakra in order to stimulate dream activity. (See page 34.) In the next experiment you will open this center again and also the third eye center. This technique can be used before the out-of-body experiment explained earlier and will make it easier to stimulate out-of-body travel. In addition, it is likely to increase the lucidity of your normal dreams should you fall asleep during the experiment.

THE THIRD EYE

The objective of these out-of-body experiments is to access information that is normally denied you. They increase your ability to recall ordinary dreams but also give you admission to the "akashic record," the cosmic register of all phenomena throughout history.

EXPERIMENT

THIRD-EYE CHAKRA EXPERIMENT

Objective: To open the chakras in order to travel in the dream body and increase the vividness of your dreams.

Step 1. Lying flat on your back, allow yourself to relax very deeply.

Step 2. Visualize a brilliant blue light unfolding at the top of the throat chakra. See it open like a lotus flower of brilliant blue light. You may feel a slight sensation in your throat as this center opens, and you may feel your head push backward into your pillow.

Step 3. Now see the light gradually move upward toward the center of the forehead. As it does, the color turns a beautiful purple. This is the color associated with the third eye, but you may also see many other splendid colors as this center unfolds.

Step 4. As this lotus unfolds, be aware of how the purple light now floods the whole head. Bathe yourself in this beautiful soothing radiance. Notice that you also feel a slight tightening around your whole head as this center gradually opens. You may

notice many beautiful multicolored lights coming from your peripheral vision.

Step 5. Once this center is activated, you can continue with the out-of-body experiment you tried previously. You will have at your disposal great quantities of psychic energy when you open this center in this way.

Step 6. Only try this experiment occasionally, as it uses a great amount of spiritual energy if you go to sleep with your third-eye center open. You may feel extremely sensitive in the morning.

Step 7. After any experiments with the chakras, is important to close them down. If you awaken after an OBE, or first thing in the morning, you should close the center as soon as you are ready. To do this, imagine that the energy in the center is quieting down. Then see it gradually fade to darkness as the lotus flower closes its petals. All is still. Light can get neither in nor out. It is closed.

Result: Doing this technique as you fall to sleep will increase the vividness of your dreams and improve your ability to project the dream body.

SHARED DREAM MEMORIES

Out-of-body travelers claim that they meet people from other regions of existence. This may include other dimensions, the afterlife spheres, the angelic kingdoms, the elemental regions of nature, and even the astral worlds of other planets. Some of this may be real, but much may be fantasy. To prove to yourself that your OBE experiences are real, do this next dream experiment with a friend or with a group of spiritually minded friends. It will sharpen your recall ability, because you and your team are going to remember the same dream!

I WILL MEET YOU IN MY DREAMS

Objective: To meet your friends in a dream. A "communicator" will bring with them a target image that is to be "seen" by the other dreamers (the "receivers").

Step 1. Choose one of your team to be the dream communicator for the night's experiment. It is best if this person is a good lucid dreamer or has had previous out-of-body dreams. The rest of the team will be dream receivers.

Step 2. Plan to meet in your dreams at a landmark known by all of you. Choose somewhere that is easily recognized yet not too busy at night. For example, you could arrange to meet in a city art gallery beside a specific painting or sculpture, at a statue in the park, or on top of a tall public building. Distance makes no difference, but it needs to be a place that is known well by all of you.

Step 3. You will now all agree to meet in your dreams at this place on a specific night. When you get there, you will all look for the communicator, who will show the rest of the team an image known only to him/her. If you have a number of people working together, you can have two or more communicators who will decide secretly in advance what the target image will be. This will increase the likelihood of someone's being at the site to transmit the target image when the receivers arrive.

Step 4. The communicators should decide the target image and go to bed knowing what it is. For example, if the chosen image is a box of corn flakes, the communicator should put a box of corn flakes beside the bed. This will reinforce the picture in the communicator's mind. You can choose anything you like that would be feasible to carry in real life: a cuddly toy, a newspaper, a cup of tea, a funny hat, a mask, and so on.

Step 5. Do the lucid dream or dream body experiments and attempt to move toward the target venue. You have only to think about the location and you will go to it. Team members should put a photograph of the place beside their bed to reinforce the image. (If you choose a well-known landmark, you could use a postcard.)

Step 6. Communicators should attempt to show the selected object to the dreamers they meet at the landmark. If they see members of the team, they should give them the object or make them aware of what it is. For example, if the target object is a box of corn flakes, the communicator should shake it so they hear it. Also, feed them some so they taste it. Hold the box in front of them and even make them touch it. Get all the senses involved so the image is shown in as many different ways as possible. If you get to the target landmark and nobody is there, leave the imaginary box of corn flakes at the location. If you are a receiver and you get to the deserted landmark, look around to see if you can see any unusual objects.

Step 7. Some of you will have very strong lucid dreams about the location. However, do not dismiss dreams that are not about the target place. The information you are looking for may be hidden in what appears to be an ordinary dream.

Step 8. When you wake up, note in your dream diary what you saw. No matter how insignificant it is, write it down. Note everything you dreamed that night, even if there appears to be no hint of the target location.

Step 9. Once you have recorded your notes, you and your friends should get together as soon as possible. Go through your dream diary entries and see if your dreams have any similarities. You are likely to discover that the dream target has been changed in some way. For example, if you were shown the box of corn flakes you may have dreamed of eating, or perhaps you dreamed that you were grocery shopping in a supermarket. You may not have seen the target image exactly but you nonetheless understood the nature of the image that was being given to you.

You may also find that many of your dreams have similar themes that have nothing to do with the target location or image. This may indicate that you and your team are developing a telepathic rapport. You are communicating thoughts but not yet traveling out of the body. When your conscious mind relaxes in sleep, your psychic abilities are at their peak. And in dreams you can communicate your inner thoughts to people you know.

RECALLING PAST LIVES

The soul in sleep gives proof of its divine nature.

MARCUS TULLIUS CICERO (106–43 B.C.)
ROMAN ORATOR AND STATESMAN

HAVE you ever thought that you may have lived before? A growing number of people now believe in reincarnation, the philosophy that says that after death the soul transmigrates and is born again in a new body. Many people today also believe in metempsychosis, which proposes that you can also be born into an animal form after death or that you may have been an animal before becoming a human. For example, if a person lives like a pig or a snake in this life the person may be reincarnated as a snake or a pig.

Belief in reincarnation has been with us a long time. The *Vedas*—the 9,000-year-old texts of the Hindus—teach that the soul (*jiva*) moves from body to body over eons of time. It may sojourn for a while in the heavenly worlds, if it has done good deeds while on earth, but it will in time reincarnate again in order to evolve spiritually. Its ultimate goal is to realize its unity with God. Many other Eastern religions believe in reincarnation. Tibetan Buddhists believe that highly evolved souls, such as the Dalai Lama, can choose which womb they will be born from for their next life. On the death of a great Lama a search is organized to discover the whereabouts of the new baby Lama. Occasionally these souls are born to Western families.

But the belief in reincarnation is not limited to the East. Orpheus, Pythagoras, Plato, and certain Gnostics and Kabbalists explicitly referred to reincarnation in their writings. Some historians believe that the early Christians may have held similar beliefs. For example, many believers in reincarnation say that the migrating soul accumulates karma. This is the potential carried by a person that dictates what good and bad things will befall the person. It is determined by the good and bad actions in this life. Similarly, the fruits of an earlier life are carried on to the next. Some argue that when Jesus said, "As you sow so shall you reap," he was referring to the cosmic laws of karma and reincarnation.

Today many spiritual and psychological techniques have been devised in order to access our lost memories of earlier existences. Regressive hypnosis, meditation, visualization exercises, aura awareness, channeling, and so on are all effective. But perhaps the simplest and safest method is the spontaneous insight that can come through dream recall.

DREAMING TO REMEMBER CHILDHOOD

One of the most mysterious qualities about dreams is their ability to recall events as if they happened only moments ago. Most of us have had dreams about our childhood. The settings, the people, and the atmosphere can be tremendously vivid. Yet if we try to recall these things in waking life they are just fuzzy and half-remembered events. We all have a number of childhood memories that are clear in our minds, but in dreams old memories come alive. In a dream we may meet our childhood friends and enemies and it feels as if not a single day has passed. Dreams open parts of the memory that are normally inaccessible.

In order to recall past lives you must first train the subconscious to recall as much of your childhood as it can. Initially you may be content with the pleasure at remembering childhood memories, but later you can push your dreams back to the time of your birth and then back even further to your past lives.

Of course you must also proceed with care. Not all childhood memories are good ones, and you may uncover the source of many of your inner fears. Proceed gently, one step at a time, and be prepared to discover both good and bad things about yourself. Approach this hidden world with a spirit of acceptance, and be honest with yourself in recognizing your strengths and weaknesses.

The thoughts and feelings you have before going to sleep can easily determine your dreams. Just as your dreams can be influenced by a television program you watched before going to bed, so too can your dreams be influenced by suggestions just before going to sleep. Before going to sleep say to yourself: "Tonight I will dream about my childhood." Say it aloud many times, as this will strengthen the suggestion. You can also reinforce the inner commands by looking at photographs of your childhood or photos of places that remind you of your childhood.

By using these techniques regularly every night you will soon start dreaming about your childhood. Influencing dreams this way is called dream incubation. The brain is like a biological computer that can be programmed. Asking your unconscious to do specific things while you sleep helps you control your feelings and worries. These techniques give you a command over the subconscious and can increase your self-confidence.

Write down any dreams that come to you and pay particular attention to dreams that remind you of your childhood. You may want to spend some time thinking about associated memories. For example, if you dream about being at school, spend some time remembering everything you can about the place. Think about your old friends, the teachers, the smells, the sounds, the times you did well, and the times you got in trouble. Take an imaginary journey down its corridors. Relive your time there as if it were only yesterday. Your dreams will help you bring the past alive and your memories will become astonishingly vivid.

DREAMING TO REMEMBER
YOUR BIRTH

Once you've established a pattern of remembering early childhood memories, the next step is to encourage your subconscious to recall your very first memories from when you were a baby and right back to the moment you were born. Look through your dream diary to see if any of your dreams relate to early childhood. You may be surprised how many there are. Dreams take no notice of time. In dreams, memories from your early years are just as vivid as the ones you can recall from yesterday.

It is a fascinating exercise to see just how much you can remember from your early life. For example, I have a hazy memory of being in the pram. I am aware of the sunshine streaming into my warm resting place. I feel wonderfully comfortable and at ease with the world and myself. Lined across the hood of the pram I can see red and yellow shapes that make a rattling sound when I hit them. I can remember my frustration at not quite being able to hit them with my tiny hands. According to my mother, four plastic ducks threaded with elastic were stretched across the hood of my pram. They were yellow and red. Beads would rattle if I hit them.

Practice remembering your childhood. Many of the techniques you have already learned can be applied to remembering long-forgotten people, events, and places from your distant past. Take another look at the section about dream recall and use the techniques to recover ordinary memories as well

as dream memories. Can you remember the wallpaper in your bedroom? What was your favorite childhood food? How many Christmas mornings and birthdays can you recall? Can you remember being reprimanded and praised?

We tend to think that we have long forgotten about the events of our own birth, but even if our conscious mind has forgotten, recorded in our unconscious is everything and every event that ever happened to us, including our birth experience. Rebirthing therapists point out that birth is a traumatic experience that is remembered by the body on a cellular level. The baby's experience of the pain of birth, the cutting of the umbilical cord, the drugs used at birth, and clinical procedures result in trauma. Memories of birth are soon repressed but will reemerge in adulthood as behavioral flaws and social maladjustment. A study done at San Quentin, a high-security prison in California, showed that over 80% of the inmates had had violent births. These included cesareans or births that involved invasive procedures and instruments.

It is claimed that recalling the trauma of birth can help you overcome many unexplained fears and anxieties. For our purpose birth recall is a stepping stone to the time before you were born and the lives you led before your spirit entered your mother's womb.

By working with the childhood memories given to you by your dreams you will also draw closer to the unconscious memories you have of birth and of being in the womb. As you did earlier, you need now to encourage your subconscious to remember this event and reveal it to you in a dream. This time, as you go to sleep say to yourself: "Tonight I will dream about my birth." Say it aloud many times to strengthen the suggestion. You have set your biological computer to run with a new program.

If you dream about your birth, you may experience the sensation of floating in the womb, being attached to the umbilical cord, being pushed down a dark tunnel, or feeling vulnerable. These dreams can be accompanied by many strange sensations that are hard to describe. Because of this, your dreams are likely to translate your birth and womb experiences into symbols such as floating in or swimming under the sea.

Here's an example from my own dream diary that I believe relates to the moment of my birth. It is a dream that has recurred throughout my life, particularly during my childhood.

> *I feel warm and secure. I have a feeling of floating and of well-being. Now there is a rumbling sound. My skin feels tight, as if my whole body is enfolded in rubber. I feel pressure all over. I have a sense of suffocation. The sounds get louder. The warm feeling of security changes to one of anxiety and resistance. I am aware of a pathway. It is lined on either side by small primrose flowers. I can hear the voices of crowds of people, as if I am in a restaurant or railway station. I am now aware of a thick rope close to my face. Now it becomes thin like fragile cotton. Again it becomes a rope. My fingers feel numb. Once more I am crushed, particularly around my head. I see an extraordinary bright, bright light. I feel fear. I wake up but cannot shake off the horrible feeling of this nightmare.*

I'm sure Freud would have had plenty to say about what my dream revealed about my resistance to life and my desire to remain in the safe waters of the womb. However, I believe that this dream is a memory of my actual birth. It is very hard to describe because so many of the sensations cannot be related to anything I know. This is likely to be the same confusion that a baby must feel. I understand the rope and cotton to be the umbilical cord, but have no idea what the primroses are. I'm sure the sensations of sound and the bright lights are memories of the moment I came into the world.

All of us retain the memory of birth somewhere in our brain. Dreams are the key to recalling this most important experience. In my extract I called the dream a nightmare. Clearly birth recall is not always a pleasant experience, but I'm sure it is of benefit to remember and integrate the experience. At one time the dream would force itself upon me. It has not reoccurred since I wrote it down.

This dream proved to me that it was possible to remember just about anything in dreams. If I could remember as far back as my birth, would it not be possible to remember even further back, to the time before I was born?

By working with your dreams in a systematic way you will gradually move back further in your memories to the time before you were born. You have already established the habit of using dreams as an aid to recalling memories from this life, so it is not a big step to shift your attention to lives before you were born. Of course some of these dreams may be fantasy, but others will ring true. Ideally you may receive some information that you can confirm by checking the public records,

REBIRTH

but in most instances the experience will be subjective.

The Tibetan Buddhist Dzogchen sect believes that it is very beneficial to remember your birth. The most important Tibetan Buddhist text that covers the subject of what lies beyond death and the means to seek a fortuitous new birth is *Bardo Thodol*, better known as *The Tibetan Book of the Dead*. (See page 91 for a discussion of this work.) *Bardo* means "intermediate state," and denotes the period between the death and rebirth. *Thodol* (pronounced "thos grol") means "liberation through understanding."

What I may have experienced in my birth dream was a memory of the sixth *bardo*, the state between death and a new birth. This is the "intermediate state," where one searches for a new birth. At the sixth *bardo* is the choice of merging with the infinite light (I would call this God) or being reincarnated again. Most of us forget this experience. However, some great souls retain their knowledge and are born into this life as fully realized and enlightened beings. The rest of us pass across the "river of forgetting" or only half-remember the glorious reality of our true nature. Birth memories bring us close to this knowledge of the infinite. It is also the *bardo* where it is possible to be totally conscious of every life that we have lived and will live in the future.

Whatever you focus your attention on grows in strength. If you spend time thinking about your childhood memories and memories of your birth, your unconscious mind will come to your aid. It is there to help you. Reading this book may also be helping you focus your attention on past-life recall. The more you think about past lives, the more likely it is that your dreams will present you with the information you are seeking.

DREAMSCAPES

I have kept dream records since I was a teenager, and some of the recurring dreams appearing in my early dream diaries may relate to past-life experiences. For example, I have often dreamt about a fishing village in a place that resembles Cornwall, in the southwestern United Kingdom. Whenever I dream of this place I have an unearthly feeling of déjà vu. The dream has occurred so many times, I now know every roll of the hills, every turn in the road, and every field and building. When I awaken from these dreams I always make a note of what I see. I have even drawn a detailed map of the area. As far as I am aware I have never been to this place. One day I may find it. I believe I have a map to prove that I once lived there in a past life.

Dreamscapes have many clues that point to memories of past lives. A dream landscape can take many forms and may have many levels of meaning. Before reading what follows, stop and think about the many landscapes that may have occurred in your dreams. If you have been keeping a dream diary, read back over your entries and particularly take notice of settings, terrains, and landscapes. You may want to make a few notes to help jog your memory about the places you have seen in your dreams. Think about the inner landscapes of the mind that are present when you dream. Consider the scenery, the backdrops, the people, and the objects that are part of your dreamscape.

These landscapes can be interpreted in a number of different ways. Most will have nothing to do with past lives, but a few may hold important cryptic information that will reveal hidden knowledge.

CHILDHOOD DREAMSCAPES

Many of your dreamscapes will link to memories from childhood. I often have dreams that are set in my childhood home or my grandfather's luscious back garden. Dreams set in childhood settings may be giving you a temporary respite from the troubles of your world. They may remind you who you really are and of your roots. These dreams may reveal deep-seated memories from childhood or be telling you that you've forgotten how to play and should develop a more carefree attitude toward life. Your dreams may also be a symbol for your potential—something that is still at an early stage of development. They could highlight immature attitudes or reveal parts of you that need reassurance and security.

Your dreams may also be helping you remember past lives, by helping you reach the deep recesses of your memory. Remembering the lost memories from this life is a stepping stone to remembering lost

THE PAST LIVES OF GEORGE S. PATTON (1885–1945)

■ George S. Patton was the American general who led the U.S. troops to breach the defenses at Normandy and led a spectacular advance to the Moselle. In the Ardennes he cleared the west bank of the Rhine, crossed it, and encircled the Ruhr. Yet, this great American general believed that he had done his military training in previous lives.

In December 1917, when he visited the Langres tank school in northeast France, a local liaison officer showed him around the town. He started to tell Patton about how the area had once been the site of a Roman military camp, but was interrupted: "You don't have to," said Patton, "I know this place. I know it well." He then directed the driver around the ruins and could point out the various landmarks. He knew the drill ground, the temples of Mars and Apollo, the forum and the amphitheater, yet he had never been to the town before in his life.

Patton believed that he had been to France before as a Roman legionnaire. He even knew the exact spot where Julius Caesar had made his camp. "It was as if someone were at my ear whispering the direction," he later told his nephew.

Patton was forthright in his conviction that his military successes were a continuation of campaigns he had waged in previous lives. He had memories of being at the walls of Tyre with Alexander the Great and of being a member of the Greek phalanx which met Cyrus II, the Persian warlord who established the Achaemenid empire in 500 B.C. He also believed he had fought at Crècy's Field during the Hundred Years' War.

During the North African campaign of World War Two, a British soldier quipped, "You would have made a great marshal for Napoleon if you'd lived in the 18th century." Patton looked back at the soldier. A wry grin broke across his face. "But I did," he replied.

memories from previous lives. There are many examples of children who remember their previous lives. Perhaps these early memories of childhood hold clues to the knowledge of past lives now forgotten.

SYMBOLIC DREAMSCAPES

Most dreamscapes will be based on your conscious memories. These may represent the way you feel about yourself and your situation. The landscape of your dream is a symbol. For example, suppose you dream of being on vacation at a place you know well. Your dream may be telling you that you need to take a break. Sometimes dreams feature anxieties, such as missing a plane or train. You may dream of carrying too much luggage. In this case your dreamscape represents the need to take it easy. It is the place where everything is relaxed and happy. It represents the goal you should set yourself.

Similarly, your dreamscape could represent your life. The roads you travel in your dream may be a metaphor for the roads you travel through life. The twists, turns, and obstacles are the difficulties you encounter in ordinary life. A fork in the road or a crossroads may represent a difficult decision you have to make.

If your dream has a symbolic meaning it is probably not a dream that recalls a past life. However, do not necessarily dismiss it. It could be saying to you, "What you are experiencing now is just like the time you were at this place…." "This place" may be somewhere from a past life.

FOREIGN DREAMSCAPES

When you dream of a strange land, do not assume that this is of a past life. Again it may be a symbol for problems that you are experiencing in this life. To dream of being in a foreign country may indicate that you are experiencing something unfamiliar in your waking life. For example, you may have recently changed jobs or may be behaving differently from your usual routine.

These dreams are often accompanied by uncomfortable feelings of loss or anxiety. Your dream may be telling you that you are not ready to leave your present life behind. Perhaps you are not prepared to deal with the circumstances that are currently dominating your life. Everything feels "foreign" to you. You are a stranger in a strange land.

Foreign dreamscapes can also represent opportunity and excitement. Positive feelings about your dreamscape may show that you are enjoying new opportunities that have been presented in your life. You may have a new job opening; new opportunities may be coming your way.

Again this dreamscape may be a symbol of your life. Despite its strangeness, it is not necessarily about a life long ago. It is most likely to be a metaphor for your life.

OBE DREAMSCAPES

Many people, including myself, believe that they have left their body during sleep. A body of light leaves the physical body and can travel across the landscape of the Earth and also to the stars and heavenly spheres. This is a very commonly reported experience.

Dreamscapes you experience during this state of awareness could be real places.

Out-of-body experiences (OBE's) may also give you access to the halls of learning in the heavenly planes. Some have called this level of vibration the "akashic record," which contains the "recording" of everything that has ever happened. It could be described as God's memory. If this information can be accessed, your past lives and the past lives of anyone can be accessed. The psychic "sleeping prophet" Edgar Cayce believed that much of the information he gave came from his ability to access the akashic record of the past lives of the people who consulted him.

The akashic record is a plane of existence storing the memories and knowledge of everything that has happened. It is like a cosmic Internet that contains the imprints of everything that has existed on the material and spiritual planes. Tune into the akashic record and you will be able to watch dinosaurs walk the earth, see the Fall of Troy, or hear Lincoln deliver the Gettysburg Address.

PAST-LIFE DREAMSCAPES

Once you have eliminated dreamscapes that have clear symbolic meaning you are left with a number of locations that cannot be explained. There's a certain "grand dream" feeling that often accompanies these dreams. Even as the dream is taking place you may have a feeling of awe and wonder. You awaken knowing that this dream is very special and that it relates to something about your distant past. There's an inescapable feeling that the dream is about a past life.

In most cases it is impossible to prove beyond doubt that a dream relates to a past-life experience. How much easier it would be if you could simply dream all the facts then

prove them with public records of births, marriages, and deaths. However, in most cases dream revelations about past lives are likely to remain unproven. I suppose it finally comes down to a gut feeling, an unshakable knowing that comes from deep within you.

There are certain dreams you are likely to have had that cannot be explained away as symbolism, metaphor, or allegory. In my own dream records I have cases I am convinced are about past lives. For example, I had many dreams about being a shaven-headed monk when I was a child. At the time I had never heard of Tibet or the doctrine of reincarnation. In particular I would have a dream about walking around in a circle on what looked like a high-walled tower. Together with other monks, I chanted mantras. The scenery was spectacular. I would awaken feeling tremendously inspired. I have also had recurring dreams about dying of exposure near a dried-up riverbed, which I now believe to be the source of the Yellow River in Mongolia, a place where there were many Tibetan monasteries. (My wife often jokes that I feel the cold too much for an incarnation of a Tibetan.)

Although I do not follow the Buddhist way today, I feel that Tibetan wisdom and teachings still influence me. It may explain why I was born with mediumistic powers and how easily I grasp Tibetan Buddhist and Bon ideas that many people find hard to understand.

Perhaps the strangest past-life dream I have had was about being chased from behind by raging dogs. A small group of people and I are near a castle. Our way is blocked by a moat. As the dogs catch up with us, soldiers start attacking us from behind with swords. There is a lot of noise and commotion. I can smell fire and blood. I feel a terrible pain in the back of my neck. There is searing pain, then nothing.

When I met my wife, Jane, who is also a medium, we talked about our dreams and were amazed to discover that we had this same dream in common—right down to the smallest detail. Neither of us knows the historical time period it relates to, although it hints at the medieval era, when mediums were persecuted as witches. It could of course all be fantasy, except that Jane, myself, and our daughter Danielle each have the same brown birth mark at the top of the neck just under the hairline. Perhaps we three are beheaded soulmates?

WHY DON'T WE REMEMBER OUR PAST LIVES?

Spontaneous recall of past lives may be a rather dubious privilege. Suppose you were now able to have unfettered access to all your past-life memories and were to discover that you were one of the worst monsters in history. What if you discovered that you were Genghis Khan, Hitler, or Stalin? Worse, perhaps, you realize you spent lifetimes as a child abuser or village idiot. How would you feel? How would you deal with the horror and belated remorse? You would probably feel so depressed and discouraged, you would have no strength to keep on.

Moreover, imagine how much karma your life now and in the future would be subject to. You would have a mountain of misfortune to deal with. How could you deal with it? Perhaps you would live in fear

of retribution for past sins. You would probably feel hopelessness, guilt, and shame and find it tremendously difficult to get on with your life. People don't like to remember things that are unpleasant or evil.

Fortunately, cosmic law protects you with forgetfulness and gives you a second chance. People need to be protected even from comparatively innocuous past lives. Take for example the story of Shanti Devi, on page 114. Twenty-five years after the events described, a reporter sought out Shanti to ask her about the case. She was working a quiet life as a government employee. She was not keen to talk about the case. "I do not wish to revive my past lives, either this one or my previous existence in Muttra," she confessed. "It has been very difficult for me to bury my desire to return to my family. I do not want to open that closed door again."

You may ask yourself the question: "What have I done in a past life to deserve this suffering?" But you forget that it was you who chose to take on the life you have today. Perhaps in a past life you were a king, queen, president, or rich person. At the end of your last life you may have decided that seeking fame, power, privilege, or wealth was a futile pursuit. You enjoyed your status and came to the end of that experience. You learned what you needed to know.

When you last died you passed down the tunnel of light and let go of everything you were. What survived is the essential you, the part of you that the Hindu philosopher Sri Aurobindo called the "psychic being." After a period of rest in the afterlife, you made the decision to take another earthly life. This time you chose new lessons to learn based on your karma and desires. You can only be free of rebirth once your path is set to the Divine.

ANCIENT MEMORIES

■ One of the best-known cases of reincarnation is that of Jumari Shanti Devi, who was born in Delhi, India, in 1926. When she was seven, she told her mother that she had lived before in a town called Muttra. She explained that she had been married to a man called Kedarnath.

"He lives in Muttra. Our house is yellow stucco with large arched doors and latticework windows. Our yard is large and filled with marigolds and jasmine. Great bowers of scarlet bougainvilleas climb over the house. We often sit on the veranda watching our little son play on the tile floor. Our sons are still there with their father."

During the next two years her memories of her previous life increased. She told the family doctor that her name had been Ludgi. Soon she was telling her parents everything about her previous life.

When she was nine, a Mr. Lal came to the door to discuss business with her father. She immediately recognized the stranger as someone she knew in her past life. "Mother! This is a cousin of my husband!" she exclaimed. "He lived not far from us in Muttra and then moved to Delhi. I am so happy to see him!"

The man did live in Muttra. He agreed that his cousin's wife, Ludgi, had died 10 years earlier. Eventually, Shanti was taken to visit her family from her previous life. When she first saw the husband she recognized him immediately and flung herself into his arms. She called him by her own pet names and used endearing phrases which only he and his wife had known.

Shanti was able to direct the carriage to Ludgi's house in Muttra and identified her father-in-law sitting in front of it. She also recognized her two eldest children and knew their names, but not the youngest, whose birth had cost Ludgi her life. Next, they visited Ludgi's elderly mother, Desh Gupta. Shanti told her that there used to be a well on the property and indicated the correct place it had been. Kedarnath then asked what Ludgi had done with several rings she had been given shortly before her death. She explained that she had hidden them in a pot in the garden of the old home. An investigating committee later excavated these.

Your task now is to fulfill the destiny you set for yourself. You must work to learn the sometimes-hard lessons you have set. You do not remember your past lives because these memories might hamper your spiritual progress. They could cause feelings of guilt or yearning for experiences past.

The memories in your unconscious are immortal. Although the memory of your past lives has vanished from your mind, if the appropriate brain cells were awakened you would be able to remember everything. Very often, these silent areas of the mind are opened during sleep and the memories awaken during dreams.

The habits you cultivated in past lives have created your physical, mental, and emotional makeup in this life. You also bring forward into this life your past karma, which determines the kind of physical form you have as well as your personality traits.

Even your sex is determined by your self-chosen tendencies in previous lives.

By knowing your past lives, you can gain an understanding of yourself and the traits that are influencing the course of your life. Most people never analyze themselves, so they are continually stuck in a rut of established behavior. They are guided by their likes and dislikes, all of which are habits brought forward from previous lives.

The objective of a self-aware person is to be in control and not to be at the mercy of his own tendencies. Knowing about your past lives can help you establish new habits and help you get out of physical, emotional, mental, and spiritual ruts. Few people try consciously to change themselves. They are stuck with preconceptions that they are sinners or are weak or temperamental, and so on. These are all habits established in past lives.

USING PAST-LIFE RECALL TO IMPROVE YOURSELF

Most people who go to fortune-tellers to discover their past lives want to be flattered. They don't want to hear that they were once evil or dull individuals. They want to be heroic figures, a great king or queen, a martyr in the French Revolution, a great sage, or famous in some way. Often the incarnations they imagine reflect their wishes and hopes, acting as an escape from their dull and banal lives. Unfortunately many false prophets tell people what they want to hear, and the grip of the illusion becomes stronger. In my own work as a Spiritualist medium, I have met a plentiful supply of ex-Nefertitis, pharaohs, Nelsons, and Queens of Sheba. It always surprises me that these great souls now incarnate as such dull and tedious individuals in this life.

If you were to truly remember who you are, you might realize that you are an immortal soul. You are Spirit and not the temporal being that walks this earth. During the day, you are tricked by your habits and false memory into believing that you are this limited physical being. However, during sleep you are free to unite with the totality of yourself. You are reminded that you are a formless Divine being. You lose all consciousness of your body and form and are reminded that you are Spirit. Your nature is bliss.

The insight that your dreams give you into your past lives can be used to bring you closer to this realization. If you remember past lives that make you feel ashamed, learn from this and rid yourself of these qualities in this life. Similarly, if your past-life recall reveals good qualities in a former life, reintroduce them into your life today. Most of all let your life be filled with happy memories from both this life and the ones before. This will keep you healthy and happy. And in particular, use your knowledge to go beyond mortal consciousness. You have come down from the Spirit to this limited world of flesh. There is no end to your consciousness. You have memories of lives that stretch back into the vast eons of time. It is all there within you. A time will come when you no longer have to make an effort to remember anything. It is all there within you in your omnipresent intuition.

Recognizing Souls from a Past Life

Why is it that you feel an immediate and deep harmony with some people when you meet them for the first time? Yet you work with others day after day for years and never really get to know them. The reason might be that the ones you feel an immediate kinship with, you knew in a past life.

Seeing them again rekindles your friendship, which continues to grow in this lifetime. Friendship is the highest relationship because it is born of free choice. Marriages that have friendship as their foundation are stronger than those based on wealth, sex, or emotion. To be a friend to all is the unfolding of God's unconditional love. Friendship can bind people together over the centuries.

If you discuss your dreams with your partner, you may find that throughout your lifetime you have held dreams in common. Of course, you may not have been friends in a past life. Sometimes your karma brings you together so you can sort out your differences. However, knowledge of dreams about your past lives will help you resolve your difficulties and generate true friendship and love. Relationships should be seen as mutual spiritual work. They should be based on soul qualities, not worldly qualities or attractions of the flesh. If you base all your friendships and relationships on spiritual values, you will attract another spiritual friend, for God now holds you in His hands.

Your dreams reveal a great deal about past relationships with people you know now. When friends, family, and enemies appear in your dreams, make a note in your dream diary. What do you remember about the setting and era in which the dream is set? Of course, in most instances your friends will be dream symbols representing the way you feel about your life at the moment. For example, friends of the same sex can represent your shadow self, the aspects of your personality you have refused to acknowledge consciously. The friendly nature suggests that you are prepared to integrate this neglected part with yourself. Dreams about family members can also represent parts of your personality. For example, if you dream about your mother, this could symbolize the motherly side of yourself, the part of you that wants to nurture and protect. A dream about your father may represent your outgoing nature and the dynamic forces within you. Even if this is not the case in reality, your dreams will cast the characters from your life in mythic, archetypal roles.

But some dreams are not symbolic. They are direct references to past incarnations. If you compare your dream notes with those of people you like the most, you may find that you have many dreams in common. As you dig deeper, you may discover that some of these dreams are too specific to be the result of chance alone. The details may reveal periods in history and lives you had in common. By working in this way you can prove to yourself that you are not a victim of your own fantasy but that your past-life memories can be substantiated through others. You may also discover that groups of your friends have dreams in common.

GROUP SOULS

A particularly interesting case of group incarnation was penned by Arthur Guirdham in his book *The Cathars and Reincarnation*. This is a factual record of a woman who, through dreams and waking impressions, remembered her previous life in the 13th century. She was burned for heresy around 1244. Guirdham, the author, was a doctor of medicine and a psychiatrist, and was trained to distinguish between fact and fantasy. At first, he was skeptical when the woman insisted she was the incarnation

■ Many top showbiz stars believe that they lived before. Many of the roles they play may reflect the characters they were in past lives:

Shirley MacLaine

She is perhaps the most well-known believer in reincarnation. She believes she was a maidservant in ancient Egypt and a model for Toulouse-Lautrec in France.

Sylvester Stallone

The star of *Rambo* and other blockbusters is convinced he lived during the French Revolution. He believes he was guillotined.

Engelbert Humperdinck

This singer believes he was a Roman emperor in a past life.

Tina Turner

This singer is so convinced she has lived before, she searched for evidence of a past life in Egypt. Her quest began after a Californian psychic told her she was the reincarnation of Hatshepsut, a woman pharaoh of ancient Egypt.

John Travolta

The star of the film *Saturday Night Fever* and more recently *Phenomenon* believes he was an actor in a past life, perhaps even Rudolf Valentino.

Martin Sheen

Sheen is a firm believer in reincarnation and believes that families do not come together by chance. "Our children," he says, "come to us to make up for indiscretions in past lives. They are holdovers from lifetimes we have not solved."

of a heretic Cathar who lived in France during the 13th century. However, her dreams revealed knowledge of the times that only a specialist scholar would know. Guirdham decided to investigate the places mentioned and the historic records to check the patient's statements.

Remarkably, he discovered that this woman's dreams gave accurate historical information that she could not have known. Her dreams were full of precise detail about the Cathars. She asserted that Cathar priests wore blue, not black, which proved to be correct. She was able to place accurately in their family and social relationships people who were not historical characters but who, with a great deal of research, could be traced through public records. But it was the little things that gave weight to her story. For example, her dreams revealed that she had given her lover loaf sugar when he was ill. Careful research revealed that loaf sugar was regarded as a medicine at the time.

As Guirdham continued his research, he discovered that he too could retrieve memories from an incarnation as a Cathar. As the book unfolds, the dreams reveals a whole network of people connected by a common spiritual lineage from the when the Inquisition wiped out this pious group of Cathars. Centuries later, they were to be reborn together again, and the past forgotten, except in dreams.

HOW FAR BACK CAN YOU REMEMBER?

Studies of people put under hypnosis show that the mind has a remarkable ability to record huge amounts of information. Many psychologists believe that the brain may be able to remember every detail of everything that has ever happened to it. All the memories are there; most people just lack the ability to access the information. Dreams are a doorway to this treasure trove of forgotten wisdom.

As has been mentioned earlier, mystics believe that a repository of memory exists that is separate from all of us. It is called the akashic record. Much of the information you access about your past lives may come from this source. However you also have personal memories. Like the akashic record, the amount of knowledge that your mind can store may be limitless. I have had very strange dreams about what appear to be Neolithic or Stone Age times. Moreover, places like Stonehenge and the other ancient megaliths fill me with a mixture of excitement, peace, and dread that is difficult to explain. Dreams appear to reach back in times to scenarios with a familiar feel, to places I feel I once knew. Some of my dreams are even set in jungle or tribal settings.

If you work with your ability at dream recall over many years, you will access the deepest buried memories from the unconscious. Not only will you awaken your memory of human lives but of animal lives as well.

DREAM MEMORIES OF ANIMAL LIVES

More people are alive today than at any other time in human history. Given that reincarnation is true, where did all these new souls come from? The truth is, there aren't enough human souls to go around. It's a significant fact that as the human population is increasing, the animal population is decreasing. The conclusion seems to be that animal souls are all reincarnating as human beings. Carefully observe your fellow humans and you will soon see the hidden animal spirit expressing itself.

All of us, say the gurus, have had previous lives as animals and have gradually climbed the spiritual ladder of evolution to attain our present human life. It is a fact that our archaic animal past is still deeply ingrained in our everyday behavior. For "new" humans, the former animal lives are particularly apparent. First-time humans may still behave like animals: we talk of a person acting like a rat, eating like a pig, or singing like a canary. Hidden within these similes are references to previous lives.

Dreams can occasionally reveal memories from your animal past. You may have direct memories, but it is more likely that they are ingrained in your instinctive behavior. Your instinctive fears, which often appear in dreams, may also say a great deal about your former animal lives. For example, you may have a fear of snakes or spiders. Perhaps the thought of a tiger or a crocodile fills you with dread because one of these animals may have taken your life in a past animal incarnation.

Now have some fun. Answer the following questions to see what animal you were in a past life:

Are you a vegetarian?

• Most animals are herbivorous. With so many animal souls incarnating it's not surprising that vegetarianism has become fashionable. You are most likely to have been an animal such as a cow, buffalo, antelope, or perhaps even a squirrel. Avoid people who like to eat nearly raw steak or meatballs—

ANIMAL SPIRIT

these people are from another species entirely and may do you harm. Your dreams may reveal a fear of being chased.

Do you feel safer when surrounded by friends?

• A "yes" answer shows that your animal lineage is with herding animals such as sheep and with species that seek safety in numbers. Your past life may have been within a school of fish, a flock of birds, or herd of wildebeests. If you were a fish, you may have dreams about breathing underwater.

Do you like to go on the prowl?

• Gangs of thugs of course originate from pack animals such as wolves, and it's possible that many great generals were wolves in their former lives. There is no greater compliment to a Hell's Angel than to call him "the leader of the pack." Today hunting grounds are clubs and bars. These are the places where latter-day wolves like to prowl. Your dreams may be filled with violent images.

Do you feel sleepy in winter?

• You are remembering the time when you used to hibernate. Many fish, amphibians, reptiles, and mammals such as hedgehogs and bats from the colder regions of the world sleep through the winter months. You lose weight during winter, prefer colder climates, and don't feel quite yourself until spring. Your dreams may feature caves or subterranean passageways.

What animal do you look like?

• What animal features do you see when you look in the mirror? Some people have protruding teeth like a camel, tiny mouse-like eyes, or a mane of lion's hair. Have you a square-set face like a bull or a thin, stork-like appearance? Look for some time and you'll suddenly see your animal face staring back at you. Your dreams about the animals you like may reveal your own past.

What does your body language say about your animal spirit?

• Because of its instinctive origins, body language reveals a great deal about animal past lives. For example, you may stand proud like a bull or swivel your head like a prairie dog watching for predators. You may strut like a peacock or scurry along like a mouse. People who blink a lot may be incarnations of owls! Could it be that your dreams of flying are an actual memory from long ago?

What do your habits say about your animal past?

• Primitive peoples say that our totem animal dream soul influences our habits. A woman who stuffs her handbag full of junk may be displaying the hoarding instincts of a hamster or even the maternal behavior of a kangaroo. Nailbiting is a throwback to the days when you had claws, and a love of swimming shows your aquatic past life. Dreams that reveal phobias about snakes, spiders, or birds also reflect ancient animal fears.

REMEMBERING THE FUTURE

The future belongs to those who believe in their dreams.

ELEANOR ROOSEVELT (1884–1962)

THE idea that dreams can predict the future has captivated the imagination for thousands of years. The ancient Egyptians, Greeks, and Romans believed that the gods could communicate to them through dreams that often contained prophecies of the future. Some of the most well-known examples of dream precognition are in the Bible. *The Book of Genesis* tells about the dreams of Joseph, son of Jacob. Joseph told his brothers: "We were binding sheaves in the field, and lo, my sheaf arose and stood upright; and behold, your sheaves gathered  around it, and bowed down to my sheaf; … Behold, the sun, moon, and eleven stars were bowing down to me."

Outraged at Joseph's proclamations, his eleven brothers kidnapped him, and he was sold into slavery in Egypt. In prison, Joseph interpreted the dreams of his fellow inmates, predicting that one would be freed but another hanged. Two years later the freed man told the pharaoh of Joseph's remarkable ability to interpret prophetic dreams. He was summoned to court to explain the meaning of a dream that had confounded all the wise men of Egypt. The pharaoh described his dream. He stood on the bank of the Nile and watched "seven fat kine" (cows) emerge from the river. The fat cows grazed contentedly by the shoreline, but "seven other kine followed them; poor and very ill-favored and lean-fleshed, much as I have never seen in Egypt. And the ill-famed kine did eat up the fat kine." The pharaoh awoke, but later the dream continued, showing him seven full heads of grain being eaten by seven withered heads of grain.

Joseph understood the dream. It was a warning from God to say that Egypt would enjoy seven years of plenty followed by seven years of famine. The pharaoh believed Joseph and gave orders that enough grain be stored to last through the seven lean years.

Egypt and the Middle East were indeed

wracked with the predicted famine. When Joseph's father and his eleven brothers came to Egypt to buy grain they met Joseph, now elevated to an important position as reward for his insight. The brothers recalled his prophecy from long ago that his father, mother, and brothers would honor him: "Behold, the sun, moon, and eleven stars were bowing down to me."

Throughout the Bible, many prophecies come from dreams. In the Old Testament, God granted Solomon the gift of wisdom in a dream, Daniel predicted the destiny of king Nebuchadnezzar, and Jacob dreamed of a ladder of angels when God announced that Jacob's descendants would spread throughout the world like the stars in the sky. In the New Testament, the apostle Matthew wrote that four angels spoke to Joseph in a dream and that Joseph's virgin wife Mary would bear a divine child. Similarly, another dream warned Joseph and Mary of the cruel edict of Herod, enabling them to flee to Egypt with the Divine Child.

Although the philosopher Aristotle argued that precognitive dreams were impossible, he was unusual for his time. Most ancient Greeks believed dreams foretold the future. They consulted soothsayers at the temple of Apollo for interpretations of dream portents. The Romans also believed that dreams could foretell the future. If Julius Caesar had been less skeptical about them, he might have listened to the warnings about his assassination that Calpurnia, his wife, received in a dream.

The course of history has been influenced by precognitive dreams. As a young man,

Oliver Cromwell had a dream in which a huge female figure drew back the curtains around his bed. She told him he would be the greatest man in England, but not the king. The impossible came true after the English Civil War when Cromwell signed King Charles's death warrant and became Lord Protector of England—the most powerful man in the land.

The military campaigns of the French emperor Napoleon were often changed because of messages he received in dreams. Similarly, Otto von Bismarck, the militaristic German chancellor, claimed that a prophetic dream convinced him to continue his 1866 campaign against the Austrians.

Abraham Lincoln assigned prophetic value to certain dreams and dreamed of his own death in 1865. In the dream, he wandered around a "deathlike" White House and could hear the distant sound of sobbing. The sound led him to the East Room, where he saw a corpse laid out. Its face was covered and the body wrapped in funeral vestments. He asked the sobbing mourners who the dead person was, and was told "the president was killed by an assassin." A few days later the dream came horribly true when John Wilkes Booth assassinated Abraham Lincoln in a theater.

Many contemporary examples of dreams that come true are sent to me through my newspaper columns. Ordinary people who make no claim to special powers have written to say that they have seen the future. "I awoke from a bad dream at exactly 9:03. In the dream I saw my father collapse outside the hospital in Glasgow," wrote Pamela

TIME AND THE FUTURE

from Knightswood. "Exactly two months later at 9:03 a.m. my father collapsed and died at the exact spot that I had dreamt about."

Another account sent to me about precognition in a dream revealed facts of startling accuracy. "I awoke from a vivid dream and told it to my husband so that I could put it into my diary later. The dream was not pictorial; it was auditory. I had heard a name, Neville, not that unusual, but I didn't know anyone by that name. I had also dreamed of the poem 'Upon Westminster Bridge,' by the poet William Wordsworth.

"Three months later I joined a discussion group and was introduced to a Neville Westbridge. We became good friends and his ideas had a very important influence on my philosophy of life. My husband has always been very skeptical about precognition but the accuracy of this dream has made him change his tune."

Some people believe that seership is an inherited gift passed down through families and even racial groups. When a gypsy girl called at Mrs. Hollings house in County Durham she was amazed to hear how much the gypsy knew about her and her family. "She knew that my husband had bad legs and went on to predict that my son was engaged to a girl with the initial M but would marry a girl with the initial S. Their firstborn would be twins."

The gypsy's prediction came true to the letter.

Often the dreams sent to me contain foreboding messages or give warnings: "I was working on an oil rig 80 miles out in the Arabian Gulf. Because we were working 12 hour shifts most of us went to bed early," says J. W. from Portsmouth, U.K. "On a Thursday night at 7:35 p.m. I awoke

from a bad dream. I had been floating about 100 feet in the air above a street near my home, watching a car traveling along a dual carriageway. Without stopping, it drove straight across a roundabout and hit another vehicle. I sensed rather than saw that the guilty driver was my father. I told my friend about the dream.

"A week later I was flown home. My father had had an accident in exactly the way my dream had revealed. He told me that as he was driving he started thinking about me in Bahrain and wondering how I was getting on. Suddenly he hit a car at the roundabout. Luckily nobody was hurt. The time was 4:35 p.m. Between Bahrain and the U.K. is a three-hour time difference in the summertime. The accident happened at exactly the time I dreamed it."

PARANORMAL RESEARCH

I believe that everybody has psychic power lying dormant in the mind. Scientists call these powers Extra Sensory Perception (ESP). ESP subdivides into telepathy (communicating by thought), clairvoyance (seeing events without using the five senses), psychokinesis (influencing matter by thought, i.e., spoon-bending), and precognition (seeing the future).

Psychic powers have been researched since the 1930s, when Professor J. B. Rhine at Duke University in North Carolina made a systematic study in the laboratory. He presented his evidence by the statistical analysis of card-guessing games. Rhine discovered that many students randomly selected from the university campus could predict which cards would come next in a randomly shuffled pack of Zener cards (special cards for testing ESP, designed by Carl Zener). Their scores were far above what would be expected by chance alone.

Extensive sleep experiments were conducted to test whether ESP is present in dreams. Experiments were designed to see if telepathy could take place in dreams. An Italian psychic researcher named G. B. Ermacora at the turn of the 20th century undertook some of the first trials. These marked the first serious attempt at inducing dream telepathy with a preselected sender and receiver.

Other interesting experiments were conducted in the 1940s by William Daim, a Viennese psychologist. Sitting in a closed room at a considerable distance from the sleeping receiver, he randomly chose an envelope from a pile on a table. In each envelope were "target" pictures. Many of the dreams of his receivers contained similar images to those he had "sent" by telepathy.

The most extensive research into dream ESP was conducted in the late '60s and early '70s by a research team led by Montague Ullman and Stanley Krippner at the Maimonides Medical Center in Brooklyn, New York. They used techniques similar to William Daim's but had the advantage of being able to wire up their subjects to EEG machines that could detect changes in brain patterns and the onset and ending of REM periods. The best results were obtained by selecting images and paintings with strong emotional overtones. They observed that if a subject's dream "is vivid, colored, and somewhat puzzling to the dreamer and does not 'fit' into his dream pattern or reflect recent activity, then we can be alerted to the possibility that the dream is being influenced by ESP."

In their book entitled *Dream Telepathy*, Ullman and Krippner wrote, "Perhaps our most basic finding is the scientific demonstration of Freud's statement 'Sleep creates favorable conditions for telepathy.'"

The Maimonides team also made extensive research into dreams and precognition. One of their most gifted subjects was an Englishman named Malcolm Bessent, who had scored high in telepathy experiments and had been used for a number of their high-profile dream experiments. One of their most successful experiments in dream precognition lasted 16 nights, with each experiment covering two nights. On the first night, Bessent would attempt to dream about which target picture would be chosen for the following night. On the second night he would see the target and try to dream about it. On the third night a new target would be chosen and the sequence repeated.

The Maimonides team found that Bessent had, on the eight precognitive dream nights, scored seven hits. On the eight control nights, his dream images bore little or no resemblance to the target pictures. The odds of this happening by chance were an amazing 1,000 to 1.

Research into ESP continues to this day and now uses video clip "targets" instead of static imagery. ESP experiments have even been done in space. It seems ironic that experiments in precognition, which started in the ancient Greek temple of Apollo, should be secretly carried out on its namesake, the Apollo 14 space mission, by astronaut Edgar D. Mitchell in the 1960s. Experiments in precognition have been going on for centuries. Many people have this ESP gift. Perhaps you are one of them.

OTHER THEORIES ABOUT DREAM PREMONITIONS

In your normal waking life, you take it for granted that time goes in a straight direction, like an arrow pushing ever onward. It doesn't go backward, sideways, or do anything silly. It goes from the past through the present and into the future. Could it be that when you go to sleep and dream, strange things happen to time? How would it be if time did not behave in the ways you have become accustomed to, in your waking life? You are aware of the past and the present, but is it not possible that your consciousness could extend into the future also? Perhaps one of the reasons you cannot remember your dreams is that they exist in another time frame or give you access to another dimension and created memories that are hard to bring forward into your ordinary world.

Many great thinkers have wrestled with the enigma of time. Saint Augustine, Galileo, Sir Isaac Newton, Albert Einstein, and Stephen Hawking have failed to explain it. The most recent theories about time reveal some very strange scenarios. For example, it is believed that if it were possible to travel between two black holes in space, you would move through time. Scientists now talk about hyperspace and cosmic wormholes that tunnel through space–time,

leading from one region to another. Particle physics also has discovered strange subatomic particles that appear to travel backward in time or appear to be in two places at once. Einstein has also shown that time is relative. Time for one observer may be completely different from time for another. "When you sit with a nice girl for two hours, you think it's only a minute," said Einstein. "But when you sit on a hot stove for a minute, you think it's two hours. That's relativity."

If you dream of the future, it may indicate that you are in touch with an alternative reality. That's something J. W. Dunne suspected when he noticed that many of his dreams appeared to foretell the future. Dunne was a distinguished man of science and a professor of mathematics. He noticed that sometimes his dreams took an odd view of time and sometimes included disagreements about time. In one dream, he was convinced it was 4:30 in the afternoon. When he awoke he looked at his wrist to check the time but found that his watch was missing. Then he spotted it on his bedroom cabinet. It had stopped at 4:30.

Dunne was sufficiently intrigued by what happened to keep a dream diary. He kept detailed records and would sometimes compare dreams with friends. Applying the methodology that he learned from mathematics to his experiments convinced him that his dreams were foreseeing the future. He found also that prophetic thoughts could be engendered in the waking mind if one were kept in a state of receptivity. Furthermore, he suspected that most people had the ability to predict future events.

In 1927, he published his conclusions in his book *An Experiment with Time*. It became a bestseller, caused great controversy, and is still the center of much debate among contemporary researchers. Dunne's book challenged the notion that time traveled in a straight line with a definite past, present, and future. He argued that his dreams proved that time was not a continuum. He believed that if time was a fourth dimension, then the passage of time must itself take time. Therefore, if time took time, there had to be a time outside time. He called this "Time 2." "Time," he said "is not a straight line, like a stretched cord; it is more like a tangled skein of wool."

Most of our life we live in "Time 1,"which is synonymous with the passing ordinary moments of everyday life. But during sleep a part of our personality ("Observer 2") can slip into this other dimension of time and experience events in the future that are communicated to our ordinary self ("Observer 1"). In other words, past, present, and future exist as one, and we only understand it as a series of events because our consciousness organizes it in this way. Dunne concluded that under certain circumstances, past, present, and future events are accessible to us. During sleep, your rationality and logic take a back seat, so you access multilevels of time in your dreams. During dreams, you can enter this forth dimension of space–time. Hence, dreams can be not only about the past and present but about a preexistent future. Just as you can have memories of the past, so too can you have memories of the future.

So is Dunne saying that the future is predetermined? We are used to determining the outcome of our lives, and society is based on self-determination of the future. It is the backbone of the American Dream: everyone can progress through effort and ambition. A future that is completely predetermined runs against everything we hold to be true. If there's nothing we can do about our destiny then why bother trying to change things? It's fate, and we're stuck with it.

Some of Dunne's dreams of the future suggest that there is predetermination, particularly when the dreams concern newsworthy events. For example, while stationed as a soldier in South Africa during the spring of 1902 Dunne dreamed he was on an island in imminent peril from a volcano. Later he was seized by a frantic desire to save the islanders, believing that 4,000 people were in danger. Throughout the dream, he recalled trying to convince incredulous French authorities to remove the islanders to safety.

Sometime after the dream, at 8 o'clock Thursday morning, May 1902, Mount Pelée erupted, destroying St. Pierre, the main trading island of the French colony Martinique in the West Indies. Dunne read about it in the *Daily Telegraph*. His dream had come horribly true, except that his figures were wrong: 40,000 people had died, not 4,000 as his dream had predicted.

This dream clearly showed that a disaster was going to take place and there was very little anyone could do about it. However, Dunne had other dreams that did not necessarily predict the future but gave warnings that allowed him to avoid catastrophe. On one occasion in 1904 while staying in a hotel in Aachensee, Austria, Dunne dreamed he was being chased across a field by a wild horse:

"I dreamed one night that I was walking down a sort of pathway between two fields, separated from the latter by high iron railings, eight or nine feet high [2.4 or 2.7 m high], on each side of the path. My attention was suddenly attracted to a horse in the field on my left. It had apparently gone mad, and was tearing about, kicking and plunging in a most frenzied fashion. I cast a hasty glance backward and forward along the railings to see if there were any openings by which the animal could get out. Satisfied that there was none, I continued on my way. A few moments later I heard hoofs thundering behind me. Glancing back I saw, to my dismay, that the brute had somehow got out after all, and was coming full tilt after me down the pathway. It was a full-fledged nightmare—and I ran like a hare. Ahead of me the path ended at the foot of a flight of wooden steps rising upward. I was striving frantically to reach these when I awoke."

The next day Dunne went fishing with his brother near the local river and the events of the dream began to unfold. A horse that they could see across the river was behaving just as in the dream. Dunne could see the same wooden steps, but the fences were only four or five feet high. Also, the fields were ordinary small fields, whereas in the dream they had been parklike expanses. Similarly the horse was small and unlike the rampaging monster of the dream. Dunne told his brother about the dream and said, "At any rate, this horse cannot get out," and they continued with their fishing.

But there was no dodging fate. To the amazement of both men the horse suddenly got out, plunged into the river, and galloped toward the wooden steps, coming straight at them. They ran 30 yards (27 m) or so from the bank and turned around. The horse stopped, looked at them, and galloped off down the road.

Clearly, Dunne's dream had come true—well, almost true. The fact is, his dream contained many things that were not precise. This is often the case with dreams about future events. They reveal some of the facts but not all of them. Dunne theorized that dreams of the future are only a sketch of what will happen, because people have free will. It's possible to glimpse at future events but since it's also possible to act on what will happen and exercise free will, the dream you initially had of the future may prove inaccurate.

My own view is that the future is like a landscape. What you see in dreams are the roads and pathways ahead. You can travel across that landscape any way you please. You may choose a hard road or an easy road. If you see an obstacle you can travel over it or move around it. Destiny is like the landscape, your journey is your free will, and your dreams of the future are maps that guide you.

DO YOU DREAM OF THE FUTURE?

Are You a Secret Psychic?

I believe everyone is psychic to some extent, but in normal waking life the rational mind pushes the subtle impressions away. During sleep the rational mind is less active and psychic abilities are able to come alive. You have incredible powers locked within your mind just waiting to be triggered! Some are born with them, others develop them, but everyone has them. Psychic powers are part of ancient survival skills dating back to before the invention of language.

JOSEPH'S DREAM OF THE FUTURE

Our prehistoric ancestors sensed the atmosphere of good or hostile places, could orient themselves without maps, and could share thoughts by telepathy.

Even today, some cultures, such as the Aborigines, retain these skills. You may have even noticed these instinctive ESP abilities in your family pet! ESP is a natural perception, but when the rational mind became dominant, somehow these skills were lost. However, buried deep within, everyone has these ancient skills just waiting to be reanimated. You can find out just how much psychic power you possess by taking our specially devised "Psychic IQ Test." You may find that you already have many psychic qualities that you will be able to discover and enhance in your dreams.

My experience as a professional psychic suggests that ESP comes from the irrational, nonverbal, right brain hemisphere, which is also very active during dreams. Scientists know that this is the part of the brain that perceives the world as a whole rather than by dividing it into categories. It may be the source of intuition and psychic awareness. Rationalists and scientists think with their left brain, but artists and psychics think with their right.

For example, when I've demonstrated mindreading on television I've often been able to describe the content of a target location being mentally projected by the audience, but I find it infuriatingly difficult to put a name to what I see. ESP is a gut feeling. It comes directly from the intuition and bypasses verbal thinking. If you want to discover your psychic powers you must trust your intuition.

WHAT IS ESP?

The American researcher Joseph Banks Rhine, mentioned briefly earlier in this chapter, is considered the father of scientific paranormal research. In the 1930s at Duke University in North Carolina, he undertook the first systematic study of the subject and used statistics to quantify his exhaustive tests. Together with his colleague Carl Zener he designed a set of colorful cards of geometric symbols that were used in various card-guessing games. His conclusion was that many people were achieving correct guesses that were far above what would be expected from chance alone. People were receiving information from something other than the known five senses.

Rhine defined this sixth sense as "Extra Sensory Perception" and subdivided it into four basic abilities:

Telepathy

The ability to tune in to the thoughts of others or inject your own thoughts into another's mind. You may experience this if you and someone you know have exactly the same dream.

Clairvoyance

The power to see things that are not available to you by the known senses and that are not known by anyone else. A dream about finding a lost object that proves to be correct could be your clairvoyance at work.

Precognition

The skill of looking into the future and seeing events before they take place, often through the subconscious when dreaming. Many people believe that dreams reveal facts about the future.

Psychokinesis

The ability to use the power of the mind to influence matter, to move objects by thought, for example. This is a rare gift but I have spoken to people who claim they dreamed of moving an object and then found it in a different room in the morning.

THE PSYCHIC IQ TEST

How Psychic Are You?

Take this simple questionnaire to find out if you have ESP ability and potential psychic personality traits.

1. When the telephone rings do you:

A: Sometimes know exactly who's unexpectedly calling?
B: Often make a guess at who's calling?
C: Never think about who it may be?

2. When you're angry or upset at work do you:

A: Systematically deal with the task at hand and experience no problems?
B: Notice that occasionally machinery breaks down?
C: Always find that faxes jam, computers crash, and photocopiers get stuck?

3. If lost while driving in a strange town do you:

A: Immediately stop the car and consult a map?
B: Drive in what you guess is the general direction?
C: Follow your instincts and drive straight to the address?

4. Are you a person who:

A: Is the life and soul of the party?
B: Likes to express himself but not excessively?
C: Prefers to keep his counsel?

5. When things go very, very wrong do you:

A: Become withdrawn or depressed?
B: Remain anxious but hopeful?
C: Brush off your troubles and maintain a high optimism?

6. When playing board games involving chance do you:

A: Lose despite being careful?
B: Find that you're quite lucky?
C: Enjoy taking risks and feel that you influence the dice in your favor?

7. When you meet someone for the first time do you:

A: Form an immediate assessment of their personality?
B: Guess what they're really like?
C: Reserve judgement?

8. Are you:

A: Logical and systematic in your thinking?
B: Full of good, innovative ideas?
C: Extremely creative and artistic?

9. With newborn babies do you:

A: Leave the care to someone else?
B: Wake from sleep just before they need feeding?
C: Know when an absent baby is upset?

10. When you sleep do you:

A: Dream in color?
B: Never dream?
C: Occasionally dream of events that happen in reality?

11. Do you:

A: Keep an open mind about the existence of ESP?
B: Accept it as completely true?
C: Believe it's all a load of tripe?

12: When you gaze at cumulus clouds do you:

A: See the shapes of faces?
B: See a multitude of changing pictures?
C: See clouds?

Answers

Add up your score and see how psychic you really are:

1. A-3 points, B-2 points, C-1 point.

Experiments reveal that telepathy appears to work over any distance. You have a mind-to-mind link with your friends.

2. A-1 point, B-2 points, C-3 points.

Intense moods such as anger can trigger psychokinesis. You may be affecting machinery by the power of your mind.

3. A-1 point, B-2 points, C-3 points.

The clairvoyant ability to psychically perceive distant locations was dubbed "remote viewing" by the CIA, which employed psychics to spy on Soviet installations during the Cold War.

4. A-3 points, B-2 points, C-1 point.

Psychic researcher Betty Humphrey from Duke University discovered that extrovert personalities displayed better ESP abilities than introverts.

5. A-1 point, B-2 points, C-3 points.

In 1977 researcher John Palmer examined every single published experiment on neu-roticism and ESP. He demonstrated that highly neurotic people were poor ESP subjects and optimists scored better results.

6. A-1 point, B-2 points, C-3 points.

It has been shown that gamblers and risk-takers display higher ESP abilities. Some may also be able to influence the fall of dice by psychokinesis.

7. A-3 points, B-2 points, C-1 point.

Your gut feelings may be telepathy at work.

8. A-1 point, B-2 points, C-3 points.

Imaginative, creative people, and particularly artists, score better on ESP tests than systematic thinkers.

9. A-1 point, B-2 points, C-3 points.

A telepathic bond has been proved to be particularly strong between parents and young siblings. Experiments show that a mother's heartbeat increases when her baby wakes and cries, even if in a soundproof room or at another location.

10. A-2 points, B-1 point, C-3 points.

People who have intense or lucid dreams often experience precognition.

11. A-2 points, B-3 points, C-1 point.

People who believe in ESP often score better in tests than skeptics. However, some skeptics have ESP ability whether they like it or not and score significantly below chance in card tests. If no ESP were involved they would have achieved a chance score.

12. A-2 points, B-3 points, C-1 point.

Psychic people can often visually project images into random shapes. Scrying (seeing pictures in water or in a crystal ball), sand reading, and tea leaf reading all employ this technique.

DREAMING OF THE FUTURE

Having taken this fun test you may agree that there are many situations where you may have used psychic powers or you may have qualities that give you the opportunity to open your powers in the future. When you first started reading this book you probably thought that you never dreamed or dreamed only occasionally. However, if you've been following the methods outlined in this book, you are likely to be much more aware of your dreams. Discovering your psychic powers is very similar. They're there but you've forgotten about them.

One of the best ways to increase your ability to have prophetic dreams is to become aware of your psychic abilities during normal waking life. Your dreams are responsive and focus on whatever emotional, psychological, or physical state is important to you at the moment. For example, if you are preoccupied with relationship problems your dreams are likely to be about emotional anxieties and sexual issues. To increase your ability to dream about the future you need to think about the future during the day. You could read books about great seers or by good psychics

and mediums. Doing this sends a message to your subconscious to help you awaken your intuitive and ESP abilities.

DREAM INCUBATION FOR PROPHECY

There are many ways to increase your intuitive abilities in everyday life. You can make a start by increasing your awareness of people's vibrations. Can you sense a person's mood when you are with that person? What is your gut feeling? Moods are very easy to pick up by telepathy. You can use this same technique and try to ascertain what mood a person is going to be in before you meet them on a specific day of the week. Try also to guess the future. What TV commercial will come up next? What will be the headline on tomorrow's newspaper? When the telephone rings ask yourself who's calling. Before you open a letter try to sense what it's about. In this way you will increase your sensitivity to vibrations and start to open your latent predictive abilities.

When you first started to recall your dreams, I advised you to repeat to yourself affirmations such as: "Tonight I will have a dream." These simple techniques gave you faith in yourself and helped you to believe you could recall your dreams every morning. I'm sure it has worked and you are now either good at recall or, at the very least, can occasionally remember a dream. Similarly, if you have faith in your ability to use psychic powers you will discover them. Belief in the fact that it is possible to see the future will increase your ability to remember dreams about the future. It can be done. You are soon going to use your dreams to look into the future. A conscious effort to have predictive dreams will increase their frequency. It requires patience and practice but is well worth the effort.

INCUBATING FUTURE DREAM RECALL

To increase the likelihood that you will remember a dream about the future it is good to repeat an affirmation to yourself during the day. Dream incubation is a powerful method for creating dreams of prophecy and has been used since the time of the ancient Greeks.

You can make up suitable affirmations for yourself or try some of the ones listed here. When you say the affirmation, touch the center of your forehead, which is the spiritual "third-eye" center. This will help you to be conscious of this important chakra that will be active as you sleep. Here's a few affirmations you can try:

- I am a psychic person and open to the guidance I receive.
- I know it is possible for me to see into the future.
- I give myself permission to remember my dreams of the future.
- I welcome the foresight unfolding within me.
- I call on the angels to bring me a helpful dream of the future.
- The future is calling me.

PROPHECIES YOU'VE ALREADY MADE

If you keep a record of your dreams, you may have noticed already that many of your dreams foretell the future. Other dreams may have appeared to forecast the future but turned out to be incorrect. For example, dreams about death are a very common dream. However, they are rarely a prophecy. In most cases, they are a symbol that represents the way you are feeling. You may feel emotionally overwhelmed by a situation or problem. It is important not to interpret every dream as a prophecy.

Go through your dream diary and highlight with a yellow highlighter any dreams you feel may have either already come true or may be about situations yet to happen. When you read back through your diary, particularly if you keep it for a number of years, it is amazing to see how many dreams contain forecasts of the future.

Most dreams about the future are not dramatic. You are not going to be transformed into the next Nostradamus overnight. Dreams about the future are often subtle and not always easily recognized. You may dream about very ordinary things that will come true: something someone will say, a letter you will receive, or a person you will meet. You will sometimes wonder why out of all the things you could have foreseen (such as the winner of the Super Bowl) you see something banal. Nobody knows why this is so. You will often dream junk, but occasionally you will dream about something that may help you a great deal. Some people, such as those who canceled their journey on the Titanic, had their lives saved because they heeded the prompting of a dream.

Go back through the notes in your dream diary and check all your dreams to see if

SHARED DREAMS

they contain correct premonitions. If you think one is a dream about the future, write "Future?" at the top of the page. If some of the dreams entered in your dream diary are not too personal, show the most important ones to a friend or at least tell your friend about them. When your prediction comes true your friend can bear witness to your psychic powers and this will increase your self-confidence and in turn lead to even better results. Belief in yourself is paramount.

Finally, don't get too serious and don't worry unduly about your dreams. Dreams are there to help. When a dream makes a prediction it usually also shows ways you can avoid any danger. Dreams reveal the potential future—a future you can change. Dreams are there to help you find the best options for a better future. Listen to their wise advice.

EXPERIMENT

HOW TO DREAM ABOUT
THE FUTURE

HAVE you ever been bombarded with a stream of incredible images as you fall asleep? The colors are so bright and the detail of the images is so vivid, you wonder how your mind can conjure up such amazing scenes. The pictures are strange, surreal, even frightening. They rise and fall in a kaleidoscope of color and form. They stream like the most complex computer animation. Psychologists call this state of mind hypnagogic dreaming. According to psychics, the imagery that flows at this time can contain symbols and auguries of the future.

Most dreams about the future are of a personal nature rather than about world events. In this experiment, you are going to look into your own future.

Step 1. During the daytime get yourself in the mood for making a prediction. Think about the future and repeat some of the affirmations you read about earlier. Occasionally stop what you are doing and ask yourself: "What will I be doing exactly three weeks from now?" From my own experience and from asking other people who work with prediction it appears that most predictions take about three weeks to come true. The act of asking yourself what you will be doing in three weeks gets you into the mental routine of thinking about the future. You can also look around and ask yourself: "Will anything be different about this place in three weeks' time?" Similarly, you can look at the people around you and say to yourself: "I wonder what they'll be doing in three weeks' time?" Repeatedly doing this will encourage your subconscious to think about the future.

Step 2. Practice guessing the future. As I explained earlier, try guessing which commercial will be on TV next, and so on. What do you think the very last word in this chapter is?

Step 3. Before you go to sleep, write a letter to yourself in the future. Ask yourself what advice the future has for you. Having the benefit of foresight, what should you do differently? Pretend there is a real you in the future, aware of what you should be doing now, who is sending messages back to you. You could also imagine sending messages to the you in the past and giving the right advice at times when things went right for you.

According to Dunne, the self enters a multidimensional state of being when you go to sleep, so part of you really is in the future already. Something that Dunne did not say in *An Experiment with Time* but that was revealed in his later writings and interviews was that he believed that people from the spirit world could communicate through multidimensional time. (I ask my spirit guide or angel to give me a dream about what I need to know.)

Step 4. Put your letter in an envelope, write your name and address on it, and put it underneath your pillow. This may sound a bit silly, but the act of writing the request gives your subconscious mind a command. Putting it in an envelope reinforces this further. And most importantly, since you expect to get a reply from letters you send in real life, so, likewise, you anticipate a reply from your subconscious psychic powers. You could reinforce the incubation by: 1. Sending your question by e-mail to yourself last thing at night. 2. As you drop to sleep, imagine that you are speaking to your guardian angel messenger who will return in the night with the answer to your question. 3. Every time the telephone rings, pretend that it is your subconscious with a message about the future.

Step 5. Assuming that your partner has not had you put away, your dreams are more likely to contain information about the future. As usual, when you wake up in the morning, write down in the left-hand column of your dream diary everything you can remember about the dream. When you've finished and added the date, title, and so on, add the word "Future," then a short description of the question you asked in your letter. Many of my best predictions are shown to me as I'm falling asleep. If you become conscious of dreaming as you fall asleep, wake yourself up and write down as much as you can remember about the dream. Similarly, if you have mastered the lucid dream techniques from Workshop 4, ask the characters in your dream to tell you about the future.

Step 6. You have already been shown how dreams speak with symbolic language, so don't expect to see the future of your life revealed in a rational way. Your dream may be an allegory of what may happen. Sometimes it's the most uninteresting dreams that contain the most surprising predictions. Look to see if any of your dreams use imagery to represent the future. For example, you dreamed a friend was in a car crash. Nothing like that happened, but soon afterward she and her husband got a divorce. In retrospect, the dream may have been predicting her emotional crash.

Does the dream contain symbolic messages? You may dream of the actual letter you wrote. Your response to it may indicate the nature of future events. If it makes you feel good, then you feel assured about the future. If the contents cause anxiety, this may indicate that you need to take a more positive attitude. Other things that occur in the dream may represent a reply to the letter under your pillow. Dreaming of receiving a parcel or answering the telephone may represent a message from your unconscious. Similarly, a loud noise such as a bell or siren may symbolize something trying to get your attention. Perhaps there are also symbols of time in your dream—the movement of the sun across the sky, the time of day, a watch, sundial, flowing river, egg timer, and so on. These may hold clues to something your dream is saying about the future.

Consider also what the people in your dream represent about your future. They may represent past situations that remind you of your present and future conditions. Similarly, the landscape may hold clues to what's ahead. An obvious example is if you dream of a road. Where is it leading? Do you see a happy-looking landscape ahead or are there mountains to cross and problems afoot?

Of course, you must be very careful if you decide to work with these future recall methods. Not everything you dream about is going to come true. In most cases the dreams are about your emotional state and reflect your hopes and fears. Don't panic thinking that terrible things are going to happen. Also, remember that dreams tend to exaggerate when they speak about your feelings and also when they give information about your future.

THE DREAMING SOUL

Remembering your dreams is certainly worthwhile. Your dreams can give you very important insights into all aspects of your life. You've learned to remember dreams to deal with your past, present, and future situations. You now know a great many techniques to help you to get to know yourself better by understanding your hidden hopes, fears, and motives. Dreams enable you get a clearer picture of what it is you want and need from life. They can give you solutions to help you attain your goals.

Modern man has lost touch with his soul. Dreams take you in search of your lost soul and can restore meaning and purpose to life. Dreams help you fill the spiritual void and put you in touch with the higher powers of the mind. They may encourage you to ask some profound questions about life, death, and the purpose of human existence.

Everything needed to make you happy is latent within you. You have incredible innate knowledge, wisdom, energy, and transcendent understanding. It's all there and every night is expressed in dreams. All you need to do is remember.

Index to Part I

Part II
UNDERSTANDING
Dream Dictionary

 ABANDONMENT (*SEE ALSO* **REJECTION**)

Psychological Meaning This dream may express your unconcious feelings of being foresaken. Do you feel that people neglect you emotionally? Do you harbor feelings of resentment, such as an unresolved problem from childhood? The dream may be saying that you need to express your feelings and that you need to be understood by others. On another level, it may be pointing out that you need guidance with some life issue. For example, perhaps you hope for an authority figure to help you take control of your life. Many people have dreams of abandonment after the death of a loved one. Grief brings a strange mixture of emotions: anger, resentment, depression, panic, and abandonment. These feelings are all part of the healing process.

Mystical Meaning Abandoning something unpleasant indicates good financial news ahead. But the omens are bad if you abandon something or someone you cherish—destiny sees troubled times. However, if you are the one abandoned, reconciliation will happen quickly.

ABBEY

Psychological Meaning A spiritual aspect of your life is about to unfold. Buildings in dreams usually represent the dreamer, the body, or the various levels of the mind. The abbey is a holy place, ancient and free of pomp. It symbolizes the true you—your spiritual self. If the abbey is very old, consider exploring ancient wisdom, such as stories of the Celts or early Christian myths. These dreamlike tales will help trigger your spiritual awakening as you draw upon the ancient memories within the unconscious.

Mystical Meaning Generally considered a good omen but, according to superstition, a young woman dreaming of entering an abbey foretells an illness. A ruined abbey predicts that plans will fail,

and if your way to the abbey is blocked, it augers that you will be saved from a ruinous mistake. To dream of an abbot means an illness or plot is afoot, but an abbess denotes happy friendships.

ABDOMEN (LOWER BODY)

Psychological Meaning The dream may have a physiological cause, such as constipation or indigestion. Emotionally something may be worrying you, something you "cannot stomach," something you want to get out of your system. Possible sexual innuendo; in a woman it may indicate a desire for motherhood.

Mystical Meaning Traditional folklore says that dreaming of your own abdomen promises great things that you must work hard for. It can also foretell of infidelity. A shriveled abdomen warns of lies; a swollen one promises ultimate success; and blood warns of tragedy within the family.

ABYSS

Psychological Meaning Real or imagined problems may be creating anxiety. You may feel you are "falling into a pit of despair" or feel that your situation is abysmal. You may be "standing on the brink" of something and fear "taking the plunge." These feelings threaten you now, so it is important to examine your situation and discover the cause of these unpleasant emotions. A dark abyss may symbolize the unknown part of yourself. If you feel anxious, perhaps you are uncertain what you will discover about yourself and about your hidden feelings and fears. Dreams of this nature sometimes occur when you are thinking about death—not as a prediction but as a way of reminding yourself of the importance of life.

Mystical Meaning An abyss is considered an omen foretelling financial difficulties. Be extremely careful in your business dealings. Some archaic systems warn of romantic, employment, or health problems ahead. The collective advice is: proceed with great caution in all your affairs.

ACCIDENTS

I keep dreaming of car crashes. Do you think my dream is forecasting the future? I am beginning to fear driving.—A.G., California

Psychological Meaning Your dream is not necessarily a premonition of the future. Nightmares of this type reveal deep anxieties and fears. The car crash may symbolize your emotional state. Are you driving yourself too hard? Perhaps you should slow down a bit. If your life feels as if it's set for disaster, examine your mistakes and resolve to set a new and better course. If the accident happens to someone else in your dream, examine your heart. Do you feel suppressed hostility toward that person? Unexpressed jealousy, resentment, or hatred may be finding its release through your dream. Or perhaps the dream refers to accidents of a different kind, such as saying the wrong thing or accidentally forgetting your anniversary.

ASK YOURSELF

1. *Do I feel emotionally at peace with myself?* Probably not, but use the dream as a prelude to a more peaceful you. Get yourself in balance. Relax, listen to music, and take up yoga, meditation, or some other therapeutic activity. And stop punishing yourself!

2. *Have I had similar dreams before?* If yes, try to recall your emotional state at the time. Remember the lessons you learned in the past and apply them again to today's circumstances.

Mystical Meaning The soothsayers says to take care for 24 hours following the dream. Some dream traditions believe that accidents at sea pertain to love affairs but accidents on land symbolize business problems

———

ADULTERY

Psychological Meaning Don't take these dreams too literally; they usually highlight inner fears. Perhaps you are worried about your sexuality or you desire something not in your best interest. The dream is a way your unconscious expresses its sexual urges. Sometimes it does this in ways that go against what is socially acceptable or advisable.

Mystical Meaning A legal action may befall you if a man dreams of adultery. A woman dreamer will lose the affections of her husband. (Ancient dream dictionaries, written before the advent of women's rights, predicted far worse consequences for women than for men who had this dream.)

AGE (*SEE ALSO* CHILD)

Psychological Meaning The dream may highlight concerns about getting older. Try not to be dated with your opinions and be a little younger at heart. However, an old man or woman in a dream may be symbolic of superior wisdom within you. Listen to the advice and guidance your higher self brings you. If you dream of being a child, you may be drawing upon the psychological resources that are the foundation of your personality.

Mystical Meaning To dream of old people brings good luck, but to dream of growing old yourself is a sign of failure. To see a friend grow old suddenly is a warning of disappointment from that friend.

AIR (*SEE ALSO* ELEMENTS *AND* WIND)

Psychological Meaning Air represents wisdom and clarity. As an element it symbolizes spiritual concerns but in a dream it may be a

FAMOUS DREAMER

J. W. Dunne
Author

J. W. Dunne, in his book An Experiment with Time *(Macmillan 1927), said he dreamed he was on an island on which a volcano was about to erupt. He explained that he tried to warn the French authorities about the impending explosion and that 4,000 lives were in danger. On waking, he immediately made an entry into his meticulously detailed dream diary. A few days later Dunne opened his newspaper to read of the eruption of Mount Pelée on the French island of Martinique. An estimated total of 40,000 lives had been lost. (See also* Time*)* warning of the dangers of losing contact with reality. As a breeze or wind it may represent the spirit that inspires or the life force that animates.

Mystical Meaning Old dream books claim that to dream of air means your hopes will wither away.

AIRPLANE (*SEE ALSO* FLYING)

Psychological Meaning To dream of being in an airplane may show you "rising above" your troubles. An airplane is a symbol of transcendence and release from psychological or material difficulties. The sky is a symbol of the expanded consciousness of the higher self. Your airplane dream expresses your desire for greater awareness or spiritual knowledge. An **airport** or air journey may indicate a new departure in your life. This could include a new job, new relationship, or an adventure. To a Freudian psychologist an airplane is a phallic symbol by virtue of its forceful, penetrative motion. You may have high ambitions and want to progress in life swiftly to achieve your goals as quickly and directly as possible. Airplanes are the quickest way to get to a destination. Alternatively, you may simply desire to travel or have a vacation. A dream of a plane crash can show that you are overly ambitious and have set your sights too high. Materially or emotionally, you may be expecting too much and you may have doubts about your ability to reach your goals.

Mystical Meaning Most modern superstitions say that dreaming of an airplane indicates that money is on the way. If you are the pilot, you will succeed in a business adventure. If the plane crashes, a business will fail. Gypsies say that dreaming of an airplane indicates that you must share your enterprises with your relatives.

ALCHEMY

Psychological Meaning Carl Jung believed that the secret art of the alchemists was a system of symbols used to bring about the transformation of the personality from its base state (lead) to exalted spiritual consciousness (gold). Alchemical symbols are archetypal images from the uncon-

scious. If you dream of alchemy you may be experiencing a period of inner transformation. It may be painful but is most definitely for the best.

Mystical Meaning Alchemy was the medieval equivalent of modern psychology. Its strange symbolism can still invoke unconscious forces that bring about positive inner transformation.

ALIEN (*SEE ALSO* FOREIGNER *AND* UFO)

Psychological Meaning Assuming that you weren't abducted during the night, dreaming of an alien indicates an encounter with an unfamiliar part of your psyche. You may feel that this unfamiliar part of yourself is hostile or an enemy. Your first step should be to find out what it is and get to know this neglected aspect of yourself. For example, you may be behaving in ways that are "alien" to you or have feelings that are "unlike you." It is unhealthy to repress or neglect these components of your nature. What at first appears frightening because of its unfamiliarity may in time become a mentor and ally. Your alter ego may have something good to offer you. Also, the alien may represent a situation you have recently experienced. When you start a new job you may at first feel alienated or like an outsider. Alternatively, you may feel that emotionally you are in another world from everyone else.

Mystical Meaning Aliens are (arguably) a product of modern times, so no traditional folkloric interpretations exist.

ALTAR

Psychological Meaning From a religious standpoint, an altar can have a number of meanings. It is a place of sacrifice, so the dream may symbolize a personal sacrifice you have made or intend to make. Or it may mean that you have sacrificed something within yourself; something within you must die if a new, happy life is to be born. For example, you may sacrifice the ego so that more sincere feelings can manifest in your life. In addition, the altar may symbolize the wedding of the unconscious and the conscious mind—the union of opposites compensates for the development of a one-sided personality. Or it may symbolize the consecration of something you deem sacred. Many dreams express themselves with puns. Maybe the dream is suggesting that you should "alter" your plans.

Mystical Meaning To dream you are inside a church is usually considered a bad omen. It warns of error and repentance. To see a priest at the altar warns of quarrels and problems at home or in business. However to see a church from the outside brings good fortune and blessing.

ANCHOR

Psychological Meaning You may be looking for greater security, as an anchor represents a stabilizing force. It may also symbolize an influence in your life that brings greater steadfastness and strength. For a career person, it can show a desire to be the "anchorman" (or woman). Alternatively, the anchor may represent something negative that is holding you back and restraining your freedom. For example, you may feel shackled to a relationship that isn't working or feel tied to an emotional problem. A Freudian interpretation of the dream might be that you are chained to your mother and dependent on her. (The sea can symbolize the mother.)

Mystical Meaning An old superstition states that if a woman dreams of an anchor, one of her children will choose a life as a sailor. It is also favorable for a sailor to dream of an anchor. For the rest of us, it means a change of residence or foreign travel. Generally it is considered a good omen, but if the anchor is in the water or partly hidden in any way, expect disappointment.

ANGEL (SEE ALSO FLYING)

Psychological Meaning As a practicing medium I believe that the spirit world can contact people through dreams, and that angels are the higher spirit beings that help humanity progress spiritually. Since earliest times, angels have been known as messengers from God. In a psychological sense, this could be a message from parts of yourself leading to greater fulfillment and happiness. Wings suggest flight and transcendence. If the angel is sinister, recognize it as something in your life that may cause trouble. Pay attention to these things and give them expression in your life. Dreaming of the Angel of Death is not necessarily an omen of death. It may symbolize your anxiety looking for a way to express itself.

Mystical Meaning Considered a fortunate dream symbol, to dream of angels predicts good fortune in love, partnerships, and friendships. Several angels means you will receive an inheritance and, if an angel enters your home, you will be wealthy.

ANGER

Psychological Meaning Dreams give the opportunity to express feelings and emotions sometimes impossible to express in waking life. You may have some aggression within yourself that you have not acknowledged fully. The dream may be suggesting that you become more assertive and stop taking a passive attitude toward your circumstances. Perhaps you feel undervalued, rejected, or jealous or you harbor hostile wishes toward someone close to you. Someone angry with you might represent a characteristic in yourself that you dislike. Are you angry with yourself? Do you feel guilty about an issue? Psychologist Alfred Adler believed that aggressive drives motivate most people but can be sublimated and directed into creative channels.

Mystical Meaning According to some timeworn sources, anger in a dream denotes an unlawful trial that awaits you. It foretells disappointment in love and attacks on your character. However, if you are angry with a stranger, unexpected good news is on its way. An invitation is likely.

ANIMA/ANIMUS (SEE ALSO HERO/HEROINE)

Psychological Meaning The *anima* is the feminine principle in the male psyche. It is often symbolized by a beautiful young woman. She may leave the dreamer determined that he must embark on a heroic quest to meet her again. The dreamer may mistakenly look for the "girl of his dreams" in the outside world, but in reality the dream points to the motivation to discover the feminine part of himself. Integration of both the masculine and feminine sides of your nature leads to psychological health and wholeness. Similarly, the *animus* is the masculine principle in the female psyche. A woman may dream of it in the guise of a beautiful young man or a hero figure.

The *anima* (the feminine principle in a man) can also take a negative role. Instead of providing spiritual inspiration and a more balanced view of

ANIMA/ANIMUS

life, it can appear in dreams as moody, irritable, and oversensitive. If the "woman of your dreams" is like this, it may signal that these destructive characteristics are dominating your personality.

Similarly, the *animus* (the masculine principle in a woman) can also be a destructive force. According to Jung, a negative *animus* causes a woman to be opinionated, argumentative, rigid, controlling, and excessively critical of herself and others. Jung believed that everyone should strive to find a proper balance between the positive qualities associated with both the *anima* and *animus* and integrate these into the personality.

Mystical Meaning The wisdom of yore says that to dream of a young man or woman is a sign that there will be a reconciliation of family disagreements.

ANIMALS (*see also* Horse, Lion, Fish, Monkey, Bird, *etc.*)

Psychological Meaning: Animals signify primal, instinctive, and sometimes base desires. Your dream may be drawing attention to an aspect of your nature you undervalue or part of yourself you repress. Try to get in touch with the natural you. Be more spontaneous and less rational. Within everyone is a deep instinctive energy that has a transforming power. A dream of eating an animal is a classic mythical symbol that represents assimilating natural wisdom. Fighting an animal may show that you are grappling with your shadow—the hidden part of yourself that the conscious mind has rejected. Animals guarding a treasure can represent brutish passions preventing you from realizing your true spiritual potential. Animals may also express certain qualities: a dog may represent devotion, a cat may represent intuition, a tiger may represent fear, and a pig may symbolize gluttony and bad behavior. Animals can represent people (sly as a fox, slippery as a fish, strong as an ox, a lying snake, etc.).

Mystical Meaning To dream of an animal is considered an omen for the future. Peaceful cows and bulls are considered particularly good omens, but try hard never to dream of crocodiles, dogs, or cats, for these bring troubles. In the Far East, to dream of a green monkey means that a medicine will not work. Indeed, to even think about a green monkey while taking a medicine stops it from working. Next time you take a medicine, try *not* thinking about a green monkey—it's impossible, of course!

ANXIETY

Psychological Meaning Nobody knows for certain the function of sleep. Many scientists say that people sleep in order to dream—that dreams are the brain's way of bringing the emotions back into balance. Experiments have shown that people consistently deprived of dream sleep suffer from emotional disorders. Dreams resolve anxieties and restore psychological equilibrium. It's quite natural to have dreams that express anxieties and emotions that cannot be asserted in everyday life. Freud believed that anxiety dreams disguise repressed aggression or resentment. Where anxiety appears in dreams, look for repressed feelings or desires that initiate anxiety. Freud identified repressed childhood feelings of resentment, jealousy, and hostility toward parents and family as giving rise to these dreams.

Mystical Meaning Superstition says that anxiety dreams have the opposite meaning, showing that a worry will very soon be relieved. In some ways this is true, for by expressing your fears in your dreams you come a little closer to resolving your hidden fears.

APE (*see also* Monkey and Shadow)

Psychological Meaning The dream may simply be a pun: i.e., "You're making an ape of yourself." You may be making an egotistical mistake of some kind. Apes are known to be gentle, so the dream may also symbolize the part of you that wants to behave more naturally and return to a simpler archaic past. A sinister ape may symbolize the dark, repressed side of your nature.

Mystical Meaning Bad news, I'm afraid. To dream of apes means that people will deceive you, and mischief is afoot. Be particularly careful of false promises connected with business. If the ape is in a tree, someone close to you will tell lies that cause widespread trouble.

ANIMALS

APPLE

Psychological Meaning The apple may be considered a sexual symbol. It is the forbidden fruit associated with the fall of Adam and Eve in the Garden of Eden and so with sin, by which sex is usually meant. Freud pointed out that eating is connected with sexuality, because the mouth is the first erogenous zone discovered by young children. From a Freudian viewpoint apples stand for lasciviousness. Your dream may be saying that you have a sexual appetite and want to taste the fruits of life. Alternatively, apples may symbolize knowledge, since this is what Adam and Eve gained after falling from innocence. On a mundane level you may have personal associations with the symbol, such as an Apple computer or the Big Apple, or it may be as a symbol of good diet and health.

Mystical Meaning It is a good omen to dream of apples, particularly if they are red. Dreaming of ripe and sweet apples promises you will be rewarded, but if the apples are sour you are in danger of loss because of your own foolishness. Fallen apples on the ground warn of false friends. And if the apple is decayed, all your efforts will be hopeless.

ARMOR

Psychological Meaning An armored, or shielded, individual is likely to protect himself from spontaneous emotional interaction with people. In dreams, these are protective symbols against anxiety. Ask yourself what it is you want to protect yourself from. Is it an inner fear? Is there something you need to defend yourself against? Examine the causes of this feeling and you may discover you need not be so guarded. With more self-confidence, openness, and social ease, you would not have to take such extreme measures to protect yourself from the outside world. The dream may also show that you are preparing to do battle. Armor may represent the fact that you are confident and well prepared.

Mystical Meaning If you dream of wearing armor, including breastplate, chain mail, or thick leather jerkin, tradition says you are taking life too seriously. Lighten up and enjoy life. People who believe in reincarnation may interpret this dream as a reference to a past life. If historical facts are revealed within the dream, see if they are true. You

may be recalling mysterious memories from lives long ago.

ARREST (*see* Police)

ARROW

Psychological Meaning A Freudian psychologist interprets this image as a male sexual symbol. Favored by Cupid, an arrow can represent the penis in its ability to penetrate. It has associations with male violence and aggression. (In the hymn "Jerusalem" William Blake refers to "my arrows of desire.") Arrows can also represent something that goes straight to the mark. The dream shows how to reach targets you have set for yourself. Perhaps you should focus on one specific goal and set about achieving it.

Mystical Meaning "Expect journeys, entertainment, and festivals," says one medieval source. To dream of being struck by an arrow means you have a secret enemy. A broken arrow portends disappointment in love or business.

ARTIST

Psychological Meaning This may represent the creative and intuitive side of your nature. You may feel a need to express yourself and may have the urge to be more creative. If you're painting a picture it may show the way you picture your situation at the moment. You are probably starting to see things more clearly.

Mystical Meaning You may have to revise your plans in order to attain recognition. If you talk about art in your dream you may expect an upturn in your business or professional status.

ASHES

Psychological Meaning After the fire has gone, dull, lifeless ash remains. You may be feeling that the good times are over and nothing of value is left in your life. Alternatively, you may be raking over the past or dwelling upon something that is finished. Ashes may represent a failed relationship or ruinous business enterprise. In Hinduism, ashes are a symbol of the indestructible soul. After everything has been reduced by fire, ash is what remains. It is the indestructible part of yourself.

Mystical Meaning To dream of ashes is a bad omen. Crops will fail, business deals will go wrong, and children will cause problems for their parents. Gypsies, however, say it means you will finally cease to mourn lost chances of the past. Many tribal societies consider ashes to be a positive symbol of fertility and good luck. In England and the United States ashes are said to ward off evil spirits.

AUDITION

Psychological Meaning Social vulnerabilities are highlighted, and you may fear that you are unable to communicate effectively with others. You feel as if your social role in life is being tested. Dreams like this may occur soon after starting a new job or undertaking a socially challenging role. You may also dream of being unable to make yourself heard over the noise of others, of being laughed at or tongue-tied, or you may have a feeling of impending disaster. All these images express feelings of social vulnerability. An unruly audience may show your inability to get your ideas across. The absence of an audience may show a lack of recognition.

Mystical Meaning Most dreams associated with actors, actresses, and the stage are considered fortunate, but to see them wandering and penniless foretells that your good fortune will be reversed. To dream of public speaking is also fortunate, but speaking from a pulpit bodes sickness and business failure.

AVALANCHE

Psychological Meaning You may fear a disaster or failure. Perhaps your intuition has identified a flaw in your plans that needs urgent attention. Carefully examine the other images in the dream and see if you can identify the cause of the fear or warning. The issue may be emotional. Are you "as cold as ice"? Your frozen feelings may be causing you problems. Loosen up or you may cause an avalanche of out-of-control emotions.

Mystical Meaning Mystics say it is tremendously fortunate to dream of an avalanche, particularly if you are buried in the snow! It portends profit and wealth. To see others buried in an avalanche indicates a change of surroundings.

AWAKENING (*see also* Lucid Dreams)

Psychological Meaning To dream of awakening may represent a new awareness that is unfolding in your life. However, it may mean that you are on the verge of lucid dreaming. In this remarkable state of consciousness you "wake up" in the dream and realize you are dreaming *as the dream is taking place*. In this state, the dreamer can direct the dream like a film director. Lucid dreams can be used creatively or to help resolve psychological problems. For example, someone with recurrent dreams of being chased, in a lucid dream might be able to turn around, stare down the stalker, and unmask the fears hitherto run from. Native Americans have practiced lucid dreaming techniques for centuries.

Mystical Meaning To dream that you are awake and walking though a beautiful landscape denotes good times ahead after a period of difficulty. People who consciously cultivate their psychic ability use special techniques to "wake up" during dreams in order to look into the future. One method is to imagine being in a time machine. The dream moves into the future and the psychic receives a premonition of future events.

AXE

Psychological Meaning This ominous symbol can be interpreted in a number of ways. Perhaps you are worried about your job, of being "given the axe." Or do you want to chop something out of your life? If you dream of an executioner's axe, you may be feeling guilty about something you have done. In this case, the axe may represent judgment and punishment. An axe used to chop wood may show that you need to divide your problem into more manageable parts. Chopping down a tree may symbolize removing the old so that the new can sprout fresh and may necessitate a change in lifestyle or circumstances.

Mystical Meaning Apart from clearly warning of danger, the axe has some strange dream lore associated with it. To dream of a shiny axe signifies gratifying rewards, but a dull one means loss of prestige. An axe also means that you will soon hear from friends. For an unmarried woman, this dream means she will meet the man of her dreams but he will never have a cent!

BABY

Psychological Meaning A baby may represent something new in your life. Does it cry for attention? Do you feel content with this new situation? A baby can also symbolize your own inner nature, pure and uncorrupted, or may say that you are innocent of an accusation. It could show the vulnerable part of you that needs protecting, or perhaps you are nurturing some new ideas or feelings. New Age gurus speak of loving the magical child within and advise expressing the innocent carefree side of yourself. Your dream may be telling you to follow this advice. To dream of a baby, of course, may show that your maternal instincts are seeking expression; you may simply wish for a child.

Mystical Meaning Surprisingly, most old dream books believe that dreams of babies have nothing to do with prophecies of pregnancy. For example, if a woman dreams she is nursing a baby, she will be deceived by someone she trusts.

BACK

Psychological Meaning The back of the body, the back of an object, stage, or building symbolizes parts of yourself hidden from view. The back may also represent secrets you keep from other people or aspects of your personality you would prefer not to think about. If the dream gives you a feeling of unease, these hidden traits may have negative connotations. You may have pushed away feelings of guilt, shame, fear, or self-disgust.

Mystical Meaning Traditionally, evil is said to stand behind us. The preacher may say "Get thee behind me, Satan." People who believe spilling salt brings bad luck throw some over their left shoulder and into the eye of the devil. Your dream may point to an aspect of your life that is now over, a situation you have "put behind you." Maybe your dream contains some other play on words: Is someone getting your back up? Do you feel you need a pat on the back?

BACKWARD

Psychological Meaning To dream of walking or moving backward means you are taking retrograde steps in your life. What you seek from life appears to be moving away from you. You may have a feeling of failure, an inability to achieve your goals and aspirations. Alternatively, the dream may be telling you that the best policy at the moment is to retreat. Why exhaust yourself in a fruitless struggle? Rest and gather your strength so that you can try again later with renewed vigor and self-confidence.

Mystical Meaning Some tribal societies believe that evil spirits can be thwarted by a dramatic change in routine. Walking backward is one way to confuse demons that bring bad luck. To dream of walking backward therefore indicates that better luck is on its way.

BAG

Psychological Meaning The bag represents psychological qualities you carry through life. For example, if the bag is full of junk, it may represent attitudes and worries you burden yourself with. In this case, your problems are of your own making—consider ways to unload your problems. Perhaps you can lighten your load by adopting a cheerful attitude. Similarly, the bag may represent responsibility. The dream may be suggesting that you share the burden you presently carry on your own. If the bag is filled with food or items of value, the dream may be showing that you are gathering ideas or new knowledge in your waking life.

Mystical Meaning Dream superstition says that dreams of paper bags forecast financial bad luck, cloth bags bring business success, and leather bags forecast unexpected journeys. The heavier the bag, the more success you'll have.

BAKING

Psychological Meaning This dream can represent plans you are nearly ready to put into action. You should soon benefit, for bread represents the qualities of nourishment and wholesomeness. This dream can also represent pregnancy. The oven is the womb and the bread is the growing child. But don't rush off to buy a crib and baby booties. The dream is most likely a metaphor rather than a prediction of an actual birth. It may be showing the development of a new idea or a period of spiritual development.

Mystical Meaning To dream of baking brings good luck, say the old superstitions. Unfortunately this dream prophesy only applies to men.

BABY

BALDNESS

Psychological Meaning If you dream of losing your hair you may be worried about your self-image and how others perceive you. You may feel insecure and anxious. You may also feel that you do not have the power to succeed in an undertaking and may be unconsciously reminded that Samson lost his strength when his hair was cut. You may also harbor fears of aging or loss of virility. If you are losing your hair in real life, this dream expresses your anxieties about it. Surrender some of your vanity and your stress level will decrease.

Mystical Meaning European and American cultures hold that to dream of being bald is a signal of financial loss. However, this belief is reversed in the Batoro tribe, whose people live between lakes Albert and Edward in East Africa. Fertility and prosperity are guaranteed the Batoro bride only if every hair on her head and body is shaved before she marries. The bride is then covered with copious quantities of oil. To dream of being bald is therefore an auspicious sign.

BALLOON

Psychological Meaning If the balloon flies freely in the sky, this dream may be expressing your desire for freedom or escape from an oppressive situation. You seek to rise above the conflicts of daily life. Festive balloons can also represent a celebration of some kind or a personal achievement. However, the dream can also have a negative connotation. Do you have an inflated opinion of yourself? Be careful, for a balloon full of wind can easily burst—and so can your ego.

Mystical Meaning Traditional interpretations say that to dream of traveling in a hot-air balloon warns of an unfortunate journey. Alternatively, it may indicate that you can see the way ahead. Look at the landscape. Does it represent the landscape and pathway of your future?

BANK

Psychological Meaning A bank, and particularly the vault, represents your inner storehouse of psychological potential. Your unconscious is telling you to start using your inner reserves of skill and energy. It's no good locking your talents away. The dream symbolism may be more literal than this. The dream may show your practical need for financial security. You are being shown that your circumstances are more secure financially than you fear. However, if you dream of robbing a bank, it may suggest that you are expending too much energy and are in danger of depleting you inner resources.

Mystical Meaning If you dream of putting money into the bank it means money is coming your way. If you dream that the coffers are empty, it forecasts financial doom.

BAPTISM

Psychological Meaning The baby or adult being baptized is you. The next stage of your life, your plans, and your hopes are all being blessed by your higher self. You are being reborn into something new and better. A baby being baptized may represent a new way of being, a new attitude toward life, or a new approach toward others. Immersion in water represents death, and emergence represents resurrection and new life. The old, negative, you has died, and it is likely that this new you will be successful. Your new attitude will bring positive things to you. The dream may also be spiritual. Your faith in God has been renewed and you are coming closer to self-realization and spiritual fulfillment.

Mystical Meaning If you dream of drinking water from a baptism, you will be a great and famous singer.

BAT

Psychological Meaning The early Christians considered bats birds of the devil because of their association with darkness and their similarity to rats. Bats share the sexual lust of the devil. (The devil is a corruption of the cloven-footed god Pan, who played his pipes in celebration of nature and sexuality.) In particular, vampire bats, which take human form in Bram Stoker's *Dracula*, represent predatory sexuality, for it is only virgins' blood that they can drink. Maurice Richardson, in *Psychoanalysis of Ghost Stories*, observes that Dracula, with his dark heroism and superhuman image, has an unconscious erotic appeal for women. He argues that the story only makes sense analyzed from a Freudian standpoint. Alternatively, a vampire bat may represent a person in your life who is depleting you of self-confidence or resources.

Mystical Meaning To dream of one of these universally loathed creatures is a portent of disaster. They are considered omens of injury or death. Because of their blindness, bats are also considered prophecies warning of danger to the eyes. Fortunately, superstition also has an antidote for these terrible dreams: Carry a bat bone in your pocket and you'll come to no harm. In parts of Europe people believe that a bat's right eye carried in a waistcoat pocket will make a person invisible.

BATH

Psychological Meaning Bathing represents psychological cleansing. You are trying to get rid of old attitudes. Water can symbolize your emotional nature. You may be trying to cleanse yourself of negativity. Perhaps you have feelings of guilt or are uncomfortable with your feelings. You may feel that your natural sexual feelings are dirty thoughts. It has also been suggested that a bath symbolizes the waters of the womb and represents a desire to escape back to the security of the amniotic waters.

Mystical Meaning It was once believed that the act of washing cleansed a person not only of the dirt from the body but also of the sins from the heart. But to dream of bathing is a mixed blessing, for in many countries it is believed to wash away your good luck.

BEARD

Psychological Meaning A beard symbolizes the wild and primitive man within you—your untamed sexual side. According to Freud, a man who dreams of having his beard cut fears castration; beard-cutting symbolizes loss of sexual confidence. If a woman dreams of growing a beard it may show her desire to play a man's role—to have a more powerful job or be more assertive. Long beards are associated with old age and wisdom. A wizened old man with a long, gray beard represents the insight that comes from the unconscious. It is your own higher self that can guide you to greater knowledge and understanding.

Mystical Meaning An Arab will not thank you if you pull his beard, for this is considered a terrible insult. Wars have been waged over lesser sins. Similarly, in Europe and America to dream of a beard signifies a fierce battle ahead.

BEREAVEMENT (SEE DEATH)

BIRD

Psychological Meaning Because of their ability to fly, birds universally represent spirituality. The sky is the unfettered realm of the spirit and, like the winged gods of old, birds show that some process within your psyche is bringing you wholeness, healing, and balance. Birds are the soul's desire for transcendence. They may also show your desire to escape from something you consider to be banal and commonplace. You may want to be free of a situation and have a desire to take wing. Or is it a habitual attachment or negative attitude you want to rise above? In mythology, birds are often messengers from the gods. In psychological terms it may show that the unconscious is offering you new insight and solutions to your problems. To dream of freeing a bird from captivity relates to releasing your own emotions or primal energies.

Birds can also symbolize aspects of relationships. Thieving birds, such as magpies, may suggest adultery or some other threat to a relationship. Territorial birds, such as blackbirds, can represent jealousy. According to Freud, birds are sexual symbols that represent the penis. Many people still call attractive young women birds. Finally, a flock of birds may represent your need to be one of a group that you admire and identify with.

Mystical Meaning For centuries it has been considered a good omen to dream of birds. Here are a few of the most common superstitions: albatross, good luck coming; buzzard, beware of gossip; cock, if it crows you will receive good news soon; dove, a peaceful solution to your problems will be found; eagle, business success; geese, improvements ahead; hawk, a bright future awaits you; magpie, a change of plan in matters of the heart; owl, beware of disappointment; stork, family problems are imminent; turkey, bad luck unless you dream of killing or eating it.

BIRTH

Psychological Meaning For a woman, dreams about birth may simply reflect your thoughts and feelings regarding motherhood. As a symbol, birth can represent the possibility of a new beginning or a period of personal growth. The same imagery is used in everyday language: "giving birth to a new idea," you may refer to a project as your baby. Sometimes bringing something new into your life can be a painful process.

For Jung, dreams about birth were important because they represented a stage in the individuation process. Put simply, this is the growth of the human psyche to maturation and wholeness. Birth therefore represents the start of an important new phase in your life and personal psychological development.

Mystical Meaning To dream of giving birth brings good luck to married people but trouble to single women.

BITE (*SEE ALSO* FOOD)

Psychological Meaning Young children sometimes bite in order to express aggressiveness. You may have unexpressed, perhaps childish, feelings of anger or resentment that need to be recognized and perhaps expressed. If you are the one being bitten, it may illustrate that you feel pestered by a problem or difficulty. If an animal bites you, consider what aspect of your instinctive nature it represents. The dream may also point to an outer problem. For example, being bitten by a shark may be a play on words telling you something like "be careful of that loan shark."

Mystical Meaning To dream of biting means you will suffer a loss because of an enemy—or so they say.

BLACK (*SEE* COLORS)

BLIND

Psychological Meaning If you dream of being blind, it may represent your refusal to see the truth. Perhaps you reject something about yourself or your situation. Do you feel you have lost your sense of direction in waking life? Or are you so bigoted in your opinions that you refuse to see any other point of view except your own? Perhaps your religious experiences are one of "blind faith" rather than tolerance and spiritual inquiry? Truth frees you from the painful bondage of ignorance. Open your eyes!

Mystical Meaning In mythology Wotan sacrificed an eye to get the runes. Similarly, the visionary Tiresias in ancient Greece was blind. Blindness as a mystical dream symbol represents

swapping outer vision for inner vision. The dream may therefore represent wisdom and self-knowledge

BLOOD

Psychological Meaning Blood is a symbol of life. If you dream of losing blood, you may be suffering from exhaustion or may feel emotionally drained by a situation. Blood can also symbolize passion, especially love, anger, or even violence. Women sometimes dream of blood at the start of their menstruation.

Mystical Meaning In many ancient rituals, participants drank the blood of sacrificial animals. This represented sharing the power and strength of the gods. Similarly, to dream of drinking blood may be a grisly symbol for receiving new vitality.

BLUE (*SEE* COLORS)

BOAT

Psychological Meaning A boat may represent traveling through emotional times. In particular, water may be a symbol for the emotions. If the water is rough, you may be feeling emotionally fraught in waking life. If all is calm and still, you may feel that your emotional life at this time is "smooth sailing." To dream of missing the boat may show you've missed an opportunity.

Mystical Meaning In mythology, boats, such as the ferry across the river Styx, could represent the transition from this world to the next. As a symbol, it may represent the passing from one phase of life to another. You may be making a clean break with the past.

BOMB

Psychological Meaning The dream may be telling you something about a potentially explosive situation you have to deal with in your waking life. Alternatively, it could be something within yourself, such as a desire to explode with anger about an issue that's affecting you. Similarly, the bomb could represent repressed desires and drives that are likely to explode if not dealt with. Proceed with caution and exercise inner calm. Why not take up meditation? It will help defuse this inner time bomb.

Mystical Meaning A heated argument will have a happy ending if you dream of a bomb, says dream superstition.

BONDAGE

Psychological Meaning If you dream of being tied up it may indicate that aspects of your psychological life are too tightly controlled. You may be restricting your need for self-expression or feel that you are a prisoner of your circumstances. You may have hidden potential you refuse to acknowledge or you may be repressing your true feelings. Perhaps the dream shows that you are held captive by the banal and commonplace, that you have a need for the inner freedom that comes with spirituality. You may want to set yourself free. You may also fear that a forthcoming event, such as a marriage, new job, or the birth of a child, will curtail your freedom.

The dream may also show that you try to dominate others. Do you try to dominate or emotionally smother your kith and kin? Some people dominate others by placing them under an obligation; this secures dependency or indebtedness. Such a controlling attitude will never bring happiness.

Bondage of course also has erotic overtones. Freud believed that dreams of bondage were an allegory for repressed sexual fantasies. These, he said, dated back to childhood when our parents dominated us. Alternatively, it could symbolize your desire to be more sexually submissive or could illustrate that you have unacknowledged sexual passions.

Mystical Meaning To dream of being tied up means that, contrary to your better judgment, you will yield to love.

BONES (SEE ALSO SKULL)

Psychological Meaning Your dream may be showing you the "bare bones" of a situation. Being stripped or cut to the bone may signify a sudden insight or an attack on your personality. To dream of fractured limbs may represent a threat to the foundations of life, and to personal power. If you dream of broken bones, you may have discovered a fundamental weakness in your plans or psychology. Sometimes, bones refer to a skeleton in the closet.

Mystical Meaning Goddesses with strings of skulls around their necks or waists refer to the negative, devouring side of time. Perhaps you fear getting older?

BOOK

Psychological Meaning This can symbolize knowledge, wisdom, or the intellect. It may also say that you are more concerned with theory and opinion than with putting what you know into practice. A book may represent a record of the story of your life.

Mystical Meaning Shun evil in all its forms if you dream of old books, say the ancient sages of dream lore.

BOSS

Psychological Meaning Bossy dream characters were nicknamed "top dog" by Fritz Perls, founder of Gestalt therapy. They are similar to Freud's notion of the super-ego. These bullies scold and lecture other dream characters, who rapidly assume the role of what Perls called "underdog." These are aspects of your personality you are ashamed of and that you try hard to ignore. For a healthy psyche, it is important to accept all aspects of yourself and let all the inner parts of yourself come to expression. In your imagination, ask each dream character to speak to you. The answers they give may reveal a great deal about your hopes, desires, and fears.

Mystical Meaning The first dream books were of course written for the literate upper classes. And so they say that to dream of being bossed around is a sign of incompetence but to dream of being the master means you will rise to a high position in society.

BOTTLE

Psychological Meaning Are your emotions bottled up? The bottle in your dream may represent how you are pushing your feelings back inside rather than letting them express themselves in waking life. The contents of the bottle illustrate the nature of the emotions. Champagne may show your need to socialize; poison may represent evil thoughts; red wine may represent passions; and milk may show the need to nurture new ideas or feelings. If the bottle is empty, you may have exhausted your inner resources. You may be feeling drained and empty inside. Regularly recording your dreams may suggest ways to fill this inner vacuum.

Mystical Meaning In many myths the genie is kept locked in a bottle until released by the hero. In dreams, the genie may represent the powers of the psyche which at first appear dark and menacing because unconscious but are transformed when brought under conscious control. The story of Aladdin and his magic lamp was based on these very ancient myths.

BOX

Psychological Meaning By opening a box you reveal things that were once hidden. This dream may be a symbol of spiritual exploration—you are getting to know the contents of your psyche. If you find bad things in the box or opening it fills you with fear, you may be uncovering things about yourself or your environment that make you feel anxious.

Mystical Meaning In the Greek myth Pandora's box represents the negative aspect of woman. This beautiful temptress is the source of all evil, yet her name means "all-giving." As a psychological dream symbol this story illustrates a man's fear of the dark, feminine side of his own nature. It may also show the way the unconscious projects its own negative complexes and attitudes onto reality.

BREASTS

Psychological Meaning Most likely, this dream symbol is a sexual one that shows your desire for love. However, it may also represent a mother's nurturing qualities. You may be nurturing new ideas and plans. A Freudian interpretation would ask you to question whether you are too attached to your real mother—an attachment that may be preventing you from achieving your independence.

Mystical Meaning If a woman dreams of having shriveled breasts she will be disappointed in love; if they are buxom and lily white, she will be rich. The ancient books say nothing about men who have these dreams.

BRIDE/BRIDEGROOM (SEE ALSO MARRIAGE AND ANIMA/ANIMUS)

Psychological Meaning A bride may represent the peak of feminine force within us. For a man she is an anima figure, the feminine side of his nature. Similarly, a bridegroom may represent the masculine, animus, side of a woman's personality. The most psychologically healthy people are those who integrate both sides of their nature.

Mystical Meaning Most fairy tales use the same symbolism found in dreams. Many end with "They got married and lived happily ever after." This typical happy ending is a classic dream symbol for the union of the masculine and feminine forces within the psyche.

BRIDGE

Psychological Meaning A bridge may represent a critical juncture in life. You are about to leave one set of conditions and enter a landscape of new possibilities. It could be a new job, a change of home, or a new relationship. It may also represent an inner transformation, such as adopting a new set of values and leaving behind the past.

Mystical Meaning "Life is a bridge across a sea of change. Pass over it but do not build your house on it," says my guru, Sathya Sai Baba. Perhaps the bridge in your dream represents this journey of life.

BROTHER (SEE ALSO SHADOW, ANIMA/ANIMUS)

Psychological Meaning Carl Jung claimed that childhood sibling rivalry and jealousy influence the dream symbol of the brother. For a male dreamer, he may represent the shadow side of the personality that is neglected and undeveloped. Sometimes this may include anti-social qualities that are alarming. However, in a woman's dreams a brother may represent the male side of her own personality (animus).

Mystical Meaning A brother may occur as a guide in a woman's dreams and take her into a dark forest, into the depths of the earth, or to the bottom of the sea. This theme, which occurs in many myths and legends, shows that the animus can guide the ego to the cause of a psychological difficulty.

BROWN (SEE COLORS)

BRUSH

Psychological Meaning A brush may symbolize your desire to brush away problems. Perhaps you are taking a cavalier attitude to circumstances that need serious consideration? If you dream of sweeping up a mess, you may desire to be pure within or may have a fear of dirty thoughts. (Freud considered brushes to represent pubic hair. Perhaps something in your life needs to be cleaned up?

Mystical Meaning A great deal of superstition is associated with brushes and brooms. It is unlucky to step over them; they can sweep away good luck and are ridden by witches. Generally it is an unlucky symbol, but if you dream of brushing your hair you will soon meet an exciting new partner.

Common Dream

BUILDINGS

My dreams are often set in a small, decaying cellar. I always wake up feeling bad about life when this happens. What does this dream mean? —D.J, Gloucester, England

Psychological Meaning Buildings and houses are symbols of yourself. The upstairs represents your conscious mind and the lower floors and cellar your hidden self.

The cramped feeling of the cellar indicates frustration and a need to expand your activities or thinking. Decayed or crumbling buildings indicate that your self-image has suffered. Treat yourself to a few activities that make you feel good.

Different parts of a house may symbolize different times. For example, modern rooms may represent the conscious mind whereas the oldest areas may represent the ancient mind—the unconscious. The condition of the building may express how you feel about yourself. In addition it can also represent your physical health. Sometimes decayed buildings are the prelude to the onset of an illness.

ASK YOURSELF

1. *What aspect of me does the house represent?* Your mind, body, and spirit? The house may represent how you see yourself. If you recognize the need for a psychological spring cleaning, get to work straightaway.

2. *Is the house symbolic of past circumstances?* For example, your parental home may symbolize your childhood feelings. Ask yourself what personal associations the buildings in your dream have for you.

Mystical Meaning To dream of small buildings spells bad luck, says superstition, but if the building is big you will experience positive changes soon.

BULL

Psychological Meaning The bull is a symbol of male sexuality. For a man, it may represent his own sexuality and virility. For a woman, it may refer to the opposite sex. If the bull in your dreams is wild and untamed, your passions may be out of control. If you dream of bullfighting, it may be symbolic of action to control lust and negative power.

Mystical Meaning In mythology, the bull is an ancient symbol of fertility dating back to earliest times. In the great roar of the storm, man believed he heard the roar of the bull. In the ancient world, the bull was associated with the creative power of spring, as symbolized in the zodiac by Taurus. To dream of a bull has therefore been symbolic of fertility and sexual power since time immemorial.

BURIAL (SEE FUNERAL AND DEATH)

BUSINESS

Psychological Meaning Your dream may be telling you to take a more businesslike attitude to your circumstances. Perhaps you need to sell yourself, or maybe you need to be more cunning, daring, or cautious. Your dream may be showing you ways to profit from your experience. If the business is doing well you may feel pleased with your circumstances at the moment, but business problems may show that you feel insecure at this time.

Mystical Meaning Beware of dishonest people if you dream of a business, say the sages of bygone times.

BUTTERFLY

Psychological Meaning A butterfly may symbolize rebirth, inner beauty, and transformation. It may also represent romance, joy, freedom, and success. It is the essence of your true self.

Mystical Meaning An interesting philosophical question was raised by Chinese philosopher Chuang Chou, who dreamed he was a butterfly. The dream was so vivid, when he awoke he couldn't decide if he was a man dreaming of being a butterfly or a butterfly dreaming of being a man.

BUILDINGS

CACTUS

Psychological Meaning A prickly situation may be symbolized by a cactus. Perhaps you feel needled by someone's remarks or feel you need to defend yourself in some way. Clearly, cacti are also a phallic symbol. Are you afraid of being hurt by a relationship?

Mystical Meaning Mexicans consider cactus an aphrodisiac, so to dream of cactus bodes well for matters of the heart.

CAGE

Psychological Meaning A cage may be an expression of your feelings about being restricted in some way. Perhaps you feel confined by your emotional relationships or you feel that your workplace is like a prison. Part of you desperately wants to escape and feel free again. If you dream of a caged animal, this can show that you hold the instinctive side of yourself in check. You may fear the wild, primitive energies of your nature. Similarly, a caged bird may show your frustrated spiritual ambitions.

Mystical Meaning If you dream of being put into a cage of wild animals, it warns that you are in danger of an accident.

CAKE

Psychological Meaning A cake is usually divided between a number of people and may refer to something that has to be shared. For example, you may feel that you are not getting your fair share of a wage increase at work. Or the cake may refer to your emotional life. A wife, for example may feel that her husband gives too much attention to his work, children, and TV, but that she misses out. Or perhaps you're being selfish. Do you want to eat your cake and have it too?

Mystical Meaning Ancient rites involved making man-shaped cakes, which were eaten to gain the power of the god of the corn. The story of the gingerbread man may have originated from these ancient traditions.

CAMERA

Psychological Meaning This often represents a desire to cling to the past or preserve it forever.

However, it may also represent the way you "picture the situation."

Mystical Meaning Undeserved disappointment.

CANDLE

Psychological Meaning A lighted candle may represent the illuminating light of intellect. Similarly, it may symbolize enlightenment or the search for truth via contemplation or meditation. It can also suggest the passage of time and your thoughts about getting older. Freudians consider it to be a phallic symbol, of course.

Mystical Meaning If the flame burns steadily, your friends will support you. If it flickers or goes out, enemies will do you harm. In times past, a whole system of fortune telling was invented based on the flicker of a candle's flame.

CAR

Psychological Meaning Surprisingly, Freud believed that the smooth motion of a car was not a symbol of sexual wish fulfillment. Instead, it represented the progress of psychoanalysis. A car is most likely to represent yourself and your ability to control your life. Are you a good driver in your dream? If so, you may also be steering the right course in life. However, if you drive badly or have an accident, your unconscious may be warning you that you are making mistakes. You may be driving yourself too hard and heading for an emotional crash. Maybe someone else is driving the car? You may feel that this person is controlling your life or that the qualities the person represents have unreasonable influence over you. The dream may be expressing your dependence and lack of control.

Mystical Meaning The ancients didn't have cars but they did have carts, and the meaning is much the same. One source claims that to ride a vehicle is a sign that there will be changes at home or in business. If your mode of transport is broken, news from a friend tells of trouble.

CARDS

Psychological Meaning A successful game of cards relies on both luck and skill. Similarly, a successful life depends on these same qualities. Your dream may show that you should use the skills of bluff, strategy, and timing in everyday life. A game such as blackjack may show that it's time to take a chance, whereas a game of patience may show the need for patience in your dealings with others.

Mystical Meaning Diamonds indicate wealth, clubs indicate work, hearts mean you will be happy in love, but spades indicate trouble ahead

CASTLE (SEE ALSO BUILDINGS, HOUSE, AND MANDALA)

Psychological Meaning A castle represents protection and security. It may also show that your psychological defenses are isolating you from others. It can be a symbol of the self.

Mystical Meaning The castle can represent the mandala, a symmetrical pattern that symbolizes the psyche. For example, in the story of Sleeping Beauty the whole castle sleeps because its masculine and feminine halves cannot relate, resulting in a state of stagnation. The castle is also surrounded by impenetrable thorns, showing that it is as difficult to get to know the inner self as it is to storm a castle.

CASTRATION

Psychological Meaning You may have fears that you have lost your virility or you may feel sexual pressure.

Mystical Meaning The myth of Saturn castrating his father may represent the fear of maturity and the conflicting desire to supplant the father.

CAT

Psychological Meaning Animals represent the instinctive side of your nature. A cat expresses feminine qualities and may represent the positive, creative, and sensuous aspects of femininity. If the cat in your dream is aggressive, it may show that you have problems with the feminine side of yourself. You may be taking a "catty" attitude or may have a negative view of women in general.

Mystical Meaning In mythology, cats were associated with old pagan fertility gods. They were a symbol of the Earth Mother and represented the power and wisdom of nature. Cats were sacred to the Egyptians as custodians of the souls of the dead. Only with the advent of Christianity were they deemed to be the evil familiar of witches. Because of this, most dream books consider it unlucky to dream about cats.

CAVE

Psychological Meaning A cave may represent the womb or female sexuality. What you find within the cave or what comes out of it are the new qualities that the unconscious is giving birth to. The cave may also be the entrance to the ancient mind, where you can discover the wisdom that is latent within you

Mystical Meaning Mythological dragons and monsters often lived in caves and sometimes guarded great treasure in their fiery lair. This is a symbol that shows that first it is necessary to overcome the fear of the unconscious before winning spiritual treasures. In some cases the monster that guards the cave represents a traumatic childhood experience that has been banished from consciousness.

CELLAR

Psychological Meaning Buildings represent the mind, and the cellar represents its deepest levels. It is a dark, damp, and sometimes frightening place where lurk creatures that shun the light of day. A cellar may be the symbolic repository where you discard all the fears and problems you do not want to deal with. In this clandestine world, you will discover your repressed fears, worries, and feelings of guilt and shame. Once you acquaint yourself with these fears and bring them into the light of day, they will no longer have power over you.

Mystical Meaning Superstition says that to dream of a cellar full of wine means you will receive profits from a dubious source.

CEMETERY (*see* Death)

CHAINS

Psychological Meaning If you dream of being chained, some part of you is being forcefully held in check. You need to liberate the part of you that wants to express itself. If someone you know is chained, consider what aspect of yourself this person represents. Similarly, if an animal is chained, think about what aspect of your animal nature is being restrained. A bull may represent an aspect of your sexuality, a growling dog may represent your anger, and a chained elephant may show that you are unable to utilize your natural strength and wisdom.

Mystical Meaning Superstition says that to dream of being in chains means that an injustice will be done to you.

CHAMPAGNE

Psychological Meaning A freshly opened bottle of Champagne is often considered to be a symbol of ejaculation and represents the sexual act. Of course it may also symbolize a celebration or a personal achievement that you feel pleased about. The effervescence of Champagne may denote a new burst of creativity or the "bubbly" side of your personality.

Mystical Meaning Dreaming about Champagne forecasts financial difficulties ahead but predicts a happy romance if your dream is set at a wedding reception.

Common Dream

CHASE

My young son has a recurring nightmare of being chased through woods by a shadowy figure. How can I help him overcome his fears?—M.T., Perth, Australia

Psychological Meaning This is a metaphor for insecurity. Circumstances may be closing in on

him, or he may feel at the mercy of feelings that get out of control. He may have feelings of guilt or fear of being caught for something he has done. Ask him if something is upsetting him and reassure him that you will support him whatever it is.

Children who have this dream may be being bullied at school. If the problem persists and you notice unusual or extreme behavior in your child, your child's doctor can put you in touch with someone who can help.

Like dreams of falling, being chased reflects the dreamer's feelings of insecurity. The dreamer is running away from something. According to Freud, men run away from the fear of castration, and women from sexual attackers, which symbolize a woman's secret desire to be wooed.

The figure that pursues the dreamer is most likely to represent an unresolved aspect of the dreamer's circumstances or personality.

ASK YOURSELF

1. *What am I running away from?* You may feel that circumstances are closing in on you and you may feel a need to escape. Perhaps you are being emotionally victimized and you feel vulnerable as you did as a child? Your feelings may be running out of control or there may be something you're avoiding in your external life or inner self. Do you feel guilt?

2. *What am I chasing?* If you are doing the chasing, you are probably trying to banish something from your life. You may be frightened by some aspect of yourself or feel anxiety that you may never reach the goals you have set for yourself.

Mystical Meaning Native Americans believe that if you dream you are being chased, you should face your pursuer, wrestle him to the ground, and then unmask him. Follow this wise counsel and you may discover that your fears are not as terrifying as you thought.

CHEST (*see also* Box)

Psychological Meaning It is with the chest that you breathe in life-giving air, so the chest may represent the center of your vitality.

Mystical Meaning A large chest warns that you may run into debt, say the auguries of old.

CHASE

CHILD

Psychological Meaning Carl Jung claimed that the dream symbol of a child is a metaphor for the forgotten things in childhood. For example, your dream may be telling you that you've forgotten how to play or should take a more innocent, carefree attitude. The symbol of the child also represents possibilities. It paves the way for future changes in the personality. In addition, the child may represent the part of you that needs reassurance and security.

Mystical Meaning A recurrent theme in mythology is the "divine child." This theme occurs in many mythologies. This mystical figure is often a hero or a savior. For example, the child-hero Hercules strangled two threatening snakes, and the baby Jesus became the Christ who saves humanity from damnation. The divine child is the symbol of the true self, both vulnerable and possessed of great transforming power. In your dream it may represent your divine self growing to its full spiritual potential.

CHRIST

Psychological Meaning The figure of Christ may have many personal associations for you, influenced of course by your attitude to traditional religion. As well as the redeemer, the symbol of Christ can represent perfection of the self, martyrdom, worldly suffering, or resurrection. Perhaps you feel like a martyr or believe you suffer as Christ did on the cross.

Mystical Meaning There are many valid paths to spiritual truth, and the religions of the world express the many ways God is made manifest in people's lives. God is omnipresent and omnipotent and appears in many guises. Perhaps the figure of Christ is using the language of the heart to bring you to God.

CHURCH

Psychological Meaning Churches and other houses of worship stand for the spiritual side of your nature. A building usually represents the dreamer, and a church can therefore symbolize the totally integrated psyche that is centered on what you consider to be supreme truth. It alludes to your core values and the things you deem sacred. Your dream may be making you aware of innate spiritual knowledge and the part of you that is eternal. This dream may be part of a series of dreams in which you explore your inner self and gain insight into divine reality.

Mystical Meaning Holy architecture is usually built according to sacred geometry that symbolizes the unity of the soul with God. In psychological terms, such buildings are mandalas representing the wholeness of the psyche.

CIRCLE (SEE ALSO MANDALA)

Psychological Meaning A circle is the perfect mandala. It represents the perfection of the self and wholeness. You are identifying with the very center of yourself. Hold on to this inner source of strength and well-being.

Mystical Meaning The Chinese consider circles to be good *feng shui*. It is therefore fortunate to dream about them.

CIRCUS (SEE THEATER AND CLOWN)

CITY

Psychological Meaning Cities usually represent community and your social environment, including family and friends. If you dream of visiting a town that feels desolate or you feel isolated from the bustle of activity, it may reflect the way you feel about your role in society. Do you feel rejected by society or by the people around you? Alternatively, if you dream of a walled city it may show that you want to protect yourself from society. You may feel that in your waking life you need to create a little time and space for yourself. A ruined city may show that you are neglecting your social relationships. To dream of being lost shows that you feel you have lost the direction in your own life.

The city may also be a symbol of yourself. Entering the city can symbolize your intention to explore your unconscious. A city on a hill may show your lofty ambition to rise in the world, whereas an underground city or one beneath the sea may symbolize a neglected self.

Mystical Meaning Mythological cities are sometimes pictured having eight gates, with one of them sealed. Each gate represents a turning point in life, and the sealed eighth gate is the final journey of death.

CLIFF (SEE ALSO FALLING)

Psychological Meaning You may be at a critical point in your life and may fear losing control. Emotionally you may feel as if you are teetering on the brink or may feel that your life is like a cliff-hanger movie. If you dream of climbing a cliff, it may show that you are trying to overcome an obstacle. Once you are over this problem, the way ahead should be smooth and even.

Mystical Meaning To dream of climbing a cliff augers well for all projects you undertake.

CLIMBING (SEE ALSO ELEVATOR AND MOUNTAIN)

Psychological Meaning Are you climbing toward a goal or away from something you fear? You may be climbing the ladder of success and feel that something you've wanted for a long time is now nearly within your reach. You have great ambition, but are you confident as you climb or does it fill you with fear? Your unconscious may be reminding you of the adage "Pride goeth before a fall." If you remain sincerely modest despite your success, your friends, family, and colleagues will express pleasure at your success. This will increase the self-confidence you need to reach your goal. However, if you become egotistical and climb too high, eventually someone will knock you down. Most people despise arrogance, but humility wins love.

Walls and mountains to climb symbolize obstacles in life that you need to overcome. An easy climb shows success, but climbing a precarious mountain ledge means that there is an uphill struggle ahead. A meteoric rise to fame is not as easily sustained as a gradual and well-planned rise to prominence. Be cautious and take one step at a time.

Freud considered dreams of climbing to represent a longing for sexual fulfillment.

Mystical Meaning The dream oracles say that to climb a ladder to the last rung means you will succeed in business.

CLOAK

Psychological Meaning To dream of wearing a cloak can represent self-protection or protective warmth and love. Freud considered it a symbol for enveloping female sexuality. A cloak can also designate illicit concealment and secrecy. Are you hiding something from yourself or from the world at large? What is it that you cloak in secrecy?

Mystical Meaning To dream of wearing a cloak forecasts a period of uncertainty ahead. If it has a hood, be warned, for someone you trust is deceiving you.

CLOCK

Psychological Meaning A clock or watch may simply represent the passage of time and indicate whether your dream refers to past, present, or future conditions. It may also show that your life is governed by the artificial routines created by organized society. Perhaps you should live a more carefree lifestyle, less dependent on deadlines or clock watching. A clock can also stand for the human heart and, therefore, the emotional side of your life. A clock showing one minute to midnight may indicate your anxious anticipation about a situation soon to affect you. Similarly, a stopped clock may indicate a stilling of the emotions, while a fast-moving sports watch may show that your emotions are running out of control.

Mystical Meaning To hear a clock chime augers bad news, say the dream oracles.

CLOTHES (SEE ALSO UNDERCLOTHES, NUDITY, THEATER)

Psychological Meaning Clothes can express personality or hide imperfections. The colors of your dream clothes can symbolize your moods. For example, brightly colored clothes may show happiness and optimism, whereas dark clothes may indicate depression and secrets. If the clothes you wear are tattered, then you may need to discard your worn-out attitudes and habits. You may want to redesign yourself and establish a new self-image. You *can* become a new person. To dream of changing your clothes may indicate a change of lifestyle. If your clothes are tight, this can indicate that you feel restricted in some way. You may feel constrained in a relationship, held back at work, or restricted in your professional role.

Mystical Meaning Early dream dictionaries say that to dream of seeing a naked woman is lucky. It foretells that some unexpected honors await you. It was also deemed unlucky to dream of having too many clothes, for this meant you lacked the necessities of life. To dream of new clothes means that you will have a domestic tiff.

CLOUDS

CLOUDS

Psychological Meaning Clouds may represent your moods. White cumulus clouds may represent cheerfulness or spirituality, whereas dark, ominous clouds may represent depression or thunderous anger. Clouds also forecast rain and with it the release of tension.

Mystical Meaning Many mystical traditions advise clearing the "clouds of ignorance" so the light of enlightenment may shine. Similarly, clouds protected the Greek gods who lived on Mount Olympus. Only your intuition can penetrate the highest knowledge.

CLOWN (SEE ALSO HERO/HEROINE)

Psychological Meaning A clown mocks the absurdity of pretentiousness. He is a trickster whom psychologists identify as being a symbol for the first, rudimentary stage in the development of the hero myth—in which the hero is instinctual, uninhibited, and often childish.

Mystical Meaning The Fool in the Tarot cards, who becomes the joker in ordinary playing cards, represents the unconscious side of personality with all its potential for transformation.

COLORS

Psychological Meaning Color can evoke strong emotional responses, and the colors revealed in dreams can tell a great deal about emotional states. Psychologists sometimes use color tests to judge the emotional condition of their patients, and a *feng shui* expert will use color in the home to attract the best energies to bring good fortune. However color meanings can vary from individual to individual, and you may have your own personal associations with a particular color. As with all dream interpretation, trust your own gut feelings.

Red: Red represents passion and sexuality. It can also represent anger or blood—it is the color of the life force.

Orange: Orange is usually associated with balance and healing. It is the passions refined.

Yellow: Often associated with artistic inspiration, yellow is sometimes considered the color of the coward.

Green: The color of nature brings new life and hope. Its negative association is with jealousy.

Blue: Blue is the spiritual color, the color healers have in their auric field. Blue brings harmony and, like the sky, it implies freedom. And, of course, it can sometimes represent depression, as when a person gets the blues.

Purple: This is the color of royalty and profound spiritual knowledge.

Black: Usually a color associated with depression. Time to get rid of those "black" thoughts. It may also indicate unconsciousness.

Brown: The color associated with the earth promises new psychological growth.

White: White is usually a symbol of purity.

Mystical Meaning Psychics see colors in the aura, the energy field that surrounds living things. The dream meaning of colors may relate to the spiritual values traditionally associated with each color. They are: red, sensuality; orange, cleansing; yellow, inspiration; green, recovery; blue, healing; purple, clairvoyance; black, illness; brown, stability; white, spirituality.

COMPASS

Psychological Meaning Your unconscious may be showing you the way. You may need to reconsider the direction your life is going or may need to take time out to get your bearings. This is a hopeful dream that promises to end your feeling of disorientation.

Mystical Meaning In *feng shui*, the eight compass directions symbolize different qualities. South relates to fame, fortune, and recognition or reputation. Southwest relates to marriage, romantic happiness, and partnerships. West relates to children and creativity. Northwest relates to helpful people, mentors, and networking. North relates to career and business success. Northeast relates to knowledge, study, and introspection. East relates to family, elders, authority figures, and health. Southeast relates to wealth and prosperity.

CONFLICT (SEE WAR)

COOKING (SEE ALSO FOOD)

Psychological Meaning If you dream of preparing food for other people, it may indicate that you have a desire to influence others. You may want people to like you or become dependent upon you. Cooking can also symbolize your need to transform a realization of a raw truth or emotion into something more palatable. Finally, the dream may represent your awareness of plans in preparation; i.e., "something's cooking."

Mystical Meaning The dream weavers of old say that to dream of cooking means that many friends will visit you in the future.

CORNER

Psychological Meaning Perhaps you feel frustrated by events that you can do nothing about. You feel trapped. You feel cornered. You are being forced to make a decision and now must take control of the situation. However, to dream of turning a corner suggests that things have taken a turn for the better and you have taken a new, and perhaps better, direction.

Mystical Meaning Corners are usually considered places where negative energy accumulates. You need to be more positive.

CORRIDOR

Psychological Meaning Dreaming of a long corridor that has no end may show that you are desperate to escape a repetitive situation. As well as external troubles, this dream could symbolize repetitive behavior patterns that you need to be free of. In most dreams, corridors represent the passing of one phase of your life to another.

Mystical Meaning In mysticism, corridors and passageways are places where energy moves fast and cannot accumulate. To dream of a corridor may therefore show that you are in danger of losing your energy and vitality.

COUPLE (SEE ALSO ANIMA/ANIMUS)

Psychological Meaning To dream of a couple may symbolize the need to bring together the male and female parts of your psyche.

Mystical Meaning Alchemy was a spiritual tradition that sought spiritual transformation of the psyche. The Royal Couple is one of the main symbols found in *Philosophia Reformata*, written by Mylius in 1622. Their coming together and merging to become one being symbolizes spiritual wholeness.

COW (SEE ALSO MOTHER)

Psychological Meaning Cows nurture, and they are used in dreams to symbolize the mother. Perhaps you are nurturing some new ideas or a part of yourself? For a man, a cow can represent the feminine part of himself. It may also represent an easygoing attitude. Your dream may be telling you to stop rushing around and to start taking your time. Cows also suggest the qualities of dignity, strength, and passive endurance.

Mystical Meaning Cows are sacred to the Hindus because they symbolize the protective, nurturing aspect of the godhead. Krishna taught the cow herders not to worship an unseen god, but their own cows. "There is where your devotion is, and where God's blessing to you resides. Worship your cows!" The lesson is clear that "God is your highest concern."

CROCODILE

Psychological Meaning Perhaps the crocodile is you? Are you being snappy all the time? The crocodile can be a symbol of aggressiveness and the shadowy realm of the instincts. Alternatively, the dream may reveal that you have been displaying false emotions and shedding "crocodile tears" or that someone close to you has.

Mystical Meaning To dream of a crocodile was believed to mean that your best friends would deceive you.

CROSS (SEE ALSO MANDALA)

Psychological Meaning The cross was used as a symbol even before the Christian era. The Greek cross, with its four arms of equal length, is a mandala of wholeness. Similarly, Native Americans drew crosses to symbolize the quartering of the universe into active and passive units. As a Christian symbol, it can represent suffering, martyrdom, death, and sacrifice. Perhaps your dream is telling you that you have a cross to bear. Find out what it is that makes you suffer, and begin healing this condition that brings you so much pain. Similarly, the cross also indicates resurrection. The ego must be sacrificed on the cross so that you can rise to God-consciousness.

Mystical Meaning In mysticism, the cross symbolizes the fourfold divisions of nature, such as seasons, the four compass directions, and elements. In the ancient world, it was considered the ideal shape of man, the blueprint of his nature. It is also closely associated with the life-giving power of the tree.

CROSSROADS

Psychological Meaning Your life has come to a crisis point and you must now choose between a number of options. Each road represents a direction you can travel in your life at this time. The choice may be difficult and painful, but you must make your decision.

Mystical Meaning Criminals were hanged at crossroads so that the maximum number of travelers would witness the consequences of crime. As a dream symbol the crossroads can therefore represent crime, punishment, and death. However, most old dream books say that dreaming of a crossroads means an important decision ahead.

CROW

Psychological Meaning The crow may represent the dark part of your psyche that appears at first to be frightening but contains what you need for spiritual enrichment. Crows, like angels, were once believed to be the messengers of the gods. In your dream, they are messengers from your unconscious.

Mystical Meaning Associated with witchcraft, the crow is said to have the gift of prophecy. Some people believe that dreams that include crows foretell future events.

CROWD

Psychological Meaning Your dream may be telling you that you need to make some space for yourself. You need solitude occasionally to reflect on events. In these moments of quiet meditation you can recharge your energy and gain a clearer insight into what it is you truly want from life. Dreaming about a crowd may show that the worries and the problems of the world are pressing in on you.

Mystical Meaning Old dream books say it is fortunate to dream of a crowd as long as they are well dressed or wearing brightly colored clothes. It means many friends will come your way.

CRYSTAL

Psychological Meaning The mathematical symmetry of a crystal can represent unity and wholeness. The crystal may represent the quintessence of your self. It is the pure spirit, the divine cosmic plan unfolding in human form. It is the eternal part of you, unsullied by the world. If you dream of gazing into a crystal, this can show that you are looking within yourself to find your true destiny.

Mystical Meaning Crystals are associated with the healing powers of the spirit. Their vibrations resonate with the life force within the aura and bring peace, harmony, and health. To dream of a crystal reveals that these hidden potentials are also within you.

CUP

Psychological Meaning The cup is considered to be a classic female sexual symbol. It may also represent something passive from which you can draw sustenance. If the cup contains wine, your dream may have a spiritual message.

Mystical Meaning The dream may be referring to the Holy Grail and the search for spiritual sustenance. A cup can also stand for love and truth. For example, the Tarot card suit of cups symbolizes the inquirer's emotional life and is generally a fortunate augury.

CUPBOARD (SEE ALSO CLOTHES, MOTHER, MASK)

Psychological Meaning A Freudian psychologist will tell you that cupboards represent the mother and show your desire to return to the secure waters of your mother's womb. However, it may simply represent something you open in order to reveal a truth. Perhaps a skeleton is hidden in the cupboard—something about yourself you do not want to accept or reveal. As a cupboard may contain clothes, the dream may be telling you about the side of yourself you present to the world (your persona).

Mystical Meaning Dream superstition tells that if you dream of an empty cupboard you will be poor, but if it is full, good fortune will not desert you.

CURTAIN

Psychological Meaning To dream of opening curtains can show your readiness to look at what has been hidden, whereas closing curtains may show a desire to hide or repress your feelings. Theater curtains can represent the beginning or ending of something. Death has sometimes been called "the final curtain." Perhaps your behavior has been a bit of a performance, but now you've changed your ways?

Mystical Meaning Tradition has it that to dream of curtains means that an unwelcome visitor will arrive. There may be quarrels.

CUTTING

Psychological Meaning To cut is to sever and separate. Your dream may be an allegory for a broken relationship, a major change in your circumstances, or the end of an outmoded pattern of behavior.

Mystical Meaning Dream oracles tell that to dream of being cut means that a friend will betray you.

DAFFODIL (SEE ALSO MANDALA AND COLORS)

Psychological Meaning Associated with the springtime, daffodils are a symbol of renewal. This is a time of inner growth, optimism, and hope. The beautiful symmetry of flowers is reminiscent of mandalas, which can symbolize psychological wholeness. The color yellow is sometimes associated with the sun and the light of inspiration.

Mystical Meaning According to a Celtic tradition from the country of Wales, a bunch or field of daffodils means more gold than silver will come your way, but a single bloom brings misfortune.

DAGGER (SEE KNIFE)

DAM

Psychological Meaning To dream of a dam may mean that you have some pent-up emotions that need to be released. If you dream of a dam bursting, it shows that you have lost control. Your anger may have gone beyond the point of self-control. You may feel overwhelmed with emotion. There is more than one way to deal with frustrations. Be kinder to yourself and others and honestly express your feelings in a controlled and gentle way.

Mystical Meaning Victorian dream books interpret blockages, impediments, and obstacles as prophecies forecasting problems ahead that must be overcome. Dams fall into this category.

DANCE

Psychological Meaning Dance is usually a celebratory activity, something you do when you feel happy. This dream may therefore indicate that you feel pleased about the way a situation is progressing at the moment. You may feel a sense of freedom from constraining influences. Other things may also be expressed by dance. For example, if you dance with another person, this intimacy can represent sexual intercourse. A man and woman dancing together may show the union of the masculine and feminine aspects of your personality (*see* Anima/Animus).

Mystical Meaning To dream of dancing can be a mystical symbol. It can, for example, represent the eternal dance of the Hindu god Shiva, who symbolizes the eternal movement of time and the powers of creation and destruction.

DARKNESS

Psychological Meaning Light is a symbol of awareness. Darkness is the absence of light and therefore is a symbol of the unconscious. If you react with fear, you may fear the unconscious, but if the darkness is comforting, you accept this unknown part of yourself. If you dream of being lost in darkness it may represent your feelings of desperation, depression, or insecurity. If you see light, it may show that you are being guided toward wholeness and understanding.

Mystical Meaning The Chinese oracle of the *I Ching* used by Carl Jung as an aid to interpreting dreams says of darkness: "In the end it perishes of its own darkness, for evil must itself fall at the very moment when it has wholly overcome the good, and thus consumed the energy to which it owed its duration." In other words, things can only get better.

DAWN

Psychological Meaning The dawn brings with it a new beginning. A period of inner darkness is replaced by the light of realization and consciousness. At last you have hope and optimism in your heart.

Mystical Meaning The ancient Egyptians identified dawn with New Year's Day and the beginning of the world, when the eye of Atum searched the great primeval ocean. Since the earliest times humanity has worshiped the rising sun as a symbol of God, hope, and rebirth.

Common Dream

DEATH (SEE ALSO FUNERAL)

I dreamed that I was dead and everyone stood around me crying. I awoke with a feeling of abject horror. Is this dream a prediction of my death?—Jose T., Quebec, Canada

Psychological Meaning Dreams of death represent the ending of one phase so a new one can begin. They can show forthcoming finalities, such as the end of a marriage or career. These are symbolic dreams and are unlikely to forecast an actual event. If the dead person is someone you know, consider what aspect of yourself that person represents. For example, to dream of your mother dying could represent the death of the motherly side of your own nature. Perhaps you should try to be more caring and maternal, or perhaps plans you have should be nurtured rather than killed off. Alternatively, you may also be expressing your hidden feelings about the person. Do you secretly resent the person or have a desire to be independent of him or her? Dead animals may also represent aspects of yourself. They indicate that you may be rejecting or repressing your instinctive side.

Freud believed that everyone has two contending basic drives: *eros*, which is the drive toward pleasure and life, and *thanatos*, the drive toward death. If the dead person in your dream was yourself, you may want to consider the following:

ASK YOURSELF

1. *What is being expressed in the dream?* Perhaps you fear dying, and the dream is reminding you of your own mortality? It is healthy to accept that death comes to everyone; this realization broadens your spiritual perspective and loosens the grip of material craving. Everything in the world is the dust of stars, but look deep within yourself and you may find the part of yourself that is eternal.

2. *Am I trying to free myself from something?* You may want to leave your old self behind so a new you can be reborn. Free yourself of emotional burdens and open yourself to new potentials. There is no need to be a martyr. The way forward is to establish a new set of values that are beneficial to you and others.

3. *Do I feel suicidal?* There's no need to punish yourself or others because of how you feel. Everyone occasionally feels a desire to retreat from life's problems or from feelings of failure. But suffering is a blessing as well as a curse. It is through adversity that you grow and become a better person. Be like a strong tree that bends with the wind but never breaks. Better times will inevitably come again.

Mystical Meaning To dream of meeting dead people you once knew is part of the grieving process. Sometimes the feeling of loss is symbolized by being rejected, divorced, or attacked by the person you loved. You may dream that they ignore you or have traveled far away. This is all part of the process of coming to terms with the death of a loved one. However, there are some dreams that cannot be explained as symbolism, allegory, or metaphor. From the many casebooks I have collected, it appears that occasionally the dead can communicate with the living through dreams. I have cases on file where information has been given to the dreamer that could not have been known other than by paranormal means. For example, one woman wrote to say that her dead husband told her exactly where to find the missing will, and I have many instances recorded where the dead person has announced his passing via a dream.

DESCENT

Psychological Meaning In many dreams this may represent descending into the unconscious. In particular, cave entrances, wells, tombs, and cellars can represent entrances to the netherworld of the unconscious. Alternatively, you may interpret this as a downward phase in your life; you may feel "down." On the other hand, perhaps you are over the worst and everything is downhill from now on.

Mystical Meaning Legend has it that the people of ancient Crete built temples in underground caves. Here they held their strange rituals and bull-dancing ceremonies. Since the earliest times, the descent into the underground world has been a symbol of man's search for divinity and spiritual empowerment.

DETECTIVE

Psychological Meaning In real life, detectives seek out hidden truths. During sleep, you may be trying to resolve a problem and may want to know the truth about an issue that worries you. Perhaps you detect that something is wrong or that someone has been less than honest with you.

Mystical Meaning To dream of being falsely accused of a crime by a detective is a dream prophecy that fortune and honor are coming your way.

DEVIL

Psychological Meaning The devil in your dream may personify your fear or repressed desires that have been buried in the underworld of the unconscious. In reality, the unconscious mind is not full of evil demons and satanic forces; it is your inner resource that gives energy and wisdom. Your own fear of the unknown prevents you from finding the wholeness and healing that the unconscious offers. Alternatively, the Devil may symbolize evil words and deeds that you or others have been displaying in waking life. What the devil fears most is light and love. Honesty and kindness may be the right form of conduct to overcome the perceived evils that trouble you.

Mystical Meaning The figure of Satan occurs in the Jewish, Christian, and Islamic traditions. Originally Satan represented fertility and the powers of Nature. Similarly, the cloven-footed god Pan of the ancient Greeks was a god of the abundance of nature. These ancient symbols of fertility are sometimes used by the unconscious to show the inauguration of a new phase of psychological growth.

DIRT

Psychological Meaning Do you have a feeling of disgust? Dreaming of dirt could represent your emotional reaction to your instincts or self-disgust about sexuality. You may have guilt feelings that could originate from childhood. Society places too great an emphasis on sex. Accept it as a natural. It's not dirty, but also is not necessarily the all-important issue of life.

Mystical Meaning Earth and soil can represent the alchemists' *prima materia*, the unconscious content worked with in order to become enlightened.

DISEASE

Psychological Meaning Sometimes dreams spot an illness before you are aware of any symptoms. If your dream persists, get your health checked by your doctor. Alternatively, the dream may be highlighting anxieties and inner conflicts. You need to heal these inner troubles and find psychological harmony. If someone else in your dream has a disease, you may either harbor hostile feelings or fear for the person's mental equilibrium.

Mystical Meaning African superstition has simple interpretation to this one: see your witch doctor for a cure.

DISGUISE (*See also* Mask)

Psychological Meaning It is likely that you're hiding from something in your waking life. You want to "dress up" an issue and turn it into something it's not. It's time to face reality and stop hiding behind that mask. Be yourself.

Mystical Meaning Many myths and children's stories tell of people who wear masks but then to their horror realize that they can't remove them.

This is a symbol that shows that you can sometimes become the person you pretend to be but forget who you really are.

DIVING

Psychological Meaning Water and the sea often represent the unconscious. Diving into water symbolizes your descent into the unconscious. You are getting in touch with the deepest strata of your being. Alternatively, the dream may be telling you to take a chance concerning an issue from waking life. It's time to take the plunge.

Mystical Meaning There are many myths that tell of heroes who dive to the bottom of the sea and bring up great treasure. In dreams, this represents the ego descending into the unconscious and finding the self.

DIVORCE

Psychological Meaning The dream may represent a hidden desire on your part to end a relationship. You may feel unhappy about your marriage or partner. Perhaps you should express your concerns and make your unhappiness known. A good relationship is both giving and taking, so don't just make demands. Look for solutions that bring happiness to both of you.

Mystical Meaning The old dream oracles wisely advised that this dream was a warning and that you should cultivate a more congenial domestic atmosphere.

DOG

Psychological Meaning Dogs helped man hunt and herd his flock. They are therefore a symbol of the right inner relationship between you and your animal nature. They may also symbolize loyalty and guidance. Alternatively, if the dog is ferocious, you have an inner conflict with the animal side of your nature. A dog straining on its leash may indicate that your emotions are at the end of their tether. Perhaps you need to express your anger about an issue that upsets you.

Mystical Meaning One dream oracle warns that to dream of a bloodhound is an omen for your imminent downfall. You'd be barking mad to believe that.

DOLL

Psychological Meaning To dream of playing with dolls may symbolize that you are trying to come to terms with an infantile aspect of yourself. This can sometimes indicate a lack of communication between the conscious and unconscious levels of the mind. It can symbolize that you have an immature attitude toward the opposite sex. Are you behaving like an adult, or do you sometimes resort to childish behavior? Alternatively, Jung believed that dolls represented the Anima or Animus, the qualities of the opposite sex within yourself.

Mystical Meaning Tribal magicians use mannequins to inaugurate their sympathetic magic. Sticking pins into a voodoo doll of your enemy, telling your troubles to a worry doll, and worshiping the corn doll are rituals that express a multitude of needs, desires, fears, and hopes. Children will confess to a doll things they would never tell an adult. Similarly, you may tell the doll of your dream your most secret fears and wishes.

DOLPHIN

Psychological Meaning Dolphins that leap in and out of the sea may represent communication between the unconscious and the conscious mind.

Mystical Meaning There will be a change of government!

DOOR

Psychological Meaning If a door opens outward, it may show that you have a need to be more accessible to others. However, an inward-opening door may represent your desire for inner exploration and self-discovery. A door may also represent a new opening in your waking life or a desire to open up your feelings. If the door is locked, you may feel that opportunities are being denied you, or alternatively it can represent closing the door to the past.

Mystical Meaning There are lots of dream oracles for this one: a doorknob means unexpected good luck; hinges bring family problems; locked doors show missed opportunities; an open door predicts good fortune; a revolving door means a monotonous period ahead; and a trapdoor predicts shocking news.

DRAGON

Psychological Meaning The dragon sometimes guards the entrance to a cave full of treasure. It symbolizes the fears you must overcome before realizing the true self. Sometimes the dragon can represent a guardian of the spirit. A Freudian psychologist interprets the dragon symbol to represent the devouring aspect of the mother. It is the resistance that prevents a man from realizing the

feminine aspect of his nature. Your dream could also be saying something about your sex drive. Dragons have a strong association with fire and, therefore, passion.

Mystical Meaning In China, the symbol of the dragon is quite different from its Western counterpart. It has amazing power, is highly spiritual, and symbolizes the wisdom of the mind. To dream about dragons is very auspicious.

DRAWING

Psychological Meaning The dream may simply mean that you may have latent artistic abilities that should be given expression. Are you drawing on inner resources, or is your bank account overdrawn? What you draw is also important, as it can show the plans, problems, and worries that you are trying to resolve.

Mystical Meaning A strange superstition says that if a woman dreams of drawing with a pencil and then rubs out what she drew, her lover will be unfaithful.

FAMOUS DREAMER

Mark Twain
Novelist

For four years during the 1850s, Mark Twain, author of The Adventures of Huckleberry Finn, *worked with his brother Henry as a steamboat pilot on the Mississippi River. One night Twain dreamed that Henry died. He saw him laid in a metal coffin that was resting on two chairs. Across his chest lay a white bouquet with a single crimson flower at its center.*

A few weeks later Henry died, when the Pennsylvania's boilers exploded. The dead crew were placed in wooden coffins. Only Henry had a metal coffin. Twain was reminded of his dream when he went to view his brother. He saw the metal coffin and noted that there was no bouquet on it.

Moments later, a woman entered the room and placed a bouquet of white flowers on Henry's chest. At its center was a single red rose.

DROWNING

DROWNING

Psychological Meaning Dreams of drowning or struggling in treacherous waters may represent your fear of being swallowed by forces hidden in the depths of your unconscious. You may be proceeding too quickly in opening your unconscious. It may be helpful to talk your problems and fears through with a friend who can throw you a lifeline and help you keep your head above water. The dream also shows that you are overwhelmed by your emotions. You may fear sinking financially, or you may be drowning in your difficulties. Do you feel that in your waking life you are being sucked into something you would rather not be a part of? Pause for a while and make sure you have your feet firmly on solid ground before you make any major decision.

Mystical Meaning A business will founder if you dream of drowning but will succeed if you are rescued.

DRUNK

Psychological Meaning Are you intoxicated by your own success or do you want to escape from reality? The dream suggests that you are not seeing your circumstances clearly and need to take a more sober view of things.

Mystical Meaning The Gypsies believe that if you dream you see a drunk you will be given a small but pleasant surprise.

DUEL

Psychological Meaning It is likely you are experiencing an inner conflict. You need to find a middle way between the extreme views and the solutions you are considering. Similarly, the conflict could be between your conscious thoughts and your instinctive feelings. You will not know peace until you stop this inner conflict. Stop seeing things only in black and white. A compromise is necessary.

Mystical Meaning Children's stories and fairy tales often illustrate psychological processes and are rich in dream symbols. In Lewis Carroll's *Through the Looking Glass*, Tweedledum and Tweedledee typify the childlike inner conflicts that can occur within the psyche.

DUMB

Psychological Meaning To dream of a person who is unable to speak or who refuses to speak represents an undeveloped function within the self. Psychologist Carl Jung said that these silent figures represent an imbalance between emotion and intellect. One side of the personality overpowers the other, rendering it speechless or impotent. Some people suffer from sleep paralysis. They wake up before the back part of the brain has started to function. This area stops the body from acting out dreams and prevents the dreamer from thrashing around while sleeping. The dreamer may "wake up" but be completely paralyzed. If this happens to you, you may want to speak, cry out, or scream but find that you can't. Don't panic. Relax until your whole brain starts working.

Mystical Meaning To dream of being dumb means that you are unable to convince people of the worth of your plans. However, a dumb person who dreams of being dumb must beware of false friends!

DUST

Psychological Meaning Dust implies neglect and something that has not been touched for a long time. Your dream therefore represents aspects of yourself that have been ignored or forgotten. It could be an ambition from the past or something you once treasured but have until now overlooked. Is the whole of your personality being expressed in your waking life? Similarly, it may be a neglected talent, such as an artistic, musical, or creative ability, that the dream draws your attention to. The objects covered in dust will give you a clue to the dream's meaning.

Mystical Meaning The Gypsies say that the more dust you see in a dream, the more minor irritations you will need to deal with.

DWARF

Psychological Meaning A dwarf can represent some quality that you have not fully developed or expressed. It may also represent the neglected or repressed parts of yourself—aspects of your personality that were unable to grow to their full potential.

Mystical Meaning Gold is a symbol of the true self and, as in the story of Snow White, is often mined by dwarfs. Dwarfs can therefore symbolize your quest for self-knowledge.

EAGLE

Psychological Meaning The eagle is a powerful bird that may represent powerful intellectual or spiritual abilities. For a Christian it may represent John the Evangelist, and for an American it may be the symbol of your country.

Mystical Meaning Early man considered eagles messengers from the sun god. In a dream, an eagle may be a messenger from your unconscious. Mythology often has stories of the eagle and the lion or the eagle and the snake. These stories are dream symbols that represent psychological opposites such as spiritual/animal, male/female, conscious/unconscious, and thought/instinct. Superstition says that to dream of an eagle is an omen for fame and fortune.

EAR

Psychological Meaning An ear may be telling you to listen to what you are being told. The advice may be coming from people you know in waking life or from your own inner self. Perhaps you should listen to the voice of your conscience?

Mystical Meaning You will hear news soon, but if your ears ache, do not trust the person who tells you.

EARTH

Psychological Meaning Dreams associated with the earth, such as lying on the ground, may show that you need to be realistic. The dream may be telling you to keep your feet on the ground. You may need to concentrate on earthly matters rather than becoming overly involved in otherworldly concerns or flights of fancy. To dream of the planet Earth may be a symbol of your true self that is yet unrealized. Sometimes, dreams are not symbolic, but can be real experiences of paranormal travel. Psychologist Carl Jung in his autobiography, *Memories Dreams Reflections*, confesses that in 1944 he had an out-of-body experience and saw the Earth from a vantage point in space. "It seemed to me that I was high up in space. Far below I saw the globe of the earth, bathed in gloriously blue light."

Mystical Meaning Mother Earth represents the unconscious mind. She is the womb that contains potential for further development. Myths about descending into the earth are allegories to describe the descent into the dark realms of the unconscious. If Mother Earth comes in a fearful guise, this may show that you fear being overwhelmed by chaotic unconscious forces that threaten the order in your life. Mother Earth was of course a fertility symbol. To dream of a barren earth means that you need to sow new seeds of life for the future.

EARTHQUAKE

Psychological Meaning Something is upsetting you that has destroyed your feeling of security. You may feel that your whole world is falling apart. You may "quake" with fear. Similarly, something may be threatening you from below the surface of your awareness. It may be repressed fear or anxiety that you have pushed underground into the depths of your unconscious.

Mystical Meaning Dream superstition interprets earthquakes as a symbol of a change of circumstance.

EAST

Psychological Meaning The sun rises in the East. This direction may therefore represent a new dawn and rebirth. You may also be interested in the philosophy and spiritual wisdom that comes from the great cultures of the East.

Mystical Meaning Your plans will be canceled, say the old dream superstitions.

EATING (SEE ALSO FOOD)

Psychological Meaning Freud considered the mouth to be the primary erogenous zone. Dreams of eating are therefore closely associated with sexuality. If you dream of gorging yourself, it can indicate that you have an indulgent sexuality, whereas dreaming of fasting or starvation may indicate that you deny your sexual needs. Eating out at restaurants is often part of couples' courting rituals. In dreams, meals that have an enjoyable atmosphere reflect a confirmation of intimacy with others and good social relationships. Dreaming of eating in uncomfortable or threatening surroundings may represent frigidity and unhappiness with your relationships. An alternative explanation is that eating symbolizes qualities that you are making part of yourself. For example, you may be digesting some new ideas or perhaps a problem is "eating at you."

Mystical Meaning To dream of eating generally warns of a quarrel or business loss. Seers claim that it is particularly bad to dream of eating salt or lard, as these signify a serious argument.

ECLIPSE (SEE MOON)

EGG (SEE ALSO SHELLS)

Psychological Meaning To dream of an egg promises that something new is about to happen in your life. You may be "hatching" a new idea or plan. After a period of waiting, wonderful new possibilities will open to you. At this stage you will need to carefully nurture your plans, as eggs are delicate things and can be easily broken. The egg could also symbolize inner potential that is developing within you. You may be learning new skills or feel that you are developing into a new and better person. You need time to incubate this new side of yourself. Soon you will be able to break out of your shell.

Mystical Meaning According to the *Oneirocriticon*, by Astrampsychus (c. 350 A.D.), "to hold an egg symbolizes vexation."

ELEMENTS (SEE ALSO AIR, EARTH, FIRE, WATER)

Psychological Meaning The elements are symbols for the sum total of the universe, including man. These are divided into solid (Earth), liquid (Water), and vapor (Air) and these three are transformed into one another through the agency of energy (Fire). Psychological qualities can be represented by each of the elements. If these are in balance, then it represents psychological wholeness and well-being.

Mystical Meaning In astrology the elements symbolize the four essential qualities of mankind: Earth, for fertility and steadfastness; Water, for imagination; Air, for intelligence; and Fire, for ambition and will. In addition, the mystics believed in a fifth element called Ether, an intangible fluid state of existence that alchemists claimed permeated everything. Today, many psychics believe that ether is the medium by which the spirit travels out of the body during sleep.

ELEPHANT

Psychological Meaning Elephants can symbolize inner strength and wisdom. They may also represent memory. Jung believed they represented the self. The defensive nature of an elephant may represent an introverted nature.

Mystical Meaning To a Hindu the elephant-headed god Ganesha represents God's power to remove obstacles. Similarly, Western dream interpretation has always considered dreams of elephants to bring great good luck.

ELEVATOR (SEE ALSO LIFT)

Psychological Meaning You may feel that you are going up in the world. As no effort is required to make your ascent, you may feel that someone is helping you or that destiny is working in your favor. You may also have raised your consciousness and may see the world from an elevated standpoint. As you transcend the lower planes and perhaps become more cerebral in your thinking, remember not to lose touch with your instinctive and intuitive nature. If the elevator is descending, it can indicate the descent of the conscious ego into the unconscious in order to explore this hidden world. Alternatively, it may represent the decline of your personal power and status. In both instances, remember it's who you are, not what you are, that counts.

Mystical Meaning They didn't have elevators in the good old days. However, it was always considered a good omen to dream to make an ascent without any obstacles and without stumbling.

EMBARRASSMENT

Psychological Meaning Dreams often expose your hidden weaknesses and fears. You may feel that your self-confidence has been undermined, or you may feel insecure about your sexuality.

Mystical Meaning Some old dream superstitions say that dreams represent the opposite of what they appear to mean. In this case, the greater the embarrassment you feel, the greater your success will be!

EMOTIONS (SEE ALSO SHADOW)

Psychological Meaning Some psychologists believe that people dream in order to allow the emotions to settle down. Without dreams, you would simply overheat. Dreams can sometimes express very powerful emotions, ones that most people wouldn't dare express in waking life. Dreams can act as an emotional safety valve to help release tension. Jung pointed out that emotions come from the "Shadow," the undeveloped, inferior functions of the psyche. Many people refuse to recognize these emotions as their own and project them onto someone else.

Mystical Meaning Some superstitions say to reverse the emotional meaning of the dream. For example, to dream of being angry or crying means that you will soon hear some good news.

EMPTY

Psychological Meaning You feel that something is missing in your life. To dream of an empty room, box, house, or vessel may be to express feelings of emotional emptiness. Freud believed that these feelings were the result of repression.

Mystical Meaning Ventures undertaken at this time will be futile, say the dream oracles.

ENEMY

Psychological Meaning The enemy may be the enemy within. Do you have inner conflicts that need resolving? You may have rejected parts of yourself that are struggling with you to find expression. The shadow side of yourself may contain the qualities you need for personal wholeness. Alternatively the enemy may represent problems with a real-life enemy and your dream may give you clues to reconciliation.

FAMOUS DREAMER

Marie Antoinette
Queen of France

Some time before the French Revolution, Queen Marie Antoinette, the wife of Louis XVI of France, dreamed of a glowing red sun rising above a column, like a temple pillar. She heard a loud "crack" as the column split in two and fell to the ground. The dream was understood to be a symbol representing the fall of the monarchy. She was guillotined in 1793.

Mystical Meaning They say that if you dream of enemies, it means you will have helpful friends.

ESCAPE (SEE ALSO CHASE)

Psychological Meaning You may want to escape from a restrictive attitude or situation that is preventing your psychological growth. Alternatively, you may be taking an escapist attitude and refusing to face up to problems that continue to pursue you.

Mystical Meaning The oracles say: A man who dreams of trying to escape from danger will soon face serious trouble.

ETHER (SEE ELEMENTS)

EVIL

Psychological Meaning Everyone has a dark side. The evil that occurs in dreams usually represents something about yourself. It may represent destructive psychological forces such as anger, jealousy, revenge, or hatred. If you recognize these tendencies within yourself, first accept them, then practice the opposite in waking life. For example, if you dream of hatred, practice love; if you dream of revenge, practice forgiveness; and if you dream of jealousy, practice giving.

Mystical Meaning The ancient Chinese oracle the *I Ching*, often used for dream interpretation, says: "The best way to overcome evil is by energetic perseverance in the good"

EXAMINATION

Psychological Meaning Dreaming of sitting for an examination may express a fear of failure. Examinations are very stressful experiences in which you are made to face up to your shortcomings. To dream of failing an exam, being late for one, or being unprepared shows that you feel unprepared for the challenges of waking life. Do not fear failure. Always do your very best and you will never have regrets.

Mystical Meaning Ancient dream guides tell that to dream of passing an examination forecasts success in life, but that failing an exam means failing in life. However, other sources say that to dream of failure augers success. So who knows what the correct answer to this dream interpretation is?

EXCREMENT

Psychological Meaning Excrement represents something you need to be rid of. This may be a negative attitude, an outdated mode of behavior, or destructive influence from the past. Rid yourself of these negative emotions. Alternatively, practical worries in waking life may make you feel like you've put your foot in it.

Mystical Meaning If you dream of treading in dog's mess while walking down the street, it means you'll have unexpected good luck financially. (You'll be stinking rich!)

EXPLOSION (*SEE* BOMB)

EYES

Psychological Meaning These "windows to the soul" give clues to the state of your spiritual health and well-being. Bright eyes suggest a healthy inner life. They may also represent insight or psychic awareness. The eye can be a symbol of wisdom and clear perception of your circumstances. It can show your way of looking at things. Are the eyes happy, sad, kind, judgmental, or enlightened? The nature of the eye may say a great deal about the way you perceive your circumstances. For example, a green eye may symbolize that you have feelings of jealousy. If you dream of the evil eye, this can represent your super-ego, the internal censor that passes judgment on your thoughts and desires. In extreme cases, to dream of a sinister eye may indicate that you harbor feelings of paranoia.

Mystical Meaning Within mystical traditions, eyes are considered to be a symbol of higher consciousness. It is believed that people have a third eye just above the eyebrows, in the center of the forehead. This spiritual center can perceive other dimensions and spiritual realities. Directly in line with this center, in the middle of the brain, lies the pineal gland, which releases chemicals that may control higher consciousness. It is believed that this was once an eye, and that over the centuries it became buried in the center of the brain. The Tuatara lizard of New Zealand still has a vestigial eye at to the top of the head that is sensitive to light.

FACE (*SEE ALSO* MASK)

Psychological Meaning If you dream of your own face it may represent the face you show to the world as opposed to the real you. This is particularly the case if you dream of putting on makeup. The dream may also contain puns. For example, are you "facing up" to your problems, or should you address an enemy "face-to-face"?

Mystical Meaning The dream oracles say that to dream of seeing your face in a mirror means that a secret will be discovered. If your face is swollen, you will receive money but if it is pale, disappointment will follow.

FAILURE

Psychological Meaning Fear of failure may originate in childhood and stem from fears of punishment or withdrawal of love. Failure themes can occur in dreams about missing trains, muddled words, or failing an examination. Too many people program themselves with failure habits. Instead of focusing on where you go wrong, emphasize the things you get right. Give yourself permission to succeed.

Mystical Meaning If you dream of failing in business or love, you will succeed in both, say the dream books of bygone days.

FAIRY

Psychological Meaning Fairy tales are full of rich psychological symbolism, and telling them can help children and adults express their innermost fears and hopes. For a man a fairy may symbolize the female aspect of his personality that can be integrated for better psychic balance. Similarly, for a woman a fairy may represent either her femininity or her motherly side.

Mystical Meaning Some cultures believe that fairies are real beings that tend and direct the powers of nature. The Findhorn organization calls them Devas and may have proved their existence by demonstrating that barren land can be made to bloom by calling for faireis' help. In dreams, it may actually be possible to communicate with these elemental powers.

FALLING

Common Dream

Many times as I'm going to sleep, I dream that I am walking along the road and suddenly trip up and fall toward the pavement. I always wake up before I hit the ground. Why do I dream this?—J.H., London, England

Psychological Meaning Dreams about falling usually occur as you are "falling off" to sleep. They may be triggered by a drop in blood pressure, a movement of the fluid in the middle ear, or a limb dangling off the side of the bed.

Some psychologists believe that these are archaic memories from the time when the ancestors of humans were tree-dwelling primates. The ape-men that survived their fall passed on their genes with the memory of the event. The dead ones did not. And that's why so often you dream of falling but of never hitting the ground.

As a symbol, falling highlights a loss of emotional equilibrium or self-control. You may fear "letting go" in real life. Anxiety usually accompanies this dream. It may represent your insecurity, a lack of self-confidence, a fear of failure, or an inability to cope with a situation. There could also be a literal interpretation. You may have noticed something unsafe—a loose stair rail, a wobbly ladder, or an insecure window. Check it out. The dream may be a warning.

ASK YOURSELF

1. *Am I over-ambitious?* Perhaps you have climbed above your station and are experiencing the pride before a fall? You may have to lower your sights somewhat and set yourself goals that are more realistic.

2. *Do I fear letting go?* The dream may be urging you to stop resisting an impulse from the unconscious. Psychologist Strephon Kaplan-Williams suggests that you relive the dream in your imagination and let the fall complete itself. In this way, you will find out what is frightening you and get to the bottom of the problem.

Mystical Meaning Some sources claim that if you dream of falling into mud, someone has told lies about you. Other dreams about falling forecast monetary loss.

FAMOUS

Psychological Meaning People who appear in your dreams represent aspects of your own self that you may be unaware of. Famous people usually represent the person you would like to be. Ask yourself what psychological characteristics and traits this person symbolizes for you. These may be the qualities that you need to integrate into your own personality. If you dream of being famous yourself, it may show your need to be admired by the people around you.

Mystical Meaning It is said that to dream of being famous means that you are trying to grasp something beyond your reach.

FATHER (*see also* Mother)

Psychological Meaning As an archetype, the father represents the protector, lawgiver, or ruler. He may appear in dreams as a king, emperor, wise old man, or as the sun, a weapon, or a phallus. Jung considered this important symbol to play a crucial psychological role in the destiny of the individual. Sometimes this figure may represent the conscience and show your conventional moral opinions. If the father plays the role of protector, it may symbolize the need to become more self-reliant and depend on your own resources. Many people dream of hostility toward their father. This shows that the unconscious is dethroning the father in order to enable you to achieve a proper sense of yourself and be a person in your own right.

Mystical Meaning Freud considered the ancient Greek myth of Oedipus to symbolize the psychological development of an individual. He claimed that failure to achieve freedom from parental influence resulted in an Oedipus complex. Children (usually between four and seven years old) go through a phase where they develop an incestuous desire for the parent of the opposite sex. The complex occurs when the young boy has feelings of resentment toward his father, whom he sees as his rival. Perhaps the father may punish him by castration? Normally the Oedipus complex resolves itself before puberty.

FEAR

Psychological Meaning Bad memories, feelings of guilt, self-doubt, worries, anger, desires, insecurities, and anxieties are often pushed out of your waking thoughts and repressed. Nightmares occur when these hidden fears force you to pay attention to them. This is an opportunity to discover what part of you is threatening to destroy your inner peace. What is it that you fear so much that you have to push it away into the darkness of the unconscious?

Mystical Meaning The superstitions come close to modern psychology with this one: If you overcome whatever frightens you in your dreams, you will also overcome the things that frighten you in waking life.

FEAST

Psychological Meaning You have the emotional need to gorge yourself. This may not necessarily be on food—you may have a ravenous sexual appetite. Consider whether there is an imbalance in your life that needs redressing. Alternatively, perhaps you are over-indulging in feelings of self-pity or are greedy for material things. You may need to set limits upon your desires.

Mystical Meaning All is well as long as you enjoy the food. If the food tastes bad or you are refused food, then you will soon experience disappointments.

FEATHER

Psychological Meaning Feathers can represent a gift that expresses your desire to show warmth and tenderness to someone close to you. A feather floating in the air may show your desire to ascend to higher spiritual knowledge or intellectual ambition. The lightness of a feather also implies lightheartedness and enjoyment of the good things in life. You may benefit if you surrender for a while to the benevolent winds of fortune. Go with the flow.

Mystical Meaning Many cultures, such as the Incas and Native Americans, used feathered headdresses to represent spiritual authority and wisdom.

FENCE

Psychological Meaning You may feel that there are barriers in your way. You feel fenced in and restricted in what you can do or can express. Perhaps your relationship is unsatisfactory because you feel that your partner does not allow you to be the person you really are. Similarly,

you may feel that your job or circumstances are restrictive to your personal growth. It's time to pull down these fences and be yourself.

Mystical Meaning A fence is an obstacle and is therefore interpreted by the ancient dream seers as difficulties ahead.

FIELDS

Psychological Meaning The openness of a field may express your desire to be free. A field is also a fertile place and may therefore symbolize personal growth. The earth can symbolize the mother, which in turn represents the instinctive levels of your being, from which this growth may come. Alternatively, the dream may simply represent your love of and desire to be with nature. In times of trouble, a short break spent with nature can be very therapeutic. Many of society's ills are caused by losing touch with nature's restorative and nurturing powers.

Mystical Meaning The Gypsies believe that to dream of a field means a great deal of hard work ahead. A field of weeds will have little reward, but if it is full of clover you will soon make wealthy friends.

FIGHTING (SEE WAR)

FILM

Psychological Meaning What you watched on TV or saw at the cinema before going to bed can influence your dreams. You may have unconsciously felt an empathy for something you saw. To dream of watching a film may demonstrate that you are contemplating your thoughts in an unattached way. You are able to view yourself and your life without becoming emotionally involved.

Mystical Meaning Medieval sources of course do not list this one, but more modern superstitions say that to dream of handling film signifies that you will receive a gratifying gift.

FINGERS

Psychological Meaning If you subscribe to Freud's theories, then fingers are clearly phallic symbols. Alternatively, they may represent dexterity or its opposite, ineptitude, and being "all thumbs." A finger pointing at you can imply self-blame. Alternatively, it may point to indicate a direction. In this case, your dream may be solving problems for you and may be suggesting what you should do. Consider what aspect of yourself or your situation the dream has pointed out and give it your attention.

Mystical Meaning It is fortunate to dream of cutting your finger, but only if it bleeds. And if you dream of having an extra finger, you will receive an inheritance.

FIRE

Psychological Meaning Fire destroys, but it also cleanses and purifies. It can illuminate, but it also causes pain. Its energy is a potent symbol of eternal life or eternal damnation. Fire is a powerful yet ambivalent dream symbol.

In dreams, it can signal a new beginning, spiritual illumination, sexual passion, or disruptive emotions, such as the flames of passion or envy. For example, to dream of a house burning down or a forest fire warns that you are consumed by passion. Consider whether your emotions are getting out of control and whether you need to calm the flames. Are you being a hothead? Do you have a fiery temper? Be careful or your burning passion may spark a flaming argument!

Fire can also be a symbol of security. To dream of a cozy fire in the hearth shows that you are comfortable with your circumstances and at ease with your life. Freud said that fire was a symbol of the libido (the passions), and to dream of poking a fire represented arousing sexual passion.

Mystical Meaning Jung said that fire represents the process of psychological transformation. Just as the alchemists used fire to transform base metal into gold, so the symbol fire is the trigger for the inner transformation. It purges the decay of the past, yet gives light and spiritual truth. It is the eternal flame in the temple of the soul. It is from the fire that the phoenix of hope arises.

FISH

Psychological Meaning Fish can represent insights into the unconscious. (The unconscious is represented by the sea.) Jung said that fish are often symbols used by the dream to describe psychic happenings or experiences that suddenly dart out of the unconscious and have a frightening or redeeming effect. Fish caught in a net and brought to the surface may represent insights emerging into the light of consciousness. Fish are also a common symbol of fertility. Your dream may be indicating that you are experiencing a period of personal growth. Fish are a product of the emotions and intuition, as opposed to the materialistic, earthbound approach to life.

Mystical Meaning A fish is a symbol for Christ. Fish have also been used as a symbol by many other religions to represent divinity. They represent the spiritual abundance that feeds everyone. Your dream may be a mystical insight into your divine potential.

FLOATING

Psychological Meaning In order to float you have to relax and accept the support of the water. In psychological terms, this means that you have accepted the feminine side of your psyche and are carried forward by it. Floating implies acceptance; you have let go of your problems, worries, and restrictions and can now enjoy just being yourself. Go with the flow.

Mystical Meaning To dream of floating means tremendous success will come your way, but if you struggle to stay afloat there will be delays.

FLOOD

Psychological Meaning Water symbolizes the emotional side of the unconscious. To dream of a flood or of being swept away by water indicates that you feel emotionally overwhelmed. These dreams also hint at baptism and rebirth. The fertile, nourishing effect of floodwater may be implied. This dream could therefore represent the start of a new phase of life and of renewed personal growth.

Mystical Meaning The story of Noah's ark, the *Epic of Gilgamesh*, and other myths about floods represent a purging that prepares the way for something better. Everything in your life has been swept away so that you may start anew.

FLOWER (SEE ALSO MANDALA)

Psychological Meaning A flower is a symbol of the true spiritual self. Its symmetry and perfection show how beautiful you really are.

Mystical Meaning At first the Buddha felt that enlightenment was impossible to convey to the

FLYING

world. Then he saw a pond of lotus flowers at different stages of unfolding. He understood that all people are at different stages of spiritual development. Like the flowers, some remain in the mud of desire, but others raise themselves and gradually open to the light. Inspired by what he saw, the Buddha began his mission.

Common Dream

FLYING

I dreamed I could fly in the air, rose above the town below, and flew high into the night sky. It felt wonderful. I had no fear and could float gently down to earth whenever I wanted.—Charles N., New York

Psychological Meaning To dream of flying is usually a pleasant experience accompanied by a sense of exhilaration and freedom. It usually feels completely natural, something you've always known how to do. Rarely is the dream accompanied by a fear of heights or of falling. Flying may symbolize liberation from something that has been troubling you. The obstructions and shackles that have held you down have been released, and you can now experience the same sense of freedom seen in the birds that soar in the sky. The sky may symbolize consciousness and spirituality, so to dream of flying can represent the expansion of your awareness and the unfolding of your higher self. (To Freud, flying dreams represented sexual release.)

Nevertheless, flying also has its perils. The ancient Greek myth of Icarus warns against flying too high. Your dream may show that you are being overly ambitious.

ASK YOURSELF

1. *What is it I am being released from?* Think about the things that have been troubling you of late. Perhaps the difficulty or emotional problem that has grounded you for so long is not as bad as you thought. Sometimes it is important to tread the paths of life lightly. Let the freedom, gentleness, and carefree feeling of the dream be expressed in your behavior.

2. *Do I feel anxiety or fear?* You may thrill at the feeling of risk that your dream gives you. If so, you

may want to take more risks in your life, for example, with your work or a relationship. If you feel trepidation and alarm, you may be overreaching yourself and may need to get a firmer footing in your life. Your dreams and ambitions may be too grandiose and not in accord with what you can realistically expect to achieve.

Mystical Meaning In ancient times, a person who dreamed of flying was considered to have entered the realm of the immortal gods. Native Americans, Babylonians, Hindus, Tibetan Buddhists, and many others claim that all people have a light body that can leave the physical body during sleep. The light body can travel great distances and even into other dimensions that mystics call the astral planes. Here it is possible to talk to friends who also travel the dimensions, communicate with the people of the spirit world, or learn from the advanced souls once called gods and angels. Many scientists believe that there is empirical proof that out-of-body travel is possible. For example, Dr Michael Sabom in *Recollections of Death* published six in-depth descriptions by patients of their surgical operations as purportedly viewed by them while out of the body. He substantiated their claims by comparing their reports with the surgeon's notes and other eyewitness testimony.

FOG (SEE ALSO BLIND AND CLOUDS)

Psychological Meaning You are not seeing things as they really are. You may be disoriented in waking life and have lost your sense of direction. It's time to finish with this foggy thinking. Be clear about what you want and what direction you want your life to take. Decisiveness will improve your inner clarity.

Mystical Meaning If the fog is thick, this is a very bad omen, say the dream oracles, but if you dream of it clearing, you will have great success.

FOOD (SEE ALSO EATING)

Psychological Meaning Food represents the qualities you take into yourself, and for Sigmund Freud it symbolized sexuality (see Eating). The different types of food you dream about can symbolize a variety of things. Fruit can symbolize sensuality, but it can also represent receiving rewards or abundance. To dream of bitter fruits such as lemons may indicate that you feel bitter-

FOOD

ness about a situation or person influencing your life. Are you the one with the sour attitude? Milk can symbolize human kindness; sugar, sweet words; and frozen food may indicate that you have frozen emotions. There are thousands of possible qualities symbolized by food. You will need to examine what your personal associations are with the food featured in your dream. For example, Freud considered that chocolate or any luxurious food represented self-reward. Do you get a feeling of guilt when you look at a cake? And could it therefore represent guilt in your dreams?

Mystical Meaning Since the times of the Ancient Greeks to dream of food was interpreted in sexual terms. Peaches and other succulent fruits stood for lasciviousness, while others, such as pomegranates, symbolized fertility. It was an apple the caused Adam and Eve to be booted out of the Garden of Eden. Food such as bread symbolized a more restrained, fertility-orientated sexuality, and many cultures believe that if you eat meat you will take on the spiritual qualities of that particular animal.

FOOT

Psychological Meaning Your dream may be telling you to be practical and sensible. "Keep your feet squarely on the ground," says your unconscious. Alternatively, you may be reconsidering your direction in life or questioning what your life is based on. For a Christian, dreaming of washing feet is a symbol of forgiveness. In India, the feet of the guru are considered the holiest part of the body and a symbol of the divine.

Mystical Meaning In China they say: "All great journeys begin with a single step." Your dream may be advising you to move forward one step at a time.

FOREIGN COUNTRIES

Psychological Meaning To dream of being in foreign countries means that you are experiencing something unfamiliar in your waking life. For example, you may have changed your job or may be behaving in ways that are different from your usual routine. If the surroundings make you feel lost or anxious, your dream may be telling you that you are not yet ready to leave your old way of life behind. You are not yet prepared to deal with a new set of circumstances that are influencing your life. However, if you feel excitement at discovering something new, your dream is reflecting your pleasure at finding new openings in your waking life. Now is the time to take advantage of new opportunities that are presenting themselves to you.

Mystical Meaning If you have patience, your wishes will come true.

FOREIGNER

Psychological Meaning A foreigner may represent a part of the psyche that is unfamiliar to you. You may be neglecting important feelings or talents that you need to get acquainted with.

Mystical Meaning Superstition tells that a friendly foreigner predicts good luck.

FOREST

Psychological Meaning The forest is often a symbol of the unconscious. Its animals and birds can be symbols for the instincts and emotions. To dream of trying to find your way through a dark forest may represent that you are searching for a breakthrough in your waking life.

Mystical Meaning Many fairy tales such as *Hansel and Gretel* and *Snow White* are set in the forest. Just like dreams, these stories represent exploring the world of the unconscious mind.

FAMOUS DREAMER

Adolf Hitler
Nazi dictator

During the First World War, 28-year-old Adolf Hitler was a corporal in the German Infantry fighting in the trenches on the French front. One night, he dreamed of being buried beneath an avalanche of earth and molten iron. He could feel the terrible pain of being fatally wounded. He woke up and felt compelled to leave the trench. As soon as he was clear of the dugout, he heard a loud explosion behind him. The trench he had been sleeping in only moments before was now a smoldering pile of dirt, hot metal, and blood. This event convinced Hitler he was invincible and destined for greatness.

FOUNTAIN (SEE ALSO MANDALA AND WATER)

Psychological Meaning A fountain is a symbol of the life force. It may represent the source of your vitality, the spiritual center from which you draw your inspiration and joy. Fountains that are symmetrical or are built upon a circular pool are mandalas symbolizing the unity of the self.

Mystical Meaning Predicts a happy, fulfilled period ahead, but if the fountain runs dry there will be problems.

FRAUD

Psychological Meaning You may feel that you have been cheated of the worldly success that you rightly deserve. Alternatively, it may be you who are the fraud by not expressing your true sentiments. Or perhaps you are simply taking advantage of people in your waking life. Honesty is your best policy.

Mystical Meaning To dream of unmasking a fraud or of catching a thief promises good fortune.

FRIEND

can represent your shadow self—the aspects of your personality that you have rejected. However, the shadow self in this dream is not portrayed as something sinister or threatening. You may be prepared to integrate this neglected part of yourself and restore inner harmony.

Mystical Meaning To dream that you have a friend who is always true is a promise of good news. If you dream that a friend is in trouble there will be worrying news.

FRUIT (SEE FOOD)

FRUSTRATION

Psychological Meaning If you dream of missing a train, being unable to read an important message, searching in vain for something, or failing to convince someone of the truth of an argument, your dream is expressing deep-set frustrations. You may be concerned that your life is not going in the direction you want, or may feel a repressed anger at the stubbornness of the people in your life. It is important that you discover why you feel so frustrated so that you can deal more effectively with its causes.

Mystical Meaning Dream superstition takes frustrations to mean the opposite—all your plans will succeed.

FUNERAL (SEE ALSO DEATH)

Psychological Meaning Don't take this one too literally. The person being buried may represent an aspect of yourself you are trying to repress. Is there something you want removed from your life? Perhaps you have feelings, desires, or thoughts that scare you. You may be worrying too much about your health, or perhaps you want to bury the past. The only constant in life is change. The past is dead and buried, so embrace the present and look forward to the future.

Who is being buried? Do you feel resentment toward this person, or does the person symbolize something happening in your life or something about yourself? If you are being buried in the dream, you may have a fear about being overwhelmed by your emotional troubles or by unconscious forces. First, get in touch with these hidden feelings and find out what they are. What happened recently (or a long time ago) to give rise to these emotions? Don't keep burying them. Start by examining them, then accept them, and finally start to control them. The problems you try to bury are probably not as bad as you think.

Mystical Meaning Occasionally dreams of funerals do foretell the future. For example, Abraham Lincoln dreamed of his own death just days before he was assassinated. He saw his own shrouded corpse laid in state in a room of the White House. However, in the vast majority of cases, dreams of funerals are a metaphor for your own state of mind.

FUTURE

Psychological Meaning To dream of being in the future may represent the way you hope or fear things will turn out. Your dream may be saying, "If you carry on behaving the way you are, this is the situation you're likely to find yourself in." However, your dream may not necessarily be a premonition of actual events to come.

Mystical Meaning J. W. Dunne in his famous book *An Experiment with Time* proposed that dreams can tell of future events and cited many examples from his dream diaries. However, it is wise not to take these dreams too literally, for the unconscious can distort the information it receives. For example, Dunne dreamed of being *killed* by a bull. In the next few days he was *chased* by a bull but certainly not killed.

GAG

Psychological Meaning The dream may be saying that you cannot express the way you really feel about an issue. There are important things that need saying but you don't know how to say them. Alternatively, the dream may be saying the opposite. Your unconscious may be warning you to keep quiet.

Mystical Meaning An obstacle dream that suggests difficulties with communications may lead to misunderstanding. Beware of gossip.

GAMBLING

Psychological Meaning You may be involved in some kind of risk-taking in waking life. Weigh the odds and decide which option is the best. Occasionally, I have interviewed people who have dreamed of a winning horse or a run of numbers that wins a prize. However, I have also heard from many more people who have placed bets because of a dream and then lost! Don't be reckless if you bet.

Mystical Meaning Superstition says to reverse this dream. To dream of winning brings a loss, but to dream of losing brings a gain.

GARBAGE

Psychological Meaning This often symbolizes the unwanted traits, attitudes, fears, or memories that you want to discard. It may also symbolize a duty or responsibility that you want nothing to do with. Perhaps you feel you have now disposed of the junk in your life that has been preventing you from progressing. If the garbage is rotten, it implies that these difficulties have been with you for a long time.

Mystical Meaning Superstition says that dreaming of garbage means your wildest dreams will come true.

GARDEN

Psychological Meaning A garden is a promising dream symbol that may show inner growth and stability. Sometimes dream gardens are symmetrical with a central point. This mandala symbol represents the inner wholeness of your true self. Pools, water, and fountains show the pure spiritual energies that constitute your nature. This dream may indicate inner healing after a period of discord and unease.

Mystical Meaning Some sources claim that to dream of a garden foretells a marriage to a very beautiful woman or a handsome man.

GATE

Psychological Meaning Walking through a gateway may represent moving into a new phase of life. New opportunities may await you.

Mystical Meaning An open gate represents changes for the better, but a closed gate means problems ahead.

GHOST

Psychological Meaning The shadowy ghosts of your dream represent those aspects of yourself that you fear. But it is fear itself that makes them frightening. Expose these dark pursuing forces to the light of day and you will discover that it is only your own fear that turns them into nightmares. You must realize that many different energies make up your psyche. Accept them all as valid parts of yourself. Your dream may also reflect your own fears about death and dying. For Freud a ghost was a symbol of the mother.

Mystical Meaning In most cases ghosts are representations of the dark forces within yourself that you have not accepted. However, as a medium I have spoken to many people who claim to have met the dead in their dreams. In some cases, the spirit gave evidence that proved it to be the real spirit of someone from the next world. Only spirits that truly care for you can communicate in this way.

GIANT

Psychological Meaning Giants can represent awe-inspiring powers that are dominating you or forcing you to take notice of them. Mythological giants are often connected with sex, and the club they often carry is considered by many psychologists to be a phallic symbol. For a man, to dream of a giant can indicate that sexual needs are disproportionate to the opportunities to gratify them. For a woman, to dream of a giant may indicate guilt or fear regarding sex. To adults a giant may be a recollection of childhood, when all adults towered above us. They may represent a protective or feared father figure.

GATE

Mystical Meaning To dream of a giant is a lucky omen that predicts commercial success.

GIFT

Psychological Meaning This dream shows how you interact with other people. If you receive many gifts, it may show that others hold you in esteem. If you are the giver, it may show that you desire to be generous to others. You may want to express your feelings or have something awkward to say that has to be carefully packaged. Does it show the way you disguise the things you say and do? What's inside the box may represent your true motives. Are they honorable?

Mystical Meaning To dream of being given a gift brings misfortune, but to dream of giving a gift means a new enterprise.

GOD

Psychological Meaning Your dream may be a truly spiritual dream. Sometimes the unconscious uses symbolism from ancient traditions to express your feelings about divinity. Put aside your material concerns and focus on higher things. It was a wise man who wrote "In God We Trust" on United States dollar bills. Goddesses and gods can also represent the anima and animus or can be symbols for the mother and father.

Mystical Meaning Most old dream books avoid this one because they were written in less tolerant times. To dream of the Christian God means you will achieve peace, but to dream of graven images signifies sexual pleasure.

GOLD

Psychological Meaning Precious gold may symbolize those aspects of your true self that you hold dear. It can represent spiritual achievement and self-realization. Associated with the sun, it may also represent life and renewal.

Mystical Meaning For the alchemists, gold represented the spiritual treasure that was gained by transforming the spirit. In mythology, it appears as the spiritual prize that is gained once the dragons and monsters of ignorance are overcome.

GOVERNMENT

Psychological Meaning A government may represent the forces within your psyche that have most power. Are you governed by qualities such as greed, lust, and jealousy, or love, acceptance, and honesty? What factors are in charge of your life? Dreaming about government may also reflect your views about society at large and about the way you organize your life.

Mystical Meaning To dream about holding a position of power within government indicates a period of uncertainty ahead.

GRANDPARENTS

Psychological Meaning Grandparents are usually seen by children to be more sympathetic figures than parents. Parents have to be obeyed, but a grandparent's advice is listened to and voluntarily applied. In dreams, they can represent wisdom that has stood the test of time. This wisdom may be the superior knowledge of the unconscious.

Mystical Meaning Even the wackiest of dream books agree that grandparents are a symbol of wisdom and security.

GRAVE

Psychological Meaning Something within you has died. You must discover what it is and why it has been returned to the unconscious, here symbolized by the earth. Alternatively, the grave may be a pun, suggesting that you are facing a "grave situation," or it could simply be a reflection of your own thoughts about death and mortality.

Mystical Meaning Superstitions say that this dream means you will experience a loss but not necessarily a death. Some superstitions say the dream foretells news of a marriage.

GREEN (*see* Colors)

GUEST

Psychological Meaning A guest may represent a previously unconscious aspect of yourself that you have invited to become part of your conscious life. Similarly, a guest may represent new challenges and interests. If you are the guest, the dream may draw your attention to circumstances in your life that are temporary. Guests don't usually stay forever, they come, are entertained, and then they go.

Mystical Meaning The *I Ching* says: "When a man is a stranger, he should not be gruff or over-

GURU

bearing....He must be cautious and reserved; in this way he protects himself from evil. If he is obliging toward others, he wins success." Perhaps your dream gives similar advice.

GUN

Psychological Meaning When Mae West said in the film *My Little Chickadee* "Is that a gun in your pocket or are you just pleased to see me?" she was talking pure Freud. In dreams guns represent aggressive sexuality. If you dream of killing someone with a gun, it may represent your desire to kill off part of yourself. If it's an animal you kill, it may show that you repress your instincts. If it's you being shot, you may feel that in waking life you are being victimized in some way.

Mystical Meaning If you hear guns in a dream, expect a quarrel with a neighbor.

GURU

Psychological Meaning The guru may represent your own higher self and the innate wisdom within you. He may take a religious form such as Buddha, Shiva, or a saint. This inner guide may also appear as an old bearded man, a priest, prophet, magician, or king. In its feminine manifestation, it may appear as the Earth Mother or a goddess. For example, the Virgin Mary appearing within dreams is a symbol of supreme compassion and selfless love; your inner guide that teaches through grace rather than power. Carl Jung called these figures "mana personalities." (Mana denotes the mysterious powers associated with the gods, or superhuman knowledge.) Because of the awe-inspiring knowledge and insight these people represent, they may sometimes appear as frightening or domineering figures. Dreams of this nature indicate that an extremely important spiritual aspect of your life is opening.

Mystical Meaning Some spiritual traditions, such as those of the Tibetan Buddhists, Hindus, and Native Americans, believe that the inner teacher is a real person who communicates to the dreamer via another realm of existence. The teacher may come from this world or from the realms of spirit. I am a follower of the Indian guru Sathya Sai Baba, whom I believe has spoken to me directly through my dreams. To some of my friends he has confirmed this, by describing the content and repeating the exact words said by him in their dreams!

GYPSY

Psychological Meaning The Gypsies are a mysterious people surrounded by legends and occult stories and may therefore represent your shadow—the undiscovered part of yourself. Alternatively, the dream may be suggesting that you look to the future. What will your circumstances be like in years to come if you continue as you are?

Mystical Meaning As Gypsies are associated with prophecy, your dream may be giving you real clues to future events. Gypsies are associated with good luck, so destiny may smile upon you yet.

HAIR

Psychological Meaning Hair often symbolizes vanity. Long hair may signify virility or male sexuality. Dreams of going bald may indicate fears about loss of self-esteem or, according to Freud, fear of castration and impotency. Dreams about losing hair can also express worries about getting older. Similarly, a strong beard can stand for vitality, while a white one can signify age or wisdom. To dream of having your hair cut may indicate that you are, like Samson, experiencing a loss of strength. You may feel that someone is trying to censor you. To shave off the hair on the head symbolizes renunciation of the earthly life in order to seek spiritual truth. If your hair is being styled or set, then your dream is highlighting your worries about your self-image. Hair blown by the wind or flowing free indicates you may need the freedom to express uninhibited feelings. You want to "let your hair down" and "hang loose."

Mystical Meaning Cutting of hair can represent conformity. In the past, it was commonplace to cut the hair of convicts, soldiers, and schoolboys. When the Beatles grew long hair in the 60s, it was an unconscious symbol that expressed the rebellion of a generation.

HALL (SEE ALSO BUILDINGS)

Psychological Meaning A hall is the center from which you can access the whole house. To dream of entering a hall may therefore represent the beginning of your adventure in self-exploration.

Mystical Meaning To dream of a long hallway predicts a period of worry ahead.

HAMMER

Psychological Meaning A Freudian interpretation of hammering a nail is that it is a symbol for the sexual act. A hammer, therefore, is a powerful male symbol of virility, power, and strength. Alternatively, it may also represent the way you are dealing with your situation at the moment. Are you being too forceful? On the other hand, perhaps you are trying to "hammer the message home."

Mystical Meaning Thursday gets its name from the Teutonic god Thor, the son of Odin, who controlled the weather and crops. He possessed a magical hammer that would return to his hand after he had thrown it. In this instance, the hammer represents divine power and spiritual strength.

HANDS

Psychological Meaning Hands can represent dexterity, artistic ability, or psychological skills. You also use them to express yourself and as extensions of your personality. A fist may represent anger or passion, folded hands can represent acceptance, joined hands can represent affection, and an upheld hand symbolizes a blessing. Consider the gesture of the hands in your dream, for it reveals the nature of the sentiments you are trying to express.

Mystical Meaning If you dream of the palm, you may be thinking about the future. Palmistry claims that the shape, lines, and mounts of the palm reveal your destiny. Your dream may be revealing a *potential* future scenario based upon your current circumstances. Fortunately you have free will, so positive actions taken now will influence the shape of things to come for the better.

HARBOR

Psychological Meaning A harbor is a sanctuary from the stormy seas. Similarly, your dream shows that you have found a safe haven where you can wait until the storms pass. For the time being, seek refuge in the familiar and thereby prepare yourself for the challenges ahead. Use this period of security to grow in strength.

Mystical Meaning Superstition claims that to dream of entering a harbor predicts a period of security ahead, but dream of leaving one and you'll break a friendship.

HARE

Psychological Meaning The hare can be a symbol of the trickster who effects transformation. It is both a messenger from the unconscious and the weak but cunning inferior function at the threshold between consciousness and unconsciousness. It can represent some personal characteristic such as rashness or shallow cleverness.

Mystical Meaning Hares were always considered unlucky because it was believed that they were sometimes witches in disguise. It was also believed that if a pregnant woman saw one, her child would be born with a harelip. However,

HANDS

some dream oracles say that to dream of a hare approaching you brings good luck.

HAT

Psychological Meaning Freud believed that hats (and gloves) represent the female genitalia because they enclose a part of the body. A hat may also represent the role you play in life. Changing hats may denote a change of attitude or direction. You may be thinking about taking on new work responsibilities or even changing your job. The type of hat is also significant: a top hat may indicate your desire for wealth; a baseball hat may represent your desire to be more athletic or younger; and a straw hat may show that you desire to adopt a more natural, carefree attitude.

Mystical Meaning Predecessors of Freud believed that if a woman dreamed of wearing a man's hat, she secretly desired to have sex with the owner. If you dream of losing your hat, yous will soon be married.

HEAD

Psychological Meaning A head may symbolize rationality and the intellect. It is the conscious self. There may also be puns in the dream such as "keeping ahead of the game" or "facing your situation head-on." In addition, the dream may be a metaphor to express what is going on in your head at the moment.

Mystical Meaning It is a sign of good news if you dream that your head is very large, say the seers of old.

HEART

Psychological Meaning The heart represents the center of emotional life. It is an archetypal symbol for love that has been with humanity from time immemorial. Your dream is describing your emotional life and the way that you are currently dealing with your feelings. If the heart is damaged, being operated on, or wounded, then you may be experiencing an emotional hurt of some kind. Examine the rest of the dream's content to see if it reveals ways to repair the emotional damage that you feel. Alternatively, if the heart is pictured in a more positive setting, then your dream is saying that you feel good about your emotion-

al life. Dare you admit that you may have fallen in love?

Mystical Meaning In India, the heart is a symbol of *prema*—divine love. It also represents innermost motivations. My guru, Sathya Sai Baba, tells us to remember to observe ourselves every time we look at our watch. "WATCH: Watch your *Words*, *Actions*, *Thoughts*, *Character*, and *Heart*."

HEAVEN

Psychological Meaning To dream of a heavenly paradise may represent your desire to find perfect happiness. You may be trying to escape from what you perceive to be a banal and depressing life. Your dream gives you a welcome break from reality and serves to restore your feelings of optimism and hope. You desire to achieve the inner balance and wholeness that is your spiritual destiny.

Mystical Meaning I have on file many cases of people who have been taken in a dream to the afterlife. Here they have met their dead loved ones. The lucidity of the dreams suggests that these dreamers may be experiencing another level of reality. I believe that, in some rare cases, the dreamer is really communicating with the dead.

HEDGE

Psychological Meaning This dream may represent the restrictions and obstacles you believe are inhibiting your progress. The restrictions that you intend to overcome may be psychological or material. If you dream of cutting a hedge, it may suggest that you have accepted an immovable obstacle and are making the best of a bad situation.

Mystical Meaning To dream of cutting a hedge means that good luck is on its way.

HELL

Psychological Meaning You may have many inner fears and repressed guilty feelings that are forcing themselves into your awareness. Take it easy on yourself and stop punishing yourself. Once you have passed through this period of inner turmoil, you will emerge as a new and better person. Be gentle and accept yourself for the person you are. It is important that you now begin to tame the repressed contents of the unconscious and transform them into something positive.

Mystical Meaning The old dream dictionaries also say that this dream arises from inner strife. However, they add that it foretells improvements in business.

HERO/HEROINE (SEE ALSO ANIMA/ANIMUS)

Psychological Meaning Whether it be Gilgamesh, Hercules, or Superman, the hero figure represents the conscious part of yourself that bravely embarks on a journey into the darkness of the unconscious to challenge its wild powers. In most myths and stories, the hero ventures into strange lands and fights monsters in order to take possession of a great treasure or win the hand of a beautiful maiden. These are symbols of the rewards you gain by probing the unconscious mind. By taming its primitive forces and using them for creative ends, you achieve psychological integration and wholeness. For a woman, a male heroic figure may represent the masculine side of herself. Similarly, if a man dreams of rescuing a maiden, it may show that he has discovered the feminine side of his own nature.

Heroic dreams awaken you to your inner strengths and weaknesses—knowledge essential for the development of a healthy personality. Although these dreams generally occur during adolescence, they can also reappear at any age. As you would expect, males tend to have more hero dreams than women do, but this is changing as women take on roles that are more assertive.

Mystical Meaning Some dream sources claim that to dream of a famous heroic figure means that someone who once disliked you will now fall in love with you.

HILL

Psychological Meaning A hill may represent an obstacle that you have to overcome in waking life. If the journey is arduous, you may be attempting something beyond your strength. However, if the journey is easy, you may now have the inner resources you need to complete your task. Move forward one step at a time and be confident.

Mystical Meaning In this case, the superstitious interpretation is the same as the psychological one. A Freudian psychologist might add that hills represent a woman's breasts—probably your mother's.

HIVE

Psychological Meaning This dream may represent your lifestyle. You are probably extremely active and working very hard at the moment. And just like the busy bees, you need to be well organized. If you dream of something upsetting the order of the hive, this represents the factors that are disrupting the smooth running of your waking-life activities.

Mystical Meaning In rural superstition, bees were always considered to be wise creatures with a special knowledge of the future. Dreams that include bees or hives may hold clues to future events.

HOLE

Psychological Meaning To a Freudian psychologist, a hole represents the vagina or womb. Your dream may therefore be about sexual issues. It may also suggest that you feel hollow and empty within. Could it be that you have indulged so much in feelings of depression that it's as if you dug yourself into a hole that you can't get out of? You may need to introduce new interests into your life in order to restore your feeling of self-worth and fulfillment. To dream of holes in clothes may indicate that you are worried about your self-image.

Mystical Meaning To dream of crawling into a hole augurs badly. You will befriend seedy and unreliable people.

HOLIDAY (SEE VACATION)

HOME

Psychological Meaning This dream may be about your need for security. You may feel that your situation is better now. Do you feel at home in your job? Is your environment homely? Perhaps you feel that after a period of struggle you are now on home ground? Your dream may also include references to your own childhood or, if you are single, thoughts about starting a family of your own.

Mystical Meaning The nomadic Gypsies claim that to dream of being forced to leave your home indicates that a favorable opportunity awaits you.

HONEY

Psychological Meaning Honey represents sweetness and feelings that bring you happiness, such as love, peace, and joy. It is the spirit or life force that sustains you. In the Far East, lies are sometimes called "poisoned honey."

Mystical Meaning Honey is the food of the gods, so this dream may be showing your desire to attain divine consciousness.

HORSE

Psychological Meaning Wild forces that have been tamed are symbolized by the horse. Horses are also a symbol of sexuality and were considered by Freud to represent the terrifying aspect of the father. To dream of riding an out-of-control horse may indicate that you are being carried away by your passions, whereas a tightly tethered horse may show that you inhibit these natural feelings. If you fear the horses in your dream, then you may fear your own instinctive nature (literally a "night mare"). In short, horses represent the wild energies of the psyche that need to be both bridled and respected.

Mystical Meaning In some myths and fairy tales, horses speak. In dreams, this represents the voice of your unconscious—a message from your innermost self. In Greek myth, horses were associated with Hades, the underworld, and death. However, dream prophecy says that to dream of horses indicates that you will receive news from a distance. And it is extremely lucky to dream of a horse being shod.

HOSPITAL

Psychological Meaning A hospital is a place of healing. Your dream may offer you cures to improve your psychological or physical health. Observe in which department your dream is set; it may give you important clues to the nature of your problem. You may need some rest or may be trying to recover from a psychological wound that requires inner healing. Or perhaps the dream is a warning about your physical health? Does the dream offer a cure? Does it suggest a healthier behavior pattern or diet? They called Edgar Cayce "The Sleeping Prophet" because he would fall asleep and answer questions put to him about the health of people he had never met. He gave startlingly accurate diagnoses, and his revolutionary treatments and cures are still being used and researched today. Hidden within dreams are the keys to spiritual, psychological, and physical health.

Mystical Meaning The Ancient Greeks believed that dreams not only give a diagnosis of a person's health but also suggest cures. In particular this was affirmed by Hippocrates, who is considered the father of medicine. Student doctors still pledge the Hippocratic Oath. Tibetan medicine also takes note of a patient's dreams in order to uncover the spiritual cause of physical ills.

HOTEL

Psychological Meaning A hotel is an impermanent abode and in dreams represents a transition from one set of circumstances to another. Your dream may highlight a feeling of impermanence or perhaps a shift or loss of personal identity. It may indicate a change in a relationship or the price that has to be paid to sustain it.

Mystical Meaning If the hotel is luxurious, failure is predicted, but if it's a seedy old motel, you will soon experience good fortune.

HOUSE (*SEE ALSO* BUILDINGS)

Psychological Meaning A house represents your psychological condition. Specific rooms in the house detail what aspect of your psychological life the dream is highlighting. Attic: the intellect. Basement: the personal unconscious. Bathroom: base feelings, childhood thoughts, and cleanliness. Bedroom: the private self and sexuality. Den: work and efficiency. Library: intellectual life. Living room: your public image. Roof: an overview of yourself. Windows: the way to interact with the world.

Mystical Meaning Dream lore has many different interpretations for this dream. Here's the simplest: country house, tranquility ahead; building a house, you will be self-confident; new house, a busy social life; empty house, low income; moving house, worries about money.

HUNGER

Psychological Meaning You may simply feel hungry. However, from a symbolic perspective this dream can represent a craving for sex, power, wealth, or fame. Perhaps you feel a lack of satisfaction and feel that your potential is not being recognized. You may be hungry for affection or an opportunity.

Mystical Meaning Superstition says that the hungrier you are, the more destiny will smile upon you.

HUNT (SEE ALSO CHASE)

Psychological Meaning The hunt represents your pursuit of what you want. You may be hunting for a solution, or perhaps you desire to achieve wealth or status. Is the dream about sexual conquest? If the hunt involves killing an animal, you may be trying to repress or destroy an instinctive aspect of yourself.

Mystical Meaning Dream lore says hunting a hare indicates trouble ahead, while a fox predicts deceit by a friend. However, if you dream of hunting a deer you will win the heart of your sweetheart.

HUSBAND

Psychological Meaning This may simply be a dream about your relationship and your unconscious feelings about him. However, you may also be projecting other qualities into this dream image. He may sometimes represent your father or the male side of your own personality (animus)

Mystical Meaning Superstition says that there will be troubles ahead if you dream of being married when you're not.

ICE (SEE ALSO WATER)

Psychological Meaning Water can show the creative flow of feelings, but as ice it shows that feelings are petrified and progress is stopped. You may feel emotionally paralyzed, so pay more attention to your emotional life and become more attuned to your affections. Perhaps you feel that a situation requires you to "break the ice"? You need to experience warm, wholesome feelings expressed with sincerity. Love will melt your frozen heart.

Mystical Meaning If you are married, this dream predicts that you will be happy, but to dream of skating bodes disaster.

ILLNESS

Psychological Meaning This dream does not necessarily presage a waking illness but may represent uncleared bad feelings. You may not be able to cope with a situation and, like a child, may take illness as an easy way out. Perhaps the dream represents a form of self-punishment.

Mystical Meaning Superstitious people believe that dreams should be reversed. This dream therefore predicts a period of good health.

INCEST

Psychological Meaning If the dream relates to real-life events, consider seeking professional advice or counseling. For a man, to dream of incest with a daughter symbolically expresses a fear of secret erotic desires. Incest with a sister or brother can represent the union of masculine and feminine sides of the dreamer. For a man, to dream of incest with his mother represents the desire he may have had for her as a small boy (see Mother) and likewise a woman's dreams of incest with her father represent her infantile desires (see Father).

Mystical Meaning The subject was so taboo, ancient dream books made no comment about these dreams.

INFIDELITY

Psychological Meaning The dream may be wish-fulfillment. Perhaps you feel unsatisfied with your relationship and feel the need for a more exotic sexual life. It is the nature of biology

INTERNET

that both sexes are tempted to be adulterous. Erotic dreams about people other than your partner may sometimes act as a safety valve to release these powerful urges. Surveys indicate that the happiest people are those with a good partnership based on faithfulness and an extended circle of friends. If you dream that your partner is unfaithful, it may indicate that you are neglecting your partner's emotional needs.

Mystical Meaning Dream superstition says that this dream means the opposite. You and your partner will be faithful to each other.

INITIATION

Psychological Meaning These dreams usually represent the transition from one psychological stage to a higher one. For example, they may represent moving from childhood to adolescence, from youth to middle age, or from middle age to old age. It can also represent the shift of interest from worldly ambitions to spiritual aspirations.

Mystical Meaning In ancient times, rituals and initiations were used as a creative dramatization of the pattern and structure of the psyche and life.

INJECTION

Psychological Meaning Clearly, a syringe can be a phallic symbol, so your dream may be saying that you need to inject more enthusiasm into your sex life. Similarly, it may be telling you to inject more fun, determination, or enthusiasm into your life. Injections imply healing and protection, so this dream may be showing you ways to become more psychologically fit.

Mystical Meaning A dream interpretation from the 1930s says that dreaming of being injected means you will be free of enemies who are plotting against you.

INSECTS

Psychological Meaning Insects symbolize the irritating minor nagging of the unconscious or daily life. You may have many irritating small problems that need to be dealt with. In Franz Kafka's book *Metamorphosis* (1912), the terrified sleeper wakes up to discover he has been transformed into a bug. Kafka worked most of his life in office jobs that he hated. Symbolically this

dream can represent how working life requires you to form a brittle shell that can eventually take over your personality completely. Here are a few of the symbolic meanings of common insects: Ants: your life may be too orderly; ants can represent social conformity. Bees: industry and work. Butterflies: the soul, spiritual transcendence. Flies: breakdown, putrefaction, and perhaps guilt. Ladybugs: happiness at work. Locusts: lack of psychological nourishment; your creativity is being destroyed. Wasps: Angry thoughts and feelings.

Mystical Meaning The ancient Egyptians worshiped the scarab beetle as a symbol of creation. In dreams, it can represent the soul. In some fairy tales, insects are called in when things have become impossibly muddled. For example, they may be asked to separate grain mixed with sand or to remove gold dust from grain. In dreams, they can represent precision and meticulous thinking.

INTERNET

Psychological Meaning Your dream may represent the need to communicate with a wider group of friends. What sites do you connect to in your dream? These represent the psychological qualities and needs that your unconscious draws your attention to. E-mail can represent messages from your unconscious.

Mystical Meaning Psychics believe that all life is interconnected by a mycelium of living energy. What happens in one place affects everywhere else. By tuning into this spiritual World Wide Web, it is possible to use clairvoyance to perceive events taking place on the other side of the world. (Remote viewing is a good example of this.) In dreams, it is sometimes possible to connect to this ethereal Internet of consciousness.

INVALID

Psychological Meaning If you dream of being an invalid you may feel that something has robbed you of your ability or self-confidence. You may feel that you are unable to act in the way you really want to. Perhaps you feel crippled by your own negative feelings or by the scorn of others? The word "invalid" may also be a pun. You may feel that something is not valid. Perhaps

somebody is not revealing his or her true feelings, or a mode of behavior has become obsolete.
Mystical Meaning Success will come slowly.

INVISIBLE

Psychological Meaning You may feel that nobody is taking notice of you, that what is important to you is of no consequence to others. Alternatively, you may feel that you want to hide from reality, or the dream could be a metaphor for shyness.

Mystical Meaning In the Ancient Greek mythology, Perseus used a cloak of invisibility. In dreams this can represent the hidden spiritual strength that is needed when exploring the unconscious.

IRON

Psychological Meaning Iron can represent inner strength but also ruthlessness. It is a metal associated with the Earth and the inferior, whereas mercury and gold are associated with spirituality. A household iron may show your desire to create order in your life. You want to "iron out the wrinkles." It may also be a dream that expresses your concerns about your self-image. A hair curling iron may show the opposite, that you want to put a bit of bounce into your life.

Mystical Meaning To dream of iron augurs badly. It is said to be an omen of distress.

ISLAND

Psychological Meaning You may have a craving for solitude if you dream a desert island. Perhaps you are surrounded by too many problems and need to make a little space for yourself? The sea often symbolizes the unconscious mind, so your desire to remain on an island may suggest a wish to cling to the conscious ego instead of venturing into these unexplored parts of yourself. The sea is also a mother symbol and can, according to Freudian psychology, symbolize relations with your mother. If the island is engulfed by the sea, this can represent a fear of being overwhelmed by too strong a mother-attachment or by unconscious forces out of your control

Mystical Meaning Comfort and easy circumstances are predicted by the ancient dream oracles.

JAM (SEE ALSO HONEY)
Psychological Meaning There is an English saying: "Jam yesterday, jam tomorrow, but never jam today." This dream may represent your feeling that you keep missing the rewards of hard work and live forever on promises. Jam may represent the sweet things in life. Alternatively the dream may be a pun. Are you "in a jam" or a "sticky mess"? If your jam is covered in wasps you may feel that your security is threatened by people or events that threaten you.

Mystical Meaning If a woman dreams of making jam, she will be surrounded by appreciative friends.

JEALOUSY

Psychological Meaning These are probably feelings that you have carried forward from your waking life. Your dream may be revealing covetous feelings that you were previously unaware of. Similarly, you may have unconsciously recognized jealousy from your family, friends, or colleagues. Your dream may be warning you.

Mystical Meaning Dream oracles warn of narrow-minded people and the clandestine influence of enemies.

JEW

Psychological Meaning You may feel that you are being persecuted by prejudiced people if you dream of being Jewish. Alternatively, your dream may be telling you to be more tolerant toward others. You may associate Jews with borrowing or lending money and careful management of funds. If you are Jewish, this dream may be about your faith and about your relationship to members of your own community

Mystical Meaning To dream of a Jew indicates that you will prosper or win legal disputes. Yiddish proverbs are full of wisdom. One of my favorites says: "Do not worry about tomorrow; you do not even know what may happen to you today."

JEWELS (SEE ALSO TREASURE)

Psychological Meaning Jewels represent something you value within yourself or in other people. This may include a valued trait such as patience, creativity,

assertiveness and so on, or it may represent core human values such as truth, non-violence, love, peace, and right conduct. Traditionally, gold and diamonds represent the incorruptible true self; rubies denote passion; emeralds, fertility; and sapphires, truth.
Mystical Meaning Predicts good luck.

JOKE

Psychological Meaning Jokes are often funny because they disrupt your normal way of perceiving the world. Your unconscious may be trying to draw your attention to a serious issue that you need to consider. Even in dreams the truest things are often said in jest.
Mystical Meaning A funny joke told in a dream means that business will boom, but if it falls flat then so will your fortunes.

FAMOUS DREAMER

Mary Shelley
Author

In the summer of 1816, Mary Shelley and her husband, the famous poet Percy Bysshe Shelley, had been staying with friends at the Villa Deodati on the shores of Lake Geneva. They spent the evening telling ghost stories. Afterward, Percy suggested that each one of them write a horror story.

That night Mary Shelley had a terrifying dream. "My imagination, unbidden, possessed and guided me," she wrote, "gifting the successive images that arose in my mind with a vividness far beyond the usual bounds of reveries....I saw the pale student of unhallowed arts kneeling beside the thing he had put together— I saw the hideous phantasm of a man stretched out, and then, on the working of some powerful engine, show signs of life, and stir with an uneasy, half-vital motion."

When Mary Shelley awoke she immediately wrote down the nightmare. "What terrified me will terrify others; and I need only describe the specter which had haunted my midnight pillow."

Inspired by this nightmare, in 1818 she wrote her most famous book, Frankenstein: the Modern Prometheus.

JOURNEY (*see also* Accidents, Airplane, Car, Train)
Psychological Meaning The act of dreaming is a journey of discovery into the center of yourself. Consequently, there are many meanings associated with this dream theme. First, the dream may represent your journey through life. An open road suggests progress, but a rocky path may show that you feel your way is arduous. Lush scenery may show that you feel happy with your circumstances, but an arid desert may indicate loneliness or a lack of creativity. Sometimes the hard path is the right way forward, or you may want to establish a more comfortable, easygoing, pattern of behavior.

Are you aware of the destination and goal of your journey? Perhaps it is to discover your true self. You may feel that you tread on hallowed ground as you come closer to your own inner divinity. Sometimes the paths take you to strange lands or unfamiliar foreign countries. This can mean that your unconscious is inviting you to explore it. In mythology, a journey to the west can symbolize the journey to old age whereas an eastward journey can indicate rejuvenation. If towns feature in your dream, consider what they represent. For example, Paris may show that you have a romantic frame of mind, whereas cold Moscow may symbolize an emotional Cold War between you and your partner. You will also have many personal associations relating to places. Ask yourself what they represent and what feelings they represent.
Mystical Meaning The old-fashioned dream interpretations correspond to the modern meanings. For example, ease of travel or obstacles reflect the ease or difficulty you will find in the future. In addition, medieval mystics said that to dream of seeing cheerful friends starting out on a journey means that you will experience a very happy period ahead.

JUDGE

Psychological Meaning A judge may represent self-reproach or guilt. You may fear getting caught or having a secret plan revealed. Your dream may be helping you decide what to do, it is helping you make a judgment of your situation. Sometimes judges can represent society and the way it judges you. Freud believed that a judge was a personification of the super-ego—the standards of conventional morality that you assimi-

JUGGLING

lated from your parents and society. This aspect of yourself may censor your instinctive feelings and desires.

Mystical Meaning Your sharp tongue will make you a new friend.

JUGGLING

Psychological Meaning The dream illustrates that you are trying to keep all the elements of your life in order and in action. You are doing too much.

Mystical Meaning Superstition says that your indecision will lead to failure.

JUMPING

Psychological Meaning If you are jumping to orders, then your dream may be telling you to be more assertive. Stop obeying the will and whims of others. Be your own master and soon you'll dream of jumping for joy.

Mystical Meaning According to superstition, if you trip while jumping you will overcome difficulties and eventually gain success.

JUNGLE

Psychological Meaning A jungle is a symbol of the unconscious and its animals represent the untamed primitive instincts. Locked away in the collective unconscious are archaic memories of primordial times. Some dreams about jungles may be million-year-old memories passed on by distant ancestors. The French painter Henri Rousseau captured the wonderful mystery of these strange dreams in paintings such as his 1907 work, *La Charmeuse de Serpents*.

Mystical Meaning Problems ahead if you get lost, but they will clear if you dream of finding your way out.

KEY

Psychological Meaning Clearly this can be a phallic symbol, and to dream of placing a key in a lock can represent sexual intercourse. Alternatively, the key may be a symbol for the solution to a problem. Your dreams may be showing you the way to unlock the door and to remove the psychological or material obstacles that block your progress.

Mystical Meaning To dream of finding a key is a symbol of good fortune, and a bunch of keys indicates profitable business dealings.

KILLING

Psychological Meaning If you murder someone in your dream, you are expressing your hatred or envy toward the person. Sometimes the person being killed can represent an aspect of your own nature that you hate. For example, if a man dreams of killing a woman, it may show that he rejects the feminine side of his nature. Similarly, if a woman dreams of killing a man, she may be rejecting her masculine side. To dream of killing animals indicates repression of your instinctive nature.

Mystical Meaning There will be arguments and you may have to make sacrifices, say the dream seers.

KING (SEE ALSO QUEEN)

Psychological Meaning A king can symbolize the self that sits on the throne of consciousness. He represents the dominant ruling power—the part of you that is in control. The king can also represent your father.

Mystical Meaning Carl Jung recognized alchemy as a system of symbolism representing the transformation of the lower self (base matter) into the divine (gold). The king is the human personification of the work. His appearance in dreams can have a number of important meanings: The king who is ill represents worn-out attitudes and sometimes the conflict between the conscious and unconscious. The decrepit king shows limited, ego-bound consciousness. If the king dissolves or returns to the mother, this shows the ego sinking back into unconsciousness. In the strange symbolism of alchemy, when a king gives birth to a hermaphrodite, it shows how the new, dominant self is born.

KISS

Psychological Meaning This could be a straightforward sexual dream. However, a kiss is also a symbol of love and affection, and so may represent those things you hold dear. Perhaps there are other connotations: the kiss of death, or the kiss of betrayal. The dream highlights the feelings that you have a closeness with at the moment.

Mystical Meaning The Gypsies believe that to dream of exchanging a kiss means that a quarrel will be over soon.

KITCHEN (SEE ALSO BUILDINGS)

Psychological Meaning In psychological terms, the food prepared in a kitchen is symbolic of the spiritual nourishment you give yourself.

Mystical Meaning If the kitchen is clean and tidy it is an auspicious dream that predicts harmony within the family.

KITE (SEE ALSO FLYING)

Psychological Meaning To dream of flying can symbolize your desire to be free of problems and to enjoy a more carefree and adventurous lifestyle. Similarly, kites symbolize the same connotations, except in a more controlled way. Just as a kite is tethered by a string, so you have not let go completely. It can also show that you desire to take control of your life. In England, a person who wants to take control of circumstances would be described as "wanting to fly his own kite." The expression often relates to self-employment or the process of setting up a business.

Mystical Meaning To dream of flying a kite denotes a great show of wealth, but if the kite crashes or the string breaks, expect financial troubles.

KNIFE

Psychological Meaning Most psychologists consider the knife or dagger a symbol of male sexuality. It can represent the penis in its ability to penetrate. It is also representative of masculinity and its associations with violence and aggression. You may be harboring a deep-seated destructive wish and may have repressed your feelings of anger. Is it you who carries the knife, or are you threatened by someone else? Identify with the possessor of the knife and discover if you are repressing angry feelings. The knife is also reminiscent of the "sword of truth" that cuts through falsity and ignorance or the will to cut away false desires.

Mystical Meaning They say that it is good luck to dream of a kitchen knife, but all other knives predict possible danger.

KNOCK

Psychological Meaning Your unconscious may be trying to attract your attention to something important you are unaware of at the moment.

Mystical Meaning To dream of someone knocking on a door indicates that soon fortune will smile on you.

KNOT

Psychological Meaning A knot may represent a problem that you're trying to untangle (a knotty problem). It can also represent the union of two people or the union of the male and female aspects of the psyche (i.e., tying the knot—a ritual that was an actual occurrence during Babylonian times, when threads from the couple's garments would be tied together).

Mystical Meaning Superstition has associated knots with problems. For example, at weddings the bridegroom should wear one of his shoes unlaced, to foil witches from untying his bride's virginity. Moreover, in Scotland it is believed that a corpse should not be put into a coffin with knots on any of its clothing or the spirit will never rest in peace. In dream superstitions, to dream knots means that you will meet with much to cause you anxiety.

LABORATORY
Psychological Meaning A laboratory may represent the transformation of the self (see Alchemy). It may also symbolize psychological experimentation and new ways of dealing with the world. You may be experimenting with ideas and perhaps even testing yourself. Could it be that you want to prove a point?
Mystical Meaning To dream of a laboratory is a warning of ill health, says superstition.

LADDER
Psychological Meaning A ladder may represent the different levels of consciousness between man and his divine self. It is a symbol of achieving personal wholeness. As a worldly symbol, climbing a ladder may represent progress such as achieving status, power, or an important goal. Descending a ladder may represent the opposite or an escape from your spiritual responsibilities.
Mystical Meaning The Biblical story of Jacob's ladder is a symbol for the communication between this world and the spiritual realm. Similarly, in Mesopotamia the Ziggurat was named "the ladder to heaven." In psychological terms this mystic symbolism can be understood as the communication between the true self and the ego. Consider this quote from Twitchell: "The higher one climbs on the spiritual ladder, the more he will grant others their own freedom and give less interference to another's state of consciousness."

LAKE
Psychological Meaning A lake may represent the unconscious mind. Water often makes a symbolic statement about your emotional state. If the lake is clear and still, it may represent your reserves of inner peace and spiritual energy. However, if the lake is disturbed in any way, you may have emotional trouble.
Mystical Meaning In Japanese Zen Buddhism the lake is a symbol of the mind. If its surface is moving you cannot see the moon's reflection. However, if the lake is allowed to be still, the moon appears. So too the mind must become still if it is to perceive enlightenment.

LAMB
Psychological Meaning Lambs may represent the part of you that is pure and innocent. It is the real you, unsullied by the troubles of this world.

Mystical Meaning The sacrificial lamb of God takes away the sins of the world. In a psychological sense, this represents a desire to find forgiveness.

LAMP
Psychological Meaning Light offers guidance and reassurance and is a symbol of the spirit. Similarly, the lamp is a positive symbol that may represent the hopes and inspiration that drive you on through dark times. If your lamp goes out, it may be a symbol that you are overwhelmed by the unconscious. You have lost your ability to find your own way.
Mystical Meaning The Hermit card from the Tarot pictures a wise old man carrying a lamp. Just like your dream, it advises you to carry your own spiritual light. It is a symbol of the wisdom that comes from free will and discrimination.

LEADING
Psychological Meaning If you dream of leading something, it shows you are taking control of factors in your life. What you are leading describes what you are taking control of. For example, if you dream of leading a dog, it may show that you are disciplining and controlling your sexual nature. If you are the one being led, consider what psychological factors you are following at the moment. Are you being led astray or toward something better?
Mystical Meaning Your dream may represent your desires. Eastern traditions teach that a person led by desire will never achieve happiness. Only by becoming the master of yourself and placing a "ceiling on desire" can you realize your innate divinity.

LECTURE
Psychological Meaning Your dream may be a continuation of your intellectual thinking and you are assimilating new knowledge that you learned during the day. However, the dream may be saying that you are becoming a bit of a bore by the way you lecture people in real life. You need to improve your communication skills. Don't be like Gladstone, a prime minister of Britain, about

whom Queen Victoria complained: "[He] talks to me as if he is addressing a public meeting."

Mystical Meaning An odd British superstition claims that if you dream of giving a lecture about a poet, all your wishes will come true.

LEFT

Psychological Meaning The right hemisphere of the brain controls the left side of the body. This part of the brain is instinctive, artistic, and intuitive. The left side of the body therefore represents these qualities.

Mystical Meaning It was once believed that the Devil stood on the left, prompting a person to do wrong.

LEGS

Psychological Meaning Legs represent your ability to progress. If they are strong, it shows your self-confidence, but if they are weak, you may feel emotionally unsteady at the moment.

Mystical Meaning According to dream lore, if you dream of having a wooden leg you will have many new worries. Fortunately, this is a very rare dream.

LETTER (*SEE ALSO* GIFT)

Psychological Meaning To receive a letter in your dream may herald an unexpected change in your life, such as a new opportunity or challenge. Your response to it indicates the nature of these anticipated events. If it makes you feel good, then you feel assured about the future, but if the contents cause anxiety, it may indicate that you need to take a more positive attitude. The letter could also be from your unconscious mind, which is trying to give you a message about your behavior or your circumstances. Take note of the great wisdom and guidance that come from this hidden source.

Mystical Meaning Some say that dreams of letters foretell unexpected news, but others claim they prophesy a marriage.

LIBRARY

Psychological Meaning A library may represent your desire to learn more and gain new knowledge. It may also represent the knowledge you have accumulated over the years. It is the world of ideas that you explore in your dreams. If people talk in the library or you fail to find the books you want, it may indicate a need for greater concentration or discrimination.

Mystical Meaning According to the wise women of yore, this dream predicts that you will deceive your friends.

LIFT (*SEE ALSO* ELEVATOR)

Psychological Meaning A lift coming up from a basement may show ideas arising from the unconscious. Going high in a lift may indicate a more elevated and detached viewpoint. You may be more rational, but be careful not to lose touch with your instinct and intuition.

Mystical Meaning The ancient sages took the stairs. However, modern superstition claims that to dream of traveling in a lift means success if it goes up, but disappointment if it goes down.

LIGHT

Psychological Meaning The appearance of light in dreams symbolizes consciousness. Light confirms that profound insights are illuminating or about to illuminate your conscious mind. Light can also take various forms. As a rainbow it symbolizes hope; as sunlight, happiness; and as moonlight, it is the guidance that comes from the unconscious, intuitive part of yourself.

Mystical Meaning The light you see may have a deep, spiritual significance. It may represent your journey toward enlightenment or be a direct experience of the inner light described by mystics. The light may have religious associations with Christ, as the light of the world; the boundless light of the Buddha's Nirvana; or the "light of ten thousand suns," as described in the yoga sutras.

LIGHTHOUSE

Psychological Meaning The lighthouse symbolizes guidance. It helps you safely journey the stormy seas of the unconscious. Consider what it is that has helped you. Perhaps you have met someone in waking life who has guided you, or you have discovered a philosophy or religion to light your way and keep you from the rocks of despair.

Mystical Meaning You will have many new opportunities to choose from, say the oracles.

LEADING

LIGHTNING

Psychological Meaning Lightning can suggest the emotional shock experienced from sudden, unexpected events. Lightning can be destructive, yet it can also show the illuminating brilliance of inspiration. You may be "struck" by a great idea or insight. Lightning also symbolizes the awesome power of nature and suggests that many of the forces governing your life remain beyond your control.

Mystical Meaning Gods of thunder and lightning have appeared in the earliest mythologies. Some authorities believe that these ancient gods were the original gods of Neolithic man preserved in the stories and legends that were passed on from generation to generation. Like many symbols in archaic myths, lightning may be a sexual symbol. When lightning strikes the ground, it represents Mother Earth being impregnated by the sky god.

LION

Psychological Meaning Lions are usually a regal dream symbol of power and pride. In a woman's dream, a lion may represent the male aspect of her psyche. A Freudian interpretation may consider lions the powerful and admired aspect of the father. It may also symbolize your animal nature or aggressiveness and will to power.

Mystical Meaning In the Tarot, the Lion is a symbol of strength that can be controlled by gentleness (symbolized by a woman dressed in white). Astrology says that Leo, the sign of the Lion, is gregarious and likes to be the center of attention. Perhaps your dream is saying that you are displaying these egocentric qualities.

LOAN

Psychological Meaning The dream may simply be about your money worries. This dream can also suggest that you draw too heavily upon your emotional resources. You may feel that you are too self-reliant and now need a little help and support from your friends.

Mystical Meaning A quaint old English superstition claims that if you dream of laughing while returning a loan, you will attract great good luck.

LOST

Psychological Meaning According to some psychologists, dreams about being lost frequently symbolize the beginning of a new phase of life and express the anxiety of leaving behind the familiar. Your dream may also express your worries about having no direction to your life. At times like this, it is wise to make a simple written list of the things that you want to achieve in life. Set yourself an attainable goal; set a deadline; and go for it!

If you dream of losing something, ask yourself what it symbolizes about yourself. For example, if you dream of losing money it may show that you feel you've lost your self-confidence or something you value about yourself.

Mystical Meaning One dusty old dream book warns that to dream of losing something means you may cut yourself by accident.

LOTTERY

Psychological Meaning To dream of winning the lottery may be your way of having an inner holiday. For a few short hours, all your material troubles are over. However, keep a careful note of the numbers—for I've met someone who dreamed of winning and did!

Mystical Meaning Most of the superstitions claim that it is unlucky to dream of the lottery.

L.S.D. (*SEE* PILL)

LUGGAGE

Psychological Meaning Luggage may represent your responsibilities. It may also symbolize the worries, habits, and attitudes you carry around with you. Perhaps you should lighten your load and become a little more carefree. If you dream of giving your luggage to someone else, it may show a need to delegate responsibility.

Mystical Meaning You may have too many material possessions, desires, worries, and needs weighing you down and slowing your spiritual progress. My guru Sathya Sai Baba says, "Less luggage gives more comfort and makes travel a pleasure. Reduce your desires, and this journey to Sai can become a real pleasure for you." Diminishing the luggage (shedding desires) is *Vairagya.* If you lessen your desires, life's journey will be comfortable.

MADNESS

Psychological Meaning Your dream may be telling you that you have been behaving in an inappropriate way. Have you recently experienced a moment of madness? Perhaps you secretly feel that you are too conventional and want to throw away the shackles of routine behavior.

Mystical Meaning Fortune smiles on you if you dream of meeting a lunatic. The oracles say it means you will meet someone of great influence who will help you become prosperous. In Japan, it is believed that if you dream your hair is on fire you will go completely bonkers.

MAN

Psychological Meaning For a man, a male figure may be a symbol for himself. For a woman, he represents the other half of her personality—the side that is rational, intellectual, competitive, aggressive, and analytical, according to Jungian dream interpretation.

Mystical Meaning If he is handsome, everything will be fine, you may even become rich; but if he's as ugly as sin, watch out—problems with friends are ahead.

MANDALA (SEE ALSO NUMBERS)

Psychological Meaning Psychologist Carl Jung noticed that many of his patients' dreams contained geometrical shapes such as triangles, squares, and circles. He realized that these had great significance. As his patients progressed toward psychological health, they dreamed of shapes progressively more symmetrical, with squares and circles radiating in intricate patterns from a central point. Jung understood that similar symbolism could be found in the geometrical patterns and religious diagrams that Tibetan Buddhists, Hindus, and Taoists used as a focus for meditation. These mandalas, as they are called in the East, represent the unity and wholeness of the psyche that is as beautiful and complex as an unfolding flower. Mandalas are your dream signposts to higher consciousness.

Mystical Meaning The mandala represents the oneness of the psyche with the cosmos. Inner and outer become the same. Tibetan Buddhists still use mandalas as a focus of concentration, and some adepts can even sustain the image of a mandala in their mind's eye as they sleep. Certain mandalas are claimed to release magical powers.

MARKET

Psychological Meaning A market may represent your career. It may show what you can offer the world. Similarly, it may illustrate what you have to trade in order to achieve your goals. For example, do you have to trade your domestic happiness for business success? The goods sold in the market may clarify the dream's theme. Antiques may represent your past; fruits and vegetables may show your potential for inner growth; and cheap goods may show that you undervalue your talents.

Mystical Meaning Superstition says that to dream of a market denotes thrift. For a young woman it foretells changes.

MARRIAGE (SEE WEDDING)

MASK

Psychological Meaning A mask represents the way that you present yourself to the world. Do you "put on a brave face" or "mask your feelings"? Psychologists call this psychological mask the *persona*. The danger comes when you forget your true identity and believe you really are the person you have been pretending to be. If you identify with it too closely, mistaking it for the real self, it will appear in your dreams as an artificial being, such as a scarecrow or robot. Ask yourself why you are wearing a mask. What does the face say about the way you present yourself to the world? The nature of the mask may reveal to you that you are pretending an emotion you do not feel or hiding your real feelings. Have the courage to be the person you really are.

Mystical Meaning Muhammad, the founder of Islam, used dreams as a way of explaining the faith. He relates in the Koran a dream in which the angel Gabriel takes him up to heaven riding a silvery-gray mare and where Allah gives him instructions. Arabic works are full of amazing dream insights. This one may help you understand your dream about masks: "He whose soul is pure is never deceived by his dreams, whereas he whose soul is blemished is continually deluded."

MAZE

Psychological Meaning To enter a maze in a dream usually relates to the descent into the unconscious part of yourself. It may show the complex defenses that your conscious mind has put up to prevent your unconscious desires from coming into the light. The path to self-discovery does not follow a straight line, but involves occasional returns to earlier starting points. Your waking life may be particularly complicated at the moment, and you may feel that you're covering the same ground repeatedly.

Mystical Meaning The maze in mythology is a place of transformation where the destructive tendencies of nature are overcome. A classical example of this inner transformation is found in the Greek myth of Theseus and Ariadne overcoming the Minotaur in the labyrinth.

MELTING

Psychological Meaning You may have met someone who is "melting your heart," or maybe you feel that you can stop being intractable and stubborn. If snow is melting, it may show that your icy feelings are becoming a little warmer. You have been emotionally cool for too long, but now you're starting to thaw out. Similarly, you may feel that a restrictive and emotionally paralyzing situation is beginning to ease.

Mystical Meaning According to superstition, melting gold brings sadness, melting silver indicates money problems, and melting ice indicates that a situation is getting out of control.

MERMAID (SEE ALSO ANIMA/ANIMUS, SEA)

Psychological Meaning The mermaid symbolizes the anima—the female aspect of the male psyche. Part woman, part fish, she embodies the mystery that haunts the male psyche. She is the bringer of secret wisdom from the depths of the unconscious, represented by the sea. She is also the seductive siren who may lure the active male energies of the conscious mind into the uncharted depths of the unconscious. A man who

dreams of a mermaid may have fears of being drowned by the feminine or by the unconscious. In a woman's dream, a mermaid might express doubts about her femininity. In some dreams, a mermaid can represent a fear of sex.

Mystical Meaning Mythology has many figures that are part human, part animal. The upper half represents the conscious ego, but the lower, fish half is still primitive, irrational, and in need of conscious attention. (A similar comparison can be made with the centaur or Pan.) These mystical symbols were invented to show that the animal and human nature are inseparable.

MESSAGE (SEE LETTER)

MICE (SEE ALSO RAT)

Psychological Meaning Mice can represent your instincts. They may also be a symbol of timidity. They can also represent the small issues that nibble away at your psychological resources.

Mystical Meaning The plague of mice and rats in the *Pied Piper of Hamelin* can be interpreted as an allegory for instincts overcoming rational thought.

MILK

Psychological Meaning This dream may represent your maternal instincts. Similarly, it may represent mother love or nurturing of ideas. If you dream of drinking milk, it may show your need for spiritual sustenance. If you dream of giving milk to others, it may show that you are teaching spiritual values or giving spiritual inspiration to others.

Mystical Meaning To dream of drinking milk is an omen of good health, particularly if it is a mother's milk.

MIRROR

Psychological Meaning What you dream of seeing in the mirror is the way you see yourself or the way that you want others to see you. You may not like what you see. Many people have the alarming dream of looking in the mirror and seeing someone else's face reflected there. This sudden fear of not knowing who you are produces an identity crisis. What face did you see? The person, animal, or object you saw will give ried by this dream. It demonstrates that you are progressing in the journey of self-discovery. You are prepared to look at yourself. Next, you may want to make changes to your behavior. However, if the person in the mirror has his or her eyes closed, then this indicates that you are unwilling to face reality.

Mystical Meaning An ancient and widespread superstition held that the reflection of a person seen in a glass was actually their soul. For this reason, Dracula has no reflection.

MIXING

Psychological Meaning To dream of mixing chemicals, potions, or even a cocktail is a metaphor to show, not the entrance of a new element to life, but a mixing of elements already there. For example, it can show the blending of opposite sides of your personality and may imply that you should adopt an attitude that is more flexible. One school of thought interprets this blending as the interaction of the left and right sides of the brain, representing logic and intuition.

Mystical Meaning The Tarot card Temperance shows an angel pouring water from one chalice to another and the Star card shows a woman pouring water into a pool and onto the land beside her. Similarly, the zodiacal sign Aquarius is represented by a water-bearer. Like your dream, these images symbolize the flow of life; the essential connection between conscious and unconscious; and the blending of male and female elements.

MONEY (SEE ALSO TREASURE)

Psychological Meaning Dreaming of a lack of money can symbolize a lack of the abilities or qualifications needed to achieve some desired goal. Hoarding money can indicate selfishness, whereas to dream of sharing money can symbolize magnanimity.

Mystical Meaning It was considered fortunate to dream of receiving or finding money, suggesting that good fortune is coming your way. Some superstitions say that to dream of finding money means a birth.

MONK

Psychological Meaning A monk may represent devotion, piety, and religious feelings. He could symbolize your need for a period of solitude. In a man's dream, he may represent the spiritual self.

Mystical Meaning Superstitions claim that to dream of a monk foretells unpleasant journeys and dissension in the family.

MONKEY

Psychological Meaning Monkeys represent your playful, mischievous side. You may feel that your dream expresses a need to be fun-loving and to stop taking life so seriously. Monkeys can also represent an immature attitude or repressed sexuality.

Mystical Meaning My Indian guru, Sathya Sai Baba, teases his followers by calling them "monkey mind" every time they give in to untamed worries, doubts, and fears. However, the constantly chattering monkey mind can be stilled by meditation. Your dream may be showing you the way to find this perfect inner peace.

MONSTER (SEE ALSO GIANT)

Psychological Meaning Towering, monstrous figures often occur in children's dreams. These figures usually represent adults in the child's life who dominate him or her with what must seem like invincible power. Children (and adults) are advised to confront these dream monsters in order to come to terms with their emotional lives.

Mystical Meaning The old dream books say that to dream of slaying a monster denotes that you will overcome enemies and rise to prominence. In ancient Tibet, wrathful monsters were considered to be guardian deities. They symbolized the powers within the self that could deter and destroy ignorance.

MOON

Psychological Meaning From time immemorial the moon has been regarded as the source of fertility, as it governs tides, rainfall, birth, and menstruation. Within dreams, it can therefore symbolize the possibility of personal growth.

The moon usually represents the feminine aspect of the self and anything hidden or mysterious. Its association with water also identifies it with the imagination. A full moon may indicate completion whereas a new moon symbolizes new beginnings. An eclipse of the moon may show that your feminine side is being overshadowed by something. A Freudian interpretation of this would say that an eclipse represents getting rid of the attachment to your mother that is detrimental to your personal growth. If the moon eclipses the sun, it may show that unconscious forces are overpowering the conscious ego.

Mystical Meaning   Palmistry tells that the lunar region of the hand (opposite the thumb) is the area where you find the lines of travel. To dream of the moon may therefore indicate a journey ahead. It is likely to be across water.

MOTHER

Psychological Meaning   The mother may symbolize the unconscious, intuitive side of yourself. However, the mother symbol can take both positive or negative forms. She may appear as a kindly mother, grandmother, or aunt or as a place, such as a cave, church, or garden. These images may represent the qualities of solicitude, growth, nourishment, and fertility. The negative mother symbol may appear as a witch or a dragon and represents dark, destructive tendencies that devour, seduce, or poison. Some people have problems freeing themselves from mother-attachment. This prevents the development of their individuality and inner self-dependence.

Mystical Meaning   Most mystical traditions have the symbol of the mother written into their legends and myths. At her most exalted, she is the divine Great Mother. At her most frightening, she is the gorgon Medusa or the Sumerian goddess Lilith. Freud believed that the Greek myths of Oedipus and Electra symbolized psychological conditions. Oedipus killed his father and married his mother. Freud claimed that this represented a boy's incestuous desire for his

mother and his jealousy toward his father. Similarly, Electra desired her father and was jealous of her mother. A girl may therefore unconsciously believe that she has been castrated by her mother and is now an incomplete male. According to Freud, this gives rise to penis-envy, said to be one of the root causes of women's feelings of inferiority.

MOUNTAIN

Psychological Meaning   Mountains represent the lofty planes of consciousness, the realm of the higher self, the part of you that has transcendent knowledge. Dreaming of being at the top of a mountain may show that you feel now that you have risen above the common routines of life and achieved something with spiritual meaning. Conversely, it may show your desire to do this. Mountains can also indicate that you are in touch with or thinking about the higher dimensions of reality. In particular you may be thinking in a positive way about death and the afterlife. On a more mundane level, climbing a mountain may symbolize your sense of achievement and the arduous effort needed for a long-term undertaking. You are on the slippery slopes to success and have the self-determination to reach the summit.

Mystical Meaning   If you dream of climbing a mountain effortlessly, then all your ventures will be successful, but if you fail in your efforts to reach the summit your plans will fail. To the Chinese, a mountain can symbolize the unshakable peace that comes from keeping the mind still during meditation.

MOUTH

Psychological Meaning   Words can heal and harm. Your dream may be saying something about harsh words that have been spoken. Or you may be reminded of something said to you recently. Perhaps you said something you shouldn't have. A mouth may also symbolize your need to express yourself or talk about an issue that's troubling you. Perhaps a part of your personality needs to express itself? Freud, of course, believed the mouth to be a sexual symbol

MONEY

representing the vagina. He also said that to dream about mouths may represent a childhood fixation marked by immature characteristics such as verbal aggression.

Mystical Meaning It is claimed that a large mouth shows riches to come but a small mouth betokens poverty. To see someone with a twisted or misshapen mouth foretells a family quarrel.

MURDER

Psychological Meaning If you dream of murdering someone you know, this dream may reveal your hidden feelings of resentment toward that person. Similarly, the person being murdered could represent an aspect of yourself you are trying to repress or destroy. What is it about yourself that you are trying to kill off? If you are the one being murdered, it may show that you are at the mercy of your emotions. Perhaps you have repressed your instincts that are now seeking vengeance.

Mystical Meaning The jury's still out on this one. Some oracles claim that this dream foretells sorrow, but others say it has no prophetic significance.

MUSEUM

Psychological Meaning A museum may represent the history of yourself and your past. It exhibits all of the important events that have made you into the person you are today. It can also represent the archaic world of the collective unconscious.

Mystical Meaning To dream of being in a museum denotes a period ahead of unhappiness and boredom, say some dream soothsayers.

MUSIC

Psychological Meaning Music is the opposite of chaos. In dreams, it represents harmony and the infinite potential of creative life. Your dream music can also express the emotions you are feeling at the moment. Is the tone happy, tragic, sad,

or threatening? Also, take note of any words and consider whether the tunes you hear have any personal associations. If the music you hear is discordant, it may suggest that your creative potential has become distorted. Many of the great composers claimed that they spontaneously heard their greatest works while dreaming or immediately after waking.

Mystical Meaning The pipes of Pan, the Pied Piper, and the haunting call of the Harpies all express the closeness of the unconscious inner realm to the world of death. Mystics also talk of the music of the spheres, the ethereal music that symbolizes the harmony of the cosmos. It is said that sometimes people hear the songs of the angels in dreams.

NAIL

Psychological Meaning A nail may represent the fact that you have resolved an issue; you have "hit the nail on the head." It could also be a phallic symbol. If nails are driven into your hands, it may show that you feel you are a martyr to your emotions or ideals. Calm, even-tempered thinking is recommended.

Mystical Meaning Since Roman times, iron has been believed to be a sacred metal. To dream of a rusty iron nail is therefore very lucky.

NAKED (SEE ALSO NUDITY)

Psychological Meaning To dream of being naked may indicate that you feel vulnerable and exposed. You may feel that you are unable to maintain your defenses against the outside world.

Mystical Meaning This dream can mean innocence or, if you are a traditional Christian, can refer to the Last Judgement.

NAMES

Psychological Meaning Names can sometimes contain puns that reveal the meaning of your dream. For example, a Mr. Swift may be your dream telling you to hurry up and put your plans into action. Dreams set in Washington may suggest you should be careful what you say. (Washing tongue!) The puns may be bad, but they reveal the hidden meaning of your dream.

Mystical Meaning There are specific superstitions associated with names. For example, if you dream that your name is George you will never be hanged. But if it's Agnes, you will go mad!

NEEDLE

Psychological Meaning Being pricked by a needle may represent the minor irritations and worries that upset you. Perhaps something is needling you? Sewing with a needle may represent your desire to repair the damage caused by a past hurt. And of course, Freud would observe that a needle is a phallic symbol.

Mystical Meaning Generally, this dream is believed to foretell a disappointment. In some parts of the world, it is said to be unlucky to mention the word needle when you wake up in the morning.

NEST

Psychological Meaning A nest may represent your home and your domestic life. It is also the place where eggs are incubated, so there's a promise that you are hatching new ideas or making new opportunities.

Mystical Meaning Dreaming of a nest full of eggs denotes that you will be prosperous. An Austrian superstition claims that to dream of a nest foretells that you will get a boil.

NIGHT

Psychological Meaning The night can represent the unconscious side of the personality. It can also symbolize ignorance, evil, or the despair of the "dark night of the soul." The process of becoming sometimes involves entering the darkness before emerging into light.

Mystical Meaning An old superstition says that you can avoid nightmares by hanging your socks or stockings over the end of the bed with a pin stuck through them. The Gypsies say that to dream of the night shows despair unless you see a wagon, campfire, or a star-studded sky.

NOISE

Psychological Meaning Noise may be your own thoughts that talk in an endless inner dialogue. Meditation techniques practiced before retiring can help to increase inner peace and still your chattering mind. Noise may also be your unconscious trying to attract your attention and make you examine an issue.

Mystical Meaning Some oracles claim that to dream of a loud noises predicts you will soon get a new job.

Common Dream

NUDITY (SEE ALSO UNDRESSED IN PUBLIC)

I dream that I am directing the traffic. To my horror, I suddenly realize that I am naked but to my surprise, nobody notices me.—B.G., Edinburgh, Scotland

NUDITY

Psychological Meaning Many sleepers are embarrassed to find themselves dreaming of being in a public place and being either naked or wearing only their underwear. These dreams often express feelings of guilt or inferiority. It is a metaphor that exposes the dreamer's perceived faults or feelings of vulnerability to some situation in life. In the above example, the fact that other people are oblivious to the dreamer's nudity indicates that the dreamer should discard as groundless any fears of being rejected if the real self is revealed. To dream of being ashamed or frightened of being naked may indicate a fear of relationships or of showing your real feelings. (Sigmund Freud once said that his favorite dream was being naked in a crowd of strangers!)

A dream of being disgusted by the nudity of another person suggests anxiety or aversion at discovering the naked truth about a person, a situation, or even about yourself. Acceptance of the nudity of others indicates that you see through people and accept them for what they are.

Nudity can also represent your longing for the lost innocence of childhood. It represents the real you stripped of pretense and imposed social conditioning. Nudity also has spiritual connotations; it is an expression of beauty and divinity. The ancient gods, such as Venus the goddess of love, Diana the goddess of the hunt, or the three Muses, who inspire the artist, are all usually depicted naked.

ASK YOURSELF

1. *Do I want people to see me for the person I really am?* It's usually the best policy to be yourself despite what you fear others may think. Examine the attitude of other people in the dream. Their behavior may reveal what attitudes are holding you back from being the person you really are.

2. *Do I feel guilty about something?* Often these dreams reveal a fear of being exposed. For example, have you been cheating in some way? Perhaps you have been putting up pretense or lying about something you fear someone may find out about.

3. *Do I fear disapproval?* You may fear that a plan will meet with disapproval from your colleagues. This may be particularly relevant if you dream of being naked at work.

Mystical Meaning Mothers used to warn their daughters that to dream of being naked meant that the dreamer would soon hear about a terrible scandal. However, the Gypsies believed that good fortune awaited the person who dreamed of being naked, particularly if it the dream was lit by the stars.

———

NUMBERS (*SEE ALSO* MANDALA)

Psychological Meaning Numbers and their corresponding geometric shapes often occur in dreams. They can represent stages of spiritual growth and archetypal energies of the collective unconscious.

Zero: Zero represents the unmanifested void. It is the ineffable vastness of space, infinite and timeless. Its symbol is the circle, the perfect mandala.

One: One is the number that initiates action. It may represent the source of life or oneness of all creation. Its associated shape is a point.

Two: Two represents diversity. It is the number of duality and divine symmetry. It represents the union of opposites such as male and female, mother and father, yin and yang, or heaven and earth.

Three: Considered by the ancient Greeks to be the perfect number, three represents the union of body, mind, and spirit. Its shape is the triangle, which may represent the creative force. Three can also symbolize the Holy Trinity.

Four: Symbolized by the square, four is the number of stability and harmony. It may also relate to the four seasons, the four elements, and Jung's four mental functions of thought, feeling, sense, and intuition.

Five: Five represents the link between the heavens and the earth. Its symbol is the five-pointed pentagram.

Six: Six symbolizes inner harmony and perfection. It may be represented by a hexagram or the six-pointed Star of David.

Seven: Seven is the symbol of completeness—an idea originating from the belief that the world was created in six days and finished by the seventh. It was believed that the soul renewed itself every seven years, and hence the belief that to break a mirror will bring seven years' bad luck, as mirrors are a reflection of the soul.

Eight: The Chinese believe that eight is very lucky and brings great good fortune. It can represent regeneration and new beginnings.

Nine: In India, this is the number of God and the yogi, who will leave the wheel of birth and death. In the West, it is also considered to be the number of eternity.

Ten: As there are Ten Commandments, the number ten was considered the number of the law.

Mystical Meaning Numerology is the study of the mystical meaning of numbers. Originally based on the Hebrew and Greek alphabets, it attributed a number to each letter, so that words and names could be studied for their mystical meaning. Holy books such as the Bible are full of numerological references. When the numerical equivalents of a person's name or birth date are added together, the numbers obtained can tell a great deal about the person's character, qualities, skills, and destiny. The art of numerology has sometimes been applied to dreams to obtain information about the future.

The human qualities associated with each name number are: *one*, initiation; *two*, attractiveness; *three*, communicator; *four*, homemaker; *five*, experience; *six*, calmness; *seven*, philosopher; *eight*, business; *nine*, freedom.

NUN

Psychological Meaning A nun may represent purity and chastity. To dream of a nun may symbolize a need to find spiritual meaning.

Mystical Meaning If you dream of being a nun you will experience disappointment in love, but if you meet a nun the reverse is true.

NUT

Psychological Meaning A nut may represent the ego that must be destroyed before the spiritual self can emerge. A green nut cannot be opened, but when a nut is ready one little tap will do. In the same way, enlightenment comes when the time is ripe.

Mystical Meaning According to superstition, to dream of nuts is a sign that money is coming.

 OBSTACLE

Psychological Meaning Dreaming of obstacles to your progress can indicate that you are uncertain of your ability to achieve your goals in life. You lack self-confidence and may feel unable to do the things you want to do. You may feel that you are being tested in some way. The barrier may or may not be self-imposed. It may represent a social distinction or some inner difficulty that is restricting your self-expression.

Mystical Meaning Ramana Maharshi said: "There are no impediments to meditation. The very thought of such obstacles is the greatest impediment." And so too with your dream: imagined obstacles always seem so much bigger than real ones.

OCEAN (*see* Sea)

OEDIPUS (*see* Mother)

OFFICE

Psychological Meaning A dream set in a working environment is most likely to be describing your conduct and the way you present yourself to the world. Offices are also organized places with everything neatly filled (we hope). The dream may be telling you to be more organized.

Mystical Meaning If you dream of being happy in an office, it is a sign of prosperity. If you are turned out of an office, expect disappointments.

OIL

Psychological Meaning You may feel that your life has ground to a halt, and oil symbolizes what it is you need to get your inner machinery moving again. The dream may be suggesting that you need to socialize or do something to break the emotional deadlock.

Mystical Meaning Superstition says that if a man dreams he is dealing in oil, he will be rich—but unsuccessful at lovemaking.

OINTMENT

Psychological Meaning This is probably a symbol of healing. Something may have entered your life that feels like a soothing balm and that relieves your bruises from the past.
Mystical Meaning Dreaming of ointment predicts that you will make new friends.

OPENING

Psychological Meaning Opening something can symbolize a new influence entering your life. You may feel inspired with new ideas soon. Ask yourself whether you are opening yourself to beneficial spiritual influences or less savory ones.
Mystical Meaning To dream of opening a door denotes slander from enemies.

OPPONENT

Psychological Meaning An opponent may be an aspect of yourself. You may have an inner conflict or be wrestling with a problem.
Mystical Meaning It is said to be unlucky to dream of triumphing over an opponent, for it shows you have malicious enemies who will succeed in harming you.

OPPOSITES

Psychological Meaning Opposites in a dream represent the opposite qualities of the psyche. This can include masculine and feminine, extrovert and introvert, active and passive, and will be represented by symbols such as light and dark, left and right, man and woman, etc. The brain is split into two distinctive hemispheres that have different functions. Dreams may help to bring these functions together as one harmonious whole.

Mystical Meaning The yogi resolves the opposites by merging with the infinite (Brahman). Reflect on the meaning of your dream in the light of this quote from the *Bhagavad Gita*: "By passion for the 'pairs of opposites.' By those twin snares of Like and Dislike, Prince, All creatures live bewildered, save some few who, quit of sins, holy in act, informed, Freed from the 'opposites' and fixed in faith, cleave unto me."

ORANGE (*see* Colors)

ORPHAN

Psychological Meaning Your dream may be saying that you feel lonely, unloved, and rejected. Alternatively, the orphan may represent some part of yourself that you have rejected.
Mystical Meaning Dreams of orphans foretell profits from rich acquaintances but unhappiness in matters of the heart.

OVEN

Psychological Meaning Something's cooking. The oven may offer a promise of nourishment in the future. For the time being you have to wait for your reward. A Freudian interpretation is that an oven represents the womb and can be a symbol for pregnancy. You may be giving birth to new ideas and may be expressing a new attitude.
Mystical Meaning To dream you are cooking at an oven is a sign of a change. If the oven is hot, the change will be for the good, but if it's cold, watch out!

OWL

Psychological Meaning An owl may symbolize the wisdom that is gained from the nocturnal world of the unconscious.
Mystical Meaning Superstition says that this is a melancholy dream predicting sadness, poverty, and sometimes disgrace.

PAIN

Psychological Meaning Your dream may be triggered by a physical ache. Dreams can reveal a great deal about health and give warnings about potential illness. As well as diagnosing, they sometimes give remedies, such as a change in diet or lifestyle. As a symbol, pain occurring in a dream may represent the emotional hurt you feel at the moment.

Mystical Meaning Some dream oracles claim that to feel pain in a dream means that a trivial transaction will cause a great deal of unhappiness. Other oracles contradict this and say that it means unexpected money is coming your way. Perhaps the key to success is to be careful.

PAINTING (SEE ALSO COLORS)

Psychological Meaning To dream of painting may symbolize your need to express your creative potential. However, it may also show the way you picture your situation. What is shown on your canvas or paper? Are the colors bright or drab? Is there a dominance of one hue? For example, reds may indicate that you are feeling aggressive, whereas blues may show a period of melancholy.

Mystical Meaning If you dream of painting, it means you will be pleased with your present occupation, but if you get any paint on your clothes you will be criticized by others.

PAPER

Psychological Meaning To dream of a clean white sheet of paper may symbolize your desire to make a new start in life. It could also represent your desire to express yourself through writing or art. If the paper is a document of some kind, it may refer to something in your past. A common anxiety dream for people in authority is to dream of a desk stacked high with papers. This suggests that you are finding it almost impossible to cope with the stress and demands that come with responsibility. Are you dealing effectively with incoming work? You may want to consider delegating some of your work load.

Mystical Meaning According to the dream oracles, to dream of blank paper foretells a period of grief. However, paper with writing on it predicts great joy concerning a love affair.

PARADISE

Psychological Meaning Paradise may represent the state of spiritual perfection that you wish to achieve. It may also be your dream's way of giving you a temporary respite from the troubles of the real world.

Mystical Meaning If your dream of paradise includes palm trees, the good fortune of this auspicious dream is doubled. Sailors believe that this is a dream of safe travel and good luck.

PARALYSIS

Psychological Meaning You may feel that you are unable to act to deal with a situation or inner problem. It is likely that your own attitudes and emotional baggage are making you unable to act. You may have fears or anxieties about a general or specific issue that are troubling you in more ways than you admit. For every problem, there is a solution. Keep a careful note of your dreams for the rest of the week; they may offer solutions to help you resolve your hidden anxieties. If you dream of someone else being paralyzed, they may represent an aspect of yourself that is not being given free expression. Similarly, if you dream of a paralyzed animal, your instincts and sexual feelings may be inhibited. (Some psychologists claim that repeatedly dreaming of paralysis is a sign that your diet needs changing.)

Mystical Meaning It was once believed that the "nightmare" was a huge spirit that sat on people while they slept. The feeling of being paralyzed was caused because of this demon. In Europe, the solution was to sleep with a knife near the bed because evil spirits feared iron and steel.

PARCEL

Psychological Meaning What you take out of the parcel may represent the parts of yourself that you are becoming aware of. This may be a time of self-discovery. It may also be a symbol for your hidden talents. You may be a very "gifted" person and should use your latent abilities.

Mystical Meaning You will have a surprise meeting with someone you've not seen for a long time if you dream of receiving a parcel.

PARTY

Psychological Meaning This dream can indicate the pleasures of life and particularly social interaction. You may simply feel that you need to get out more and enjoy the company of others. The nature of the party and your feelings will reveal your hidden hopes and fears. For example, a happy party may indicate that you feel self-confident, but a bad one may indicate that you are unsure of your social skills. A formal party may represent your working life, whereas an orgy may be expressing your sexual frustrations.

Mystical Meaning Traditional interpretations say that this dream indicates that quarrels are ahead unless the party is exceptionally enjoyable.

PASSENGER

Psychological Meaning You may feel that some of your friends and family take a parasitical attitude toward you. Are you spending too much of your available energy carrying others? If you are a passenger, it may indicate that you are not in control of your life. Are you always meekly going along with other people's decisions?

Mystical Meaning If you see passengers laden with luggage coming toward you, you will see an improvement in your situation. If they are traveling away from you, conditions will deteriorate.

PASSPORT

Psychological Meaning A passport represents your identity. It may symbolize a period of self-analysis and the need to know your true nature. A passport takes you to foreign lands and the undiscovered world of the unconscious. You may be about to embark on an inner journey of self-discovery.

Mystical Meaning According to some oracles, dreaming of passports has nothing to do with travel. It means your love life will blossom!

PATH

Psychological Meaning This dream may represent your progress and the paths you are taking through life. The references may be to both psychological and material conditions. This may be a good time to reassess your future goals and consider what you most want from life.

Mystical Meaning A broad, smooth pathway indicates emotional troubles, but a rocky road predicts a happy marriage.

PATIENT

Psychological Meaning The dream may be suggesting that you are undergoing a healing process. Alternatively, it could be a pun to say you must have more patience.

Mystical Meaning To dream of being a patient indicates that a happy surprise is coming your way.

PAYING

Psychological Meaning This dream may show that you are taking charge of your situation. You are paying your own way.

Mystical Meaning Paying may show the workings of karma—cause and effect. Everything has its cost: gluttony brings ill health; selfishness brings loneliness; material greed brings spiritual poverty; and so on. The key to happiness is to find the middle way between craving and austerity. Accept that you can possess nothing. It all belongs to God, who loans you the things of this world. Dedicate the fruits of your labor to God and you will possess nothing and yet have everything.

FAMOUS DREAMER

Napoleon Bonaparte
Emperor of France

Napoleon probably said "Not tonight, Josephine," because he was so busy scribbling down his dreams! He was said to have used them to plan his military campaigns. Before the battle of Waterloo, he supposedly had a dream about a black cat that ran between opposing armies. As it did this, he saw his own forces decimated.

On June 18, 1815, Napoleon was finally defeated at Waterloo by British, Dutch, Belgian, and German forces commanded by the Duke of Wellington.

PEN/PENCIL

Psychological Meaning Pens and pencils are probably used in your dream as phallic symbols. However, they are also symbols of self-expression. Take careful note of anything you write or see written in the dream. This may be a cryptic message from your unconscious.

Mystical Meaning Dream lore says that if you dream of a pen that will not write, you'll be charged with a serious breach of morality!

PEOPLE

Psychological Meaning If you dream of people you know, your unconscious may be making you aware of qualities and feelings that you desire. The feelings that your interaction with those people gives will be those you are becoming aware of in real life. If you dream of people you don't know, it may be a way of confronting aspects of yourself. Ask yourself what the dream says about the hidden aspects of yourself. Do you like the person in the dream? What does this person mean to you?

Mystical Meaning So long as the people you meet are friendly and well dressed, you can expect good fortune, say the dream books of old.

PHALLUS

Psychological Meaning Dreams often express sexual feelings that society would never permit in reality. Sometimes these instincts are repressed or pushed out of conscious awareness. In dreams, your primal instincts and desires (the id) try to communicate with the conscious ego. Freud says that this communication is censored by the super-ego, your moral principle. The result is that the sexual messages from the unconscious come through to the conscious mind in the disguised form of symbols. Phallic symbols can include anything long and straight that may resemble the male penis.

Mystical Meaning In many races and tribes, the phallus is the primary symbol of worship. Ancient cave paintings of the human reproductive organs have been found in countries as far apart as Senegal and Niger, Australia, France, China, Japan, and India. They are proof of the power of this symbol. For example, the Romans used phallic charms to ward off evil spirits and the god Priapus was depicted as a huge phallus with a human face. The Toltecs and Aztecs of Mexico worshiped a winged snake, and the Hindus still worship Shiva as a phallic emblem. The favorite god in Chinese homes is Shou-lao, the god of longevity. He is normally depicted with an enormous bald head that resembles a phallus.

PICTURE

Psychological Meaning A portrait or still photograph often suggests that you feel a need to preserve a relationship. You may idealize the past and want it to remain the same forever. A picture may also represent your thoughts or ideas and be a way of making you aware of something that requires your attention. The content of the picture will symbolize what this is.

Mystical Meaning Your hopes are false if you dream of a picture, says superstition. It can also mean disappointment in love, particularly if the picture is of you.

PIG

Psychological Meaning A pig may symbolize ignorance, stubbornness, greed, or just plain bad manners. It can even be a sexual symbol of bestiality and brutish lust. Perhaps you or someone close to you has been behaving like a chauvinistic pig? Of course, this dream has nothing to do with kind police officers or sensitive journalists.

Mystical Meaning Pigs have long been the subject of superstition. For example, fishermen believe that if you say the word "pig" before fishing you will have a poor catch. However, in dreams pigs denote exceptionally good news or a stroke of luck.

PILL

Psychological Meaning You may have realized something that is just the medicine you need to restore inner harmony. If you dream of taking a hallucinogenic drug, this dream may be the start of a series of lucid dreams. An addictive pill may indicate that it is your compulsive emotional behavior that harms you. Alternatively, the pill may represent the bitter pill you have to swallow.

Mystical Meaning Some people believe that hallucinogenic drugs such as LSD can awaken the higher consciousness that is found in deep meditation and sometimes also in dreams. The problem is that what goes up also has to come down. "A man who has attained certain powers through medicines, or through words, or through mortification still has desires, but that man who has attained to *Samadhi* through concentration is alone free from all desires."—Vivekananda.

PIN (SEE NEEDLE)

PLAY

Psychological Meaning Playing emphasizes that your creativity is unrestricted by an overtly serious attitude. You may have an attitude that likes to break the rules of convention. A playful attitude toward work can sometimes be more productive than the drudgery of monotonous repetition.

Mystical Meaning My Indian guru, Sathya Sai Baba, tells us that life is a divine play that the Hindus call *leela*. One of his most well-known sayings is "Life is a dream; realize it. Life is a game; play it."

POISON

Psychological Meaning If you dream of consuming something poisonous, it may indicate that you are introducing something into yourself that is harmful to your well-being. This may be bad feelings or bitterness on your part. Similarly, the poison could represent underhanded actions of others or a fear of being the target of innuendo.

Mystical Meaning As you would expect, superstition says that dreaming of poison indicates that you will suffer because of the wrongdoing of others.

POLICE

Psychological Meaning Laws, rules, and regulations represent structure and control. Dreams in which you break rules may show your urge toward self-assertion and your desire to test the limits imposed by others.

If you dream of being accused of breaking rules of whose existence you were unaware, this shows the unfairness of many life experiences. You may be frustrated by your circumstances and feel that life is unjust. Police officers can symbolize the upholding of rules of conduct. They may represent inhibition and the censorship of natural impulses by the conscious mind. (Freud claimed that police officers were a superego symbol, representing taboos stemming from childhood.)

If you dream of being arrested it may symbolize sexuality or emotions being restrained by feelings of guilt. Alternatively, your dream may be telling you to arrest your feelings and stop behaving in inappropriate or anti-social ways. If you dream of being chased by the police, you may need to face the accusations of a guilty conscience or learn from past mistakes.

Mystical Meaning Tradition says that to dream of a police officer means that you will be helped by someone you love.

PRIEST

Psychological Meaning A priest may represent traditional religion with its spiritual rules and regulations. Are you making moral judgments? Alternatively, the priest could represent your own spiritual wisdom.

Mystical Meaning Any dream concerning a priest is deemed good by superstitious people. In particular it means the end of a quarrel.

PRISON

Psychological Meaning You may feel that your life is restricted at the moment, and your dream reflects your need to change your routines. To release yourself you may need to make major changes to your waking life. Another interpretation is that you are restricted by behavior that enslaves you or you have repressed your emotions. If you dream of someone else in prison, it may represent the element of your personality that you are unable to set free.

Mystical Meaning Superstition can sometimes interpret dreams in very strange ways. One says that if you dream of seeing prisoners it is an omen that soon your dearest wish will be granted. Some sources claim that it predicts a marriage. I wonder why!

PRIZE

Psychological Meaning You may feel pleased with yourself and may be encouraged by your unconscious. You may have made significant progress in your personal development or may have achieved an important worldly goal. Your unconscious is saying, "You can do it. You can win!"

Mystical Meaning Dream of giving or receiving a prize and you'll soon be in the money.

PUNISHMENT

Psychological Meaning You may have a conscience about something that has happened or feel guilty about something. Are you be punishing yourself? Sometimes traumatic childhood experiences or overly authoritarian parents can set in motion a self-punishment cycle that can become an automatic psychological response. You may need to free yourself of the parental and social conditioning that holds you back from being your true self.

If you dream of punishing people you know, you may have a hidden resentment toward them. Alternatively, they may represent aspects of your own personality that you fear. If you dream of punishing an animal, you may feel antagonistic toward your instinctive drives and sexuality. In all instances, you must learn acceptance and forgiveness if you want to be at peace with yourself.

Mystical Meaning The Gypsies believe that to dream of being punished betrays the guilt you feel for neglecting your relations.

PUPPET

Psychological Meaning Either you are trying to control someone or someone is trying to control you. Puppets are manipulated by strings or a hidden hand. Is it you who have the power, or is someone else pulling the strings?

Mystical Meaning The oracles announce that happiness is assured because of your ability to organize people if you dream of puppets.

PURPLE (SEE COLORS)

PURSE

Psychological Meaning The purse is a common symbol for female sexuality. It can stand for both the female genitalia and the womb. According to Freud, as the purse can be both opened and closed, it sometimes represents the female power to give or withhold favors. As the purse is also a place you keep money, it may also symbolize treasure, which can be a symbol for the real self. If you dream of losing your purse, then this may be an allegory for losing touch with your real identity. To dream of an empty purse may indicate a loss of security.

Mystical Meaning If you dream you open your purse and find money in it, you will be happy, particularly if you find gold. Similarly, it is good if you find a purse. But beware if you dream that someone tells you they have found a purse, for this means you will hear bad news soon.

QUARREL

Psychological Meaning You may have an inner conflict or be trying to make a difficult emotional decision. You are divided within yourself. Just as with arguments in real life, a compromise is usually the best course. Stop seeing everything in black-and-white. Alternatively, you may be expressing emotions that you have been unable to give vent to in waking life. If you know the person you are arguing with, he or she may represent an aspect of yourself. Do you secretly resent this person in waking life?

Mystical Meaning Superstition says that this dream portends unhappiness in relationships and business.

QUARRY

Psychological Meaning A quarry is a man-made hole in the environment. Perhaps your dream indicates that you have dug yourself into an emotional hole from which you cannot escape. Have you fallen into a pit of despair? A quarry may also symbolize your desire to reveal the contents of the unconscious, symbolized by the earth. Perhaps you have uncovered something that was once hidden? In a social sense, a quarry may represent your concerns about the damage being done to the environment. (If your quarry was the pursuit of an animal, see Chase.)

Mystical Meaning A chalk quarry is an omen for financial difficulties that can be overcome by hard labor. A stone quarry predicts a journey.

QUEEN (SEE ALSO ANIMA/ANIMUS, KING, MOTHER)

Psychological Meaning Freud believed that the king and queen represent the dreamer's parents, while a prince or princess represent the dreamer. She may stand for the unconscious, intuition, nature, and the instincts. Jung saw royal figures as representations of animus (the male principle) and anima (female principle). The white queen from Lewis Carroll's *Through the Looking-Glass* (1872) runs continuously to stay at the same spot. Some authorities claim she expresses the way the earth is in a continuous state of upheaval in order to stay much the same.

Mystical Meaning Carl Jung recognized that the strange writings of the alchemists were in fact symbols for the integration of the personality. The queen personified the feminine forces within the psyche, the unconscious feeling for life.

RABBIT

Psychological Meaning Because of their reputation for breeding, rabbits may represent your sexual activity. The rabbit could also represent innocence and timidity. If you dream of it going down a hole, this could show that you are trying to escape from a problem.

Mystical Meaning It is a good omen if you dream of seeing rabbits running in green grass. If you see them in hutches, the good fortune will be lessened. Dead bunnies bode disaster.

RACE

Psychological Meaning This dream may be an allegory for the way you live. Are you in a perpetual hurry? The dream may reveal your competitive side and that you measure yourself against other people. Make a conscious decision to slow down and you may achieve more. The old story holds true—the steady progress of the tortoise beats the impulsive hare.

Mystical Meaning If you dream you are racing a car or running, this is a sign that you will soon hear news. If you win, the news will be wonderful.

RADIO

Psychological Meaning What is said or played on the radio may be messages from your unconscious. You are tuning in to its frequency. In particular, note the words of any songs played and consider what these say about the way you are feeling.

Mystical Meaning Not many ancient mystics had radios, but superstitions that are more recent say that listening to one in a dream foretells an imminent meeting.

RAGS

Psychological Meaning If you dream of wearing rags, you may be concerned about your self-image. You may feel unable to deal with responsibilities and may lack self-confidence. You may feel that your life is in tatters. Perhaps a little retail therapy will brighten you up? Buy something new and give yourself a boost.

Mystical Meaning Some oracles predict that you will suffer great losses if you dream of wearing rags. Other authorities claim that it is a sign that you will make a wise decision.

RAILROAD (SEE TRAIN)

RAIN

Psychological Meaning Rain usually represents cleansing and purification. It can also represent the release of tension that comes after a storm or a period of crying. Rain replenishes and brings fertility, so it may also symbolize that you are opening to a new phase of personal growth in your life. Your dream says, "Don't worry, for soon the gray clouds will be gone and light will shine in your life once more."

Mystical Meaning To dream of rain is generally considered a good omen unless of course the rain is falling on cattle, for this means a business loss of some kind.

RAINBOW

Psychological Meaning A rainbow symbolizes good news, hope, redemption and the end of gloom. Since the sun can be a symbol of the self, it is also associated with the magical quest for the treasure of self-knowledge. The rainbow is a bridge between heaven and earth, between your earthly self and your higher, enlightened self.

Mystical Meaning The Gypsies say that to dream of a brightly colored rainbow means a happy change is coming. If the colors become dull there will be a deterioration in your circumstances.

RAPE

Psychological Meaning For a man, this may be a sadistic expression of sexual desire. It may show feelings of vengeance toward the opposite sex. For a woman this dream may represent fears of sex or masochistic fantasies.

Mystical Meaning Even the Victorian dream books cover this topic. Superstition claims that if a woman dreams of rape, her pride will be wounded. You will hear shocking news if you dream that a friend is raped.

RAT (SEE ALSO MICE)

Psychological Meaning Rats may represent unworthy thoughts and feelings that hide from the light of day and gnaw away inside you. These may be feelings of guilt, envy, avarice, and so on, or they may be of a sexual nature. They could represent the feelings you reject. In addition, you may have thoughts about wanting to harm others or perhaps you feel that somebody in your life is, in the words of James Cagney, a "dirty rat."

Mystical Meaning An enemy will try to harm you if you dream of rats. Some superstitions believe that rats contain the souls of men, so their actions should be observed and acted upon.

REBIRTH

Psychological Meaning "On the way of true development, something old must die and something new must be born in him...."—*Collins*. A dream about rebirth shows that you are entering a new chapter of life. You may have discovered inspiring new goals, values, or a way of expressing your true self. The past is dead. Long live the future!

Mystical Meaning Most spiritual traditions use rebirth symbols or baptism to symbolize the entry into the spiritual life. One of the most beautiful symbols of rebirth is the magnificent phoenix. He is consumed by the fire he brought but is reborn from the ashes. Rebirth can represent spiritual transformation and hope.

RED (SEE COLORS)

REFUGEE

Psychological Meaning Do you feel like an outcast? Perhaps you feel that you have been socially rejected, or the dream represents the way you feel emotionally isolated. Similarly, the dream may highlight your desire to escape or dodge an issue. You will never find security if you keep running away from your problems.

Mystical Meaning Displaced people of any kind indicate that well-conceived plans will fail.

REINCARNATION

Psychological Meaning The dream may be referring to some event in your known past. However, you may also be recalling memories of lives that you have lived before. In the East they believe that memories of past lives will be revealed when the spiritual aspirant has reached a suitable level of inner development. Past lives are then spontaneously recalled during meditation or dreams.

Mystical Meaning Hollywood actor Sylvester Stallone is convinced that he lived during the French Revolution; singer Engelbert Humperdinck believes he was once a Roman emperor; and pop star Tina Turner was told by a Californian psychic that she was the incarnation of a woman pharaoh named Hatshepsut. You are not alone in believing that there are memories of lost lives locked away in the unconscious.

REJECTION (SEE ALSO ABANDONMENT)

Psychological Meaning You may be refusing to accept an influence in your life or a situation that is being imposed upon you. If you are the one rejected, it may reveal that you have hidden feelings of a lack of self-worth or alienation from others. Sometimes there are sexual undertones to this type of dream. Freud would say that it is you who are rejecting yourself. Your super-ego (conventional conscience and attitudes) is rejecting your sexual desire. You may be punishing yourself.

Mystical Meaning Some dream oracles insist that you reverse your dream. Rejection therefore means success.

RELATIONSHIPS

Psychological Meaning The people who appear in your dreams, particularly strangers, usually represent facets of yourself. It may be shocking to see the truth about yourself that is projected into the characters of the dream. Your relationships with these people illustrate how much you are in harmony with yourself and demonstrate which parts of your personality you allow to take the stage. For example, if a man dreams of very feminine women, it may show a need to accept the feminine side of his nature. Similarly, a woman who dreams of assertive men may herself need to act in a more masculine way. And, of course, the dream could be talking about real-life scenarios

and the true or repressed feelings you have for the people you know in reality.

Mystical Meaning Dream superstition says that the way people act toward you in a dream predicts events to come. If they are friendly, expect happy events to follow. If they are downright nasty, take precautions against potential disaster.

REPAIRING

Psychological Meaning Dreaming of repairing something indicates that you are recovering from something that may have upset you. You are undergoing a period of self-renewal. The item that is being repaired is a symbol of the area of your life or yourself that you are working on.

Mystical Meaning Some people believe that if you dream of sewing the clothes you are wearing it brings terrible bad luck.

RESCUE

Psychological Meaning The person or thing that you rescue may represent an aspect of yourself that has been neglected or ignored. They symbolize an aspect of yourself that is trying to find expression. If you are being rescued, then consider what the scene represents. For example, rescue from a ferocious animal may show that you fear your animal nature. Rescue from a stormy sea may show how close you came to drowning in your emotions. Who is it that rescues you? This person may represent the psychological qualities and attitudes that you should apply to your life.

Mystical Meaning Mystical traditions claim that everyone has the potential to be super human. Deep within you is a psychological resource that enables you to achieve just about anything. You can rescue any situation. Nothing is impossible.

REVOLUTION

Psychological Meaning To dream of taking part in a revolution may represent an inner revolution that is happening to your attitudes and behavior. You no longer need to conform to what society expects of you. You can be yourself.

Mystical Meaning Dreaming of a revolution may spell troubles for business affairs. If blood is spilt it is a sign that you are taking too many financial risks.

REBIRTH

RIDING

Psychological Meaning Freud advises that riding a bicycle, a motorbike, or a horse symbolizes the rhythm of the sexual act. A tame and well-controlled horse may symbolize control of your passions, whereas a runaway horse represents the opposite. The dream could also be a pun. Is your ego "riding high"?

Mystical Meaning This is deemed by superstition to be a very fortunate dream, particularly if someone you love rides with you.

RING

Psychological Meaning The dream may refer to marriage or commitment to a relationship. You may feel that you want to be loyal to your partner. Similarly, a ring could mean loyalty to your principles and ideals. It may represent a binding oath. From a spiritual perspective, a ring, being a circle with no beginning and no end, can represent eternity, wholeness, and your true self.

Mystical Meaning To dream of being given a ring augurs well, but to lose a ring is a warning of trouble. If you dream of finding a ring it means you will soon have a new friend or lover. However, some superstitions say that to dream of being given a ring means a broken promise.

RITUALS

Psychological Meaning Rituals can symbolize the transitions in life. They are also a form of drama that invites you to escape the confines of the conscious mind and pass into the world of the imagination. According to Carl Jung, images of fertility rites in dreams emerge from the collective unconscious in an attempt to abolish the separation between the conscious and unconscious minds. Your dream is putting you in touch with your instinctive self.

Mystical Meaning Shamanic rituals induce a dreamlike state and may trigger clairvoyant and prophetic powers. Make a note of your dream that you can refer to later on, as your dream may include a real prophecy.

RIVER

Psychological Meaning A river may represent the flow of the life force. In a spiritual sense, it may show your acceptance of divine will and destiny. Instead of struggling against life you "go with the flow." Crossing a river may symbolize a fundamental change of lifestyle.

Mystical Meaning Consider your dream in the light of this quotation from *Siddhartha* by Hermann Hesse: "But he learned more from the river than Vasudeva could teach him. He learned from it continually. Above all, he learned from it how to listen with a still heart, with a waiting, open soul, without passion, without desire, without judgment, without opinions."

ROADS

Psychological Meaning Your dream may be a metaphor for the roads you travel through life. The twists, turns, and obstacles are the difficulties you encounter in ordinary life. A fork in the road or a crossroads may represent a difficult decision you have to make.

Mystical Meaning Flowers or trees bordering a road predict success, say the dream books of long ago.

ROBBER

Psychological Meaning You may feel that someone has stolen your success. For example, a work colleague may have accepted the praise and honor for work that is in reality yours. Similarly, you may feel robbed of your ability to express yourself emotionally or act in a decisive way. What is it that has been stolen? This may represent the part of yourself that needs to be recovered from the unconscious.

Mystical Meaning The Gypsies believe that to dream of robbing means that you have a guilty conscience. However, if you dream of being part of a gang of robbers this means that you can count on your friends.

ROBOT

Psychological Meaning This dream may be telling you that you are behaving in a mechanical way and have lost the ability to express feelings. Is your emotional life running on automatic? Do you speak from the heart, or are your responses unnatural and rigid? Similarly, the dream may be portraying your working life. Perhaps work is making you feel like a robot?

Mystical Meaning Erich Von Daniken aside, robots have not featured in traditional mysticism. However, they have become a modern archetype. Why is it that the Daleks, Terminator, and Hal are so frightening? These machines symbolize the fear of losing the sense of humanity in this mechanical age. They can also represent the inevitability of death.

ROCK

Psychological Meaning A rock symbolizes permanence and security. It is the foundation or essence of the self. If you dream of sailing toward rocks, this is a signal that you may be encountering a dangerous situation. Perhaps you should set a different course?

Mystical Meaning The Sirens who lured sailors to their death upon the rocks with their singing are dream symbols for the negative side of the intuition. The dangerous rocks are reminders not to disregard the practical realities of the real world. Idealism should not be taken to extremes.

ROOMS (SEE ALSO BUILDINGS)

Psychological Meaning Rooms stand for different aspects of your personality. The living room represents the conscious mind; the cellars, the unconscious; and the upper rooms represent your higher aspirations and spirituality.

Mystical Meaning The variations on this theme are too numerous to list. However, one interesting superstition states that to dream of your bedroom means that you will visit faraway lands.

ROSE

Psychological Meaning A red rose has been the traditional symbol of love since Roman times. The theme of your dream is likely to be about love and the way you feel about your past and present emotional relationships. Freud considered the red rose to symbolize the female genitalia, or the blood of menstruation. In addition, the way a flower unfolds and its symmetry are reminiscent of a mandala (*see* Mandala), which is a symbol of the wholeness of the self.

Mystical Meaning The Romans believed that the rose could protect the dead from evil spirits and so decorated their tombs with the flower. As a dream symbol, it therefore meant safety and protection. Most oracles believe roses to be a favorable omen.

RUBBISH (SEE GARBAGE)

RUINS

Psychological Meaning Do you feel that your life is in ruins? Perhaps your business collapsed or a relationship has failed. This dream represents your feeling of defeat. Perhaps this demolition was necessary. You can start again to build a new life.

Mystical Meaning To dream of finding ancient ruins or holy relics may symbolize your discovery of the treasures that lie within you. You are uncovering the ancient wisdom of the unconscious.

RULES (SEE POLICE)

SACRIFICE

Psychological Meaning If you are the sacrificial victim, the dream may be a reflection of your attitude. Do you always play the martyr? Perhaps you have tendencies of self-punishment and self-denial. You may feel that other people undervalue your talents and good qualities.

If you are performing the sacrifice, consider what it is you are sacrificing. An animal may represent part of your instinctive nature, or a person you know may represent an aspect of your personality. Perhaps you are sacrificing your principles or your human values? In a spiritual context, the ego must be sacrificed so the divine self can emerge.

Mystical Meaning Ritual sacrifices were a way to appease the gods and bring fertility to the land. The individual was sacrificed for the sake of social and cosmic unity. In Hinduism, Purusha was slain to make men; in Egyptian myth, Osiris is cut to pieces by his brother, Seth; in the Greek stories, Orpheus is torn apart by women; and in Christianity Jesus is crucified. These powerful images of surrender to God still appear in the dreaming life of modern man.

SAFE

Psychological Meaning A safe may be a symbol of the things you hold dear. It may represent the innermost qualities of your true self, the treasure that lies within you. It could also represent a secret. Is there an aspect of your character that you want to hide from the world?

Mystical Meaning Dream oracles are clear about this one. If you dream that you are breaking open a safe, you will not marry the person with whom you are now in love. An empty safe indicates an early marriage and a full one predicts a late marriage.

SAILOR

Psychological Meaning A sailor represents the adventurous side of your personality. It can represent your desire to explore the unknown reaches of the unconscious as symbolized by the sea or may simply represent your desire to travel.

Mystical Meaning As well as the straightforward interpretation of travel, dream oracles advise that dreams of sailors on shore predict a new romance. If they are aboard ships, there will be news from far away. It is unlucky for a woman to dream of being a sailor.

SAINTS

Psychological Meaning A saint may be a messenger from your higher self to help you to see your situation from a spiritual perspective.

Mystical Meaning For a devout Christian, this dream may be a direct encounter with the spirit of one of the saints who are claimed to help sincere worshipers through dreams. Similarly, in India it is said that a living guru, and also those who have passed into the next life, can help the devotee through dreams. As a spiritualist medium, I believe that advanced souls can use dreams as guides.

SALT

Psychological Meaning Salt can represent the spiritual essence of life. (Salt preserves and is in itself indestructible. It is also the residue that remains after the body has decayed.) It may also represent tears, for these taste of salt, or the unconscious, as symbolized by the sea. Alternatively, your dream may be saying that someone is "rubbing salt in the wound."

Mystical Meaning Salt has also been used as a symbol for enlightenment. If salt is mixed with water, what becomes of it? The salt crystals are gone, but taste the water and you'll know it's still there. It is the same when the self merges with Nirvana. The individual is gone but the essence remains as part of the One.

SAVAGE (*SEE ALSO* SHADOW)

Psychological Meaning This dream may allude to your sexuality. The savage represents your primitive urges. In addition, the savage may be a shadow figure representing the aspects of yourself that you reject or banish to the jungles of the unconscious.

Mystical Meaning Sometimes the shadow can appear in a helpful guise. For example, in one of the oldest mythical stories in the world, Gilgamesh is helped by the dark Enkidu, lord of the forests. Similar dreamlike images are found in the noble savage, from Aldous Huxley's *Brave New World* (1932) to the story of Mowgli, in Rudyard Kipling's *Jungle Book* (1894).

SCALES

Psychological Meaning Your dream may be helping you make a decision. You are weighing the pros and cons of a situation. It may also be telling you that you need to take a balanced view of a situation and not get so emotional. If you are interested in astrology, scales may represent the zodiacal sign Libra; this may be a Libra you know or may become the characteristics of this sign that you exhibit.

Mystical Meaning Since ancient times, scales have been a symbol of Justice. Ancient Egyptian images show that the soul is weighed in the scales of Justice by the jackal-headed god Anubis. Your dream may be saying that justice will be done.

Common Dream

SCHOOL (SEE ALSO EXAMINATION)

I am now in my 70s, yet last night I dreamed that I was back at my childhood school. In the dream the teacher scolds me, and I notice that the classroom is in a state of decay.—Gary T, Leeds, England

Psychological Meaning Dreams set at school are very often reported by people from all age groups. Sometimes these dreams highlight childhood insecurities that have still not been resolved. For example, this dream, set in a decaying school building, suggests that the dreamer is carrying disappointed childhood expectations or unpleasant memories. In addition, the schoolteacher is a classic symbol for authority and may represent his father and others who have determined the course of his life. The schoolteacher may also represent the censoring aspect of his personality that keeps the chaotic impulses in control. Being scolded may indicate that the dreamer has feelings of guilt or inferiority or that he worries that his misdeeds will be found out. Alternatively, if the teacher in the dream were praising Gary, it

would indicate that Gary had self-confidence and believed in his own abilities.

Another interpretation of dreams set at school is as a metaphor for what you are learning from life over a long period. These dreams may also carry a feeling of nostalgia and reveal a hidden desire to recapture the freedom, optimism, and ambition of these formative years.

ASK YOURSELF

1. *Do I have any unresolved anxieties from my childhood?* Clearly these problems are not going to be solved overnight, but your dream may be helping you come to terms with long-standing worries that need to be addressed. Becoming aware of and identifying your anxieties is the first step in the healing process.

2. *Does the dream teach me a lesson?* The dream may be showing you what you can learn from your circumstances today. Life itself is like a school, and there are many tests. I like to think that God gives his hardest lessons to his best pupils. It may explain why the most deserving people often have the most wretched lives.

Mystical Meaning Some dream superstitions claim that to dream of teaching at school is a sign of good fortune. However, you will experience setbacks in business if you dream of being a pupil. These will be particularly bad if you dream of forgetting your lessons.

SCISSORS (SEE ALSO CUTTING)

Psychological Meaning Precise cutting indicates control and decisiveness in your waking life.

Mystical Meaning Dreams of scissors are usually interpreted by superstition dream lore to indicate that an enemy will do you harm. However, if they are clean and bright you have nothing to fear.

SEA (SEE ALSO WATER)

Psychological Meaning The sea may represent the unconscious, and your dream may show that you are now ready to explore the intuitive and instinctive aspects of yourself. Sailing on a boat or putting out to sea may represent this journey into the unknown part of you. (For a man this can represent the search for the feminine side of his nature.) The condition of the sea may depict the way you are feeling. For example, a stormy sea may indicate that you feel angry about something or threatened by forces outside your control. However, a calm sea may show inner contentment and peace of mind. Freud considered the sea and the incoming tide to be symbols of sexual union.

Mystical Meaning In primal myths, the sea existed before the creation of humanity and is therefore like a womb from which the rest of creation emerges. In the legends, the creator god wrestles with the sea goddess, who is impregnated to give birth to the world. The sea is therefore a symbol of the raw materials of existence and is associated with the creative potential of your true self. From a spiritual perspective, the sea may represent the totality of existence. It is the ultimate reality, the One of which we are all a part. Enlightenment is gained when the individual self merges with the infinite. This exalted state of consciousness is likened to a raindrop merging with the sea.

SEARCHING

Psychological Meaning What are you trying to find? Your dream search may symbolize the quest to find something physical, emotional, intellectual, or spiritual. You may be searching for a new way to solve an old problem. If you dream of searching for someone you know, you may be anxious about your relationship with that person and may want to end the emotional separation. Are you sure that this search is worthwhile, or is the dream reflecting your feeling of hopelessness?

Mystical Meaning Perhaps your dream is a spiritual search. Myths such as the quest for the Holy Grail by King Arthur's knights may be describing the inner process of spiritual transformation.

SEASONS

Psychological Meaning The seasons can represent your state of mind and prevailing psychological or material conditions. They remind you that everything is subject to change and renewal.

Here are the meanings for Northern Hemisphere countries:

Spring: Optimism and rebirth are associated with springtime. Spring may represent a new beginning for you or new projects and a new attitude toward life. It may represent youth.

Summer: Pleasure and happiness are associated with summertime, as are relaxation and vacations. It may symbolize early middle age.

Autumn: This time may represent a maturing of your ideas. It is also a time for preparation and the ending of a cycle. It is a time when the trees bear fruit, and so may represent the fruition of a plan. Autumn may symbolize late middle age.

Winter: A time of rest, but your dream may be expressing feelings that your life is barren and empty. It may symbolize old age.

Mystical Meaning The movement of the sun across the sky, the solstices, and the seasons since earliest times have come to represent the phases of human life. They also relate to the four elements: the bare earth, to winter; rain, to spring; heat and fire, to summer; and the element of air, to the winds of fall.

SEED

Psychological Meaning A seed is a symbol of potential. It may show that you have recognized an opportunity in your waking life or it may represent your potential for personal growth. For a couple planning a family, it may represent conception.

Mystical Meaning My research reveals that seeds represent increasing prosperity in most archaic dream books.

SEVEN (SEE NUMBERS)

SEX

Psychological Meaning Erotic dreams are usually a straightforward expression of sexual desire. The nature of the sex may reveal your hidden hopes and fears. For example, if you dream of having sex with someone other than your partner, it may highlight dissatisfaction with the physical side of your relationship. Your dreams may reveal patterns in your sexual relationships that you may not be aware of. If your sexual dreams are violent or perverse, you may need to be more relaxed about your sexuality. You may have sexual phobias or compulsions that need to

SEX

be recognized and brought under control. Your dreams may offer ways to help you lead a happier and more natural sexual life.

Mystical Meaning An odd superstition claims that if a man or woman dreams of visiting a brothel, there will be an improvement to domestic life. And good news for cross-dressers: there will be success within the family if you dream of changing sex.

SHADOW

Psychological Meaning The "shadow" is the dark side of your nature. It represents everything you wish not to be. It is also the unused or rejected side of yourself and your emotions. It is your dark side that you refuse to recognize. It is the repressed aspects of the self. Try to bring these hidden feelings into the light of day so that they loosen their hold over you, otherwise you are likely to project this "other self" on to other people. Do you accuse others of faults that are, in reality, your own?

Mystical Meaning Many superstitions say that the "shadow" is a part of a person's soul. To tread on it or throw stones at it is unlucky and may cause a person harm. Beware if you dream that this happens to you.

SHAPES (SEE NUMBERS AND MANDALA)

SHEEP (SEE ALSO LAMB)

Psychological Meaning Are you being a conformist? To dream of sheep may indicate that you are following a conventional way and falling in with what everyone expects of you. Perhaps you should try a less orthodox approach to your situation. Why keep following the flock? The opposite meaning is symbolized by the ram, which is an individualist. Similarly, to dream of a shepherd may represent the power of love that can unify divergent tendencies. This may apply to your world or the conflicts within yourself.

Mystical Meaning Consider this quote from the Vedas: "Come up, Lions, and shake off the delusion that you are sheep. You are souls immortal, spirits free, blest, and eternal. Ye are not matter; ye are not bodies; matter is your servant, not you the servant of matter." Also associated with the Christian "lamb of God," sheep are considered to be a lucky dream omen.

SHELLS

Psychological Meaning Shells are usually a spiritual symbol because they come from the sea, which represents the vast expanses of the unconscious mind. They are also a divine feminine symbol associated with the goddess Venus, who was born from a shell. (The shape of a shell is reminiscent of the vagina, say Freudian psychologists.) A heavy tortoise shell may represent your desire for protection. Similarly, a delicate eggshell may symbolize your feelings of vulnerability. Finally, eggshells can represents thin-skinned egotism which, like the arrogant Humpty Dumpty, is easily smashed to pieces.

Mystical Meaning According to some authorities on dream superstition, shells predict that something strange will happen to you. So if you wake to find you've been abducted by aliens or there's a flipper where your foot was, it is probably the shell dream that's to blame.

SHIP

Psychological Meaning A ship may represent the course of your life, and the type of ship may say something about your state of mind. For example, you may be in a pleasant mood when you dream about a cruise ship but may be feeling aggressive if it's a warship. A lifeboat may represent your need to be rescued from the stormy emotions and troubles that beset you, and traveling on a submarine may show your desire to explore the unconscious. Or perhaps the dream is simply encouraging about your material success by saying that your ship's come in.

Mystical Meaning A ship in dock or on a calm sea is claimed by the ancient seers to promise happiness in love. If there are storms, happiness will be delayed. There will be worrying news if you dream of a shipwreck.

SHIRT

Psychological Meaning This dream may represent your self-image and the way you present yourself to the world. A starched shirt may symbolize formal conservatism, whereas a bright or

SHADOW

unbuttoned shirt may show your unconventional free spirit.

Mystical Meaning The Gypsies believe that the more colorful the shirt you dream of, the luckier you will be.

SHOES

Psychological Meaning Freud proposed that items of clothing that can be entered by parts of the body are sexual symbols. Fairy tales often use the same language of symbols as are found in dreams. When Cinderella put her foot into the shoe, it was a symbol of her desire for sexual relations with the prince.

Mystical Meaning Superstition says that to dream of losing a shoe predicts an illness. This may originate from an old English rural superstition that says that burning a smelly old shoe in the home helps avoid infection in the house. Dusty shoes indicate an unexpected journey, and shiny ones mean happiness in love.

SHOOTING

Psychological Meaning Freud says that guns represent male sexuality, and shooting a gun is a symbol for ejaculation. This may also be saying that your plans are right on target and that you know what you are aiming for in life.

Mystical Meaning If you dream of enjoying the shoot, there will be good fortune, but if you are filled with fear there will be difficulties. Shooting stars are universally regarded as good luck and their appearance in dreams is auspicious.

SHOP

Psychological Meaning Shops can symbolize the array of opportunities and rewards that life offers. However, if you dream that the shop is closed or that you have insufficient money, this indicates that you feel the things you want from life are unattainable. Your dream may be telling you to lower your expectations and set yourself goals that are more realistic.

Mystical Meaning To a tradesman this is an unlucky dream signifying many pressing creditors. For everyone else it is an omen of prosperity, so long as you don't buy anything. You will be blessed with good fortune if you dream of working in a shop.

SHORE

Psychological Meaning As a dream symbol the shore is the place where the conscious mind meets the unconscious. The dream may also represent a journey, either an actual one or the symbolic journey of self-discovery across the sea of the unconscious.

Mystical Meaning Some authorities claim that an empty beach is a sign of opportunity. Dream of a busy beach, and you will soon feel secure.

SHOWER

Psychological Meaning A shower may symbolize spiritual energy and cleansing. You have been cleansed, your worries are washed away, and you can begin afresh.

Mystical Meaning A shower may be a symbol of healing. Here's a healing technique you can try: Stand upright and imagine that a shower of liquid light is pouring from above. It washes over you and through you. As it does, it washes away all illness, pain, and worries and replaces these dark spots with glorious, shining light. Now fill yourself with light from your toes to the top of your head. Your dream may have given you a clue to self-healing. Now try it in waking life.

SIGNPOST (SEE ALSO CITY AND CROSSROADS)

Psychological Meaning Many dreams are about problem-solving. Your dream is showing you the direction to take in life. What is the destination the sign suggests? The name of the town it points to may be a pun to represent the human qualities you need.

Mystical Meaning The Gypsies say that to dream of a wooden or stone signpost indicates that you will soon be able to say goodbye to a period of indecision.

SILVER

Psychological Meaning Silver represents something you value. This may be something such as your financial needs or your own inner emotional resources. There may be an allusion to the moon and therefore to the feminine qualities of intuition and feeling.

Mystical Meaning To dream that you have silver in your purse is a sign that you will lose money. It is not considered a lucky metal to dream about.

SINGING

Psychological Meaning Your dream is expressing your current feelings. The nature of the music and the words of the song may say something about you and your situation.

Mystical Meaning Singing can be an expression of spirituality. Consider your dream in light of this quote from Rabindranath Tagore: "God respects me when I work, but he loves me when I sing."

SINKING (*SEE ALSO* DROWNING)

Psychological Meaning You may fear being overwhelmed by your emotions or worries about a situation. You may fear that something of importance in your life is ending. For example, you may be concerned about a failing relationship or business enterprise. It could be a symbol of despair. You have a choice: sink or swim.

Mystical Meaning An acclaimed astrologer and phrenologist claims that this dream means you've been spending too much money shopping!

SISTER (*SEE ALSO* SHADOW, ANIMA/ANIMUS)

Psychological Meaning Carl Jung claimed that childhood sibling rivalry and jealousy influence the dream symbol of the sister. For a female dreamer, she may represent the shadow side of the personality that is neglected and undeveloped. Sometimes this may include anti-social qualities that are alarming. However, in a man's dreams a sister may represent the female side of his own personality (anima).

Mystical Meaning A sister may occur as a guide in a man's dreams and take him into a dark forest, into the depths of the earth, or to the bottom of the sea. This theme, which occurs in many myths and legends, shows that the anima can guide the ego to the cause of a psychological difficulty.

SITTING

Psychological Meaning Your dream may indicate that you are taking a passive position about something. Perhaps your inaction is causing problems. Instead of "sitting on the fence," you may need to act.

Mystical Meaning If you dream of sitting on a high seat, your luck will be good, but if the seat is low, expect disappointments.

SKELETON (*SEE* BONES)

SKIN

Psychological Meaning Skin is the outermost part of yourself. Your dream may be saying something about the way you present yourself to others. A skin rash may be a play on words, indicating that you are making a rash decision. Or it may simply highlight your worries about your physical appearance. Perhaps you don't like to show your emotions. Are you thick-skinned?

Mystical Meaning The Baluchi women of Oman believe that to dream of pale skin indicates that a person will receive many jewels.

SKULL (*SEE ALSO* BONES)

Psychological Meaning Carl Jung decided to become a psychologist after dreaming of discovering a skull in a deep cellar under his house. The skull represented his desire to probe the secrets of the mind. To dream of a skull may also symbolize mortality and your spiritual contemplation of the meaning of life and death. It may also refer to finality and the things in life that cannot be avoided.

Mystical Meaning To the Gypsies, a skull represents wisdom derived from their ancestors. To drink from a skull means sharing in their wisdom. In Ireland, it can be a symbol of truth, for it is believed that if a man takes an oath on a skull but is lying, he will die soon after.

SKY

Psychological Meaning If the sky is a dominant image in your dream, you may be thinking about the spiritual meaning of life and the purpose of human existence. The daytime sky represents cosmic consciousness, as opposed to ordinary awareness. It is usually associated with God. A star-studded night sky may represent the world of the unconscious. Jung saw the night sky as the most suitable place for man to project unconscious content. The symbolism of the constellations and the zodiacal signs are archetypal expressions of the inner world of the unconscious.

Mystical Meaning Most dream superstitions agree that to dream of a blue sky brings good luck, but cloudy skies spell misfortune. Some authorities claim that to dream of a red sky forecasts that a terrible disaster will befall the nation.

SLEEPING

Psychological Meaning Dreaming of being asleep may indicate that part of you needs to be jazzed up a bit. You may have become complacent or dull. From a philosophical standpoint, it may represent the nature of the human predicament. Ignorance is sleep, but to understand reality you have to awaken.

Mystical Meaning Many people report dreaming of seeing themselves asleep in bed. When it first happened to me I suddenly realized that I was actually standing outside my body. This phenomenon is known as astral traveling.

SMELL

Psychological Meaning Perfumers realize that smells trigger emotional reactions. They compose a fragrance like a piece of music, with high, middle, and low notes. What emotions are created by smells in your dream? If you feel disgust, you may be reacting again to aspects of your own nature or to the attitudes of others. Perhaps you had an argument and are still fuming, or something about your situation makes you "smell a rat"?

Mystical Meaning Each smell has a specific meaning. Here are some examples: camphor, scandal; ginger, a love affair; jasmine, a true spiritual experience; lavender, a happy relationship; nutmeg, deceit.

SMILE

Psychological Meaning Your dream may be expressing your approval of decisions you have made. You may feel pleased with your successes and achievements. There is a promise of happiness. Enjoy this nice, smug feeling.

Mystical Meaning Perhaps your dream is telling you to cheer up a bit. The Indian guru Paramahansa Yogananda in his book *Man's Eternal Quest* encourages his followers to be smile millionaires: "My smile comes from a joy deep within my being, a joy that you also may attain. Like a fragrance, it oozes out from the core of the blossoming soul. This joy calls others to bathe in its waters of divine bliss."

SMOKE

Psychological Meaning Smoke is caused when a fire is stifled. Ask yourself what part of your self needs to come to expression. Let your true self shine.

Mystical Meaning A bad omen. Smoke brings disappointment unless you dream that it annoys you.

SNAKES

Psychological Meaning The snake is one of the world's oldest symbols, found in some of the most ancient sculptures. Snakes are often used

---

FAMOUS DREAMER

Abraham Lincoln
U.S. president (1809 - 1865)

Abraham Lincoln dreamed he heard weeping coming from the East Room of the White House. He walked into the room and was shocked to realize he had interrupted a funeral service. In front of him was a corpse wrapped in funeral vestment and laid on a catafalque. It was guarded by soldiers and surrounded by a large crowd of mourners.

"Who is dead?" Lincoln asked one of the guards.

"The president," came the reply. "He was assassinated."

The weeping and wailing of the crowd became so loud that Lincoln awoke. He spent the rest of the night pale-faced as he contemplated the hidden meaning of his dream.

Abraham Lincoln died on April 15, 1865, the morning after being shot by John Wilkes Booth in a box at Ford's Theater, in Washington, D.C.

as phallic symbols and have long been linked with pagan fertility gods. Because it lives close to the ground, the snake is an emblem of the nurturing earth and also the unknown perils of the underworld. Christian imagery emphasizes the dark side of this symbol. It is considered evil, yet it is the snake, created by God, that tempts man to gain knowledge. In dreams, a snake can represent hidden fears. Falling into a pit of snakes may represent the many worries that are threatening you. Sometimes snakes can symbolize the poisonous words and innuendo of the people around you.

Mystical Meaning Entwined snakes appear on the god Mercury's caduceus, which is the symbol of the medical profession to this day. The Greeks attributed healing powers to the snake. Similar symbolism may be found in Indian Kundalini yoga, where it represents the life force that rises up the spinal chord. In particular, the cobra is a symbol of divine enlightenment and is associated with the god Shiva.

SNOW (SEE ALSO ICE)

Psychological Meaning Snow can indicate frozen emotions but can also symbolize transformation and purification. Clean, pure snow can represent a fresh start. Melting snow can indicate that obstacles and fears are dissolving, whereas an avalanche of snow can indicate that you fear being overwhelmed by emotions that have been held in check for too long. Are you cold and lacking warmth?

Mystical Meaning To dream of watching falling snow indicates that a letter will arrive shortly. Some superstitions claim it will be from the person you will marry. The truth is that most oracles consider this dream to be one of good luck.

SOLDIER

Psychological Meaning Associated with aggression and conquest, a soldier may represent the way you impose your feelings on others. You may be preparing to do battle over an issue in your waking life or may feel the need to defend yourself from an emotional attack. Be careful how you use your power.

Mystical Meaning For a man, this dream means a change at work. For a woman, it's a warning about a casual relationship. Some oracles believe it means a lawsuit, whereas the Gypsies say you will soon receive honors.

SON

Psychological Meaning A son may represent the youthful part of yourself. He may also represent your own potential. Perhaps you recognize in him the ideal and hopes that you once had. The son may of course have no symbolic meaning at all, and the dream may simply be about your own son. Are you worried about him?

Mystical Meaning According to superstition, it is fortunate to dream about your son. If you dream he is getting married, there'll be family worries.

SONG (SEE MUSIC)

SOUNDS (SEE ALSO MUSIC, FLYING)

Psychological Meaning Loud sounds can indicate that the unconscious is trying to draw your attention to an issue. A bugle being blown may show a call to arms, suggesting that you must become more alert to problems of pressing importance. A whistle may indicate that someone has exposed your clandestine plans ("blown the whistle") or it can show that you are being obedient, like a dog responding to its master's call. To hear muffled or indistinct voices indicates that you must listen more carefully to your wise inner voice. Sometimes dreams incorporate sounds such as the alarm clock or traffic outside your bedroom into the dream and weave them into the symbolism of the dream.

Mystical Meaning If the subtle body re-enters the physical body too quickly after an out-of-body experience, the dreamer may hear a loud crack, like a shotgun being fired in the room. This is very disconcerting but quite normal. It will disappear once you master the art of astral travel.

SPIDER

Psychological Meaning A spider may represent a fear. Perhaps you feel trapped in a web of deceit or entangled by emotions and fears from which you cannot escape? Alternatively, are you the spider that's spinning a web to ensnare someone else? Sigmund Freud believed that in dreams spiders represent the devouring mother who consumes her children through possessiveness or her power to arouse guilt. She is symbolized by the spider that traps and lives off her innocent victims. (Freud's mother has a lot to answer for!)

Mystical Meaning Arachnophobia may be an instinctive fear that originates from primordial times when poisonous spiders were common. Your dream draws upon these ancient memories to express the fear you have about something that is upsetting you. Superstitions dating back to the Middle Ages claim that it is lucky to dream of spiders.

SPIRAL

Psychological Meaning An upward spiral may represent advancement and progress. A downward spiral may represent despair and failure. Are things spiraling out of control?

Mystical Meaning According to the Chinese mystical tradition of *feng shui*, spirals are very auspicious symbols that stimulate health, wealth, and happiness. *Chi* energy, the life force, is said to be at its best when it moves in spirals.

SPIRITS (*SEE* GHOST)

SPIT

Psychological Meaning You may wish to be rid of something that is part of yourself. Perhaps you feel the need for inner cleansing and spiritual healing. Spitting may represent anger and contempt.

Mystical Meaning Superstitious people agree that if you have a bad dream you can rid yourself of any bad luck by simply spitting three times as soon as you wake up. Please note, this technique can also cause problems in relationships.

STAGE (*SEE* THEATER)

STARS

Psychological Meaning Stars can represent your higher states of consciousness, the exalted spiritual state that you wish to attain. They can also represent your desire for worldly success, particularly if you work in show biz! Stars may also symbolize the forces of destiny that you feel may be controlling your life at this time. Usually the stars carry a happy, favorable meaning.

Mystical Meaning The ancients believed that when a great person died, he became a star in the sky. To dream of the stars therefore implied that the spirits were guiding you. "Have patience, Candidate, as one who fears no failure, courts no success. Fix thy soul's gaze upon the star whose ray thou art, the flaming star that shines within the lightless depths of ever-being."—Blavatsky

STATION (*SEE ALSO* TRAIN *AND* JOURNEY)

Psychological Meaning A station is a point of departure. It indicates that new opportunities await you and that you are preparing for a new

---

FAMOUS DREAMER

Graham Greene
Author

Famous novelist Graham Greene got much of his inspiration from dreams. Some of Greene's dreams contained prophecies, and his diary shows that he foresaw the sinking of the Titanic. He said: "On the April night of the Titanic disaster, when I was five, I dreamt of a shipwreck. One image of the dream has remained with me for more than 60 years: a man in oilskins bent double beside a companion—way under the blow of a great wave."

At least 19 other cases of precognition through dreams and visions have been associated with the sinking of April 14, 1912. For example, London businessman J. Connon Middleton sold his tickets just before the trip because for two nights in a row he dreamed that the Titanic would sink.

and perhaps exciting venture. Railway lines run in straight lines, so your journey to your goal will be direct and on target. A station is also a public place, so it may represent your role in society.

Mystical Meaning It is fortunate to dream of meeting someone at the station, for this means that your career will be helped forward by someone with great influence. It can also signify news coming.

STATUE

Psychological Meaning A statue or bust often represents the desire to idealize someone or something. If you do this and put the person on a pedestal, you only increase the perceived feeling of remoteness and unattainability associated with this person or situation.

Mystical Meaning If you dream of a statue coming alive, it means that you will reform a broken friendship. Some oracles deem sculptors to be auspicious omens. If you see one working or dream of being one, your fortunes will change for the better.

STEALING

Psychological Meaning Do you feel that someone has cheated you, or perhaps it is you who have been less than honest? You may unconsciously feel that you have set your sights too high and feel that you cannot attain your goal without breaking the rules. The dream could also represent needs that are not being met and a lack of fulfillment.

Mystical Meaning Some superstitions say that this dream refers to matters of the heart. You may be infatuated with someone.

STICK

Psychological Meaning A stick may be an instrument of punishment or power. If you are punishing an animal with a stick, you may have negative feelings toward your instinctive nature. The people you hit with a stick may represent the part of yourself that you are in conflict with. Freud on this one: the stick is a phallic symbol.

Mystical Meaning Masters of mystical oneiromancy (predicting the future through dreams) say that to dream of sticks is an unlucky omen.

STONE

Psychological Meaning Stone can represent permanence and the things that endure. Similarly, it can represent the unchanging eternal self. However, it can also symbolize coldness, stubbornness, and a refusal to change. Perhaps it represents a weighty problem that you have to deal with?

Mystical Meaning Stones on the road symbolize awkward people who stop your progress; throwing stones indicates accusations; and some oracles say that if you dream of collecting stones you'll inherit some land. Finding precious stones is of course a symbol of good luck.

STORM

Psychological Meaning A storm may indicate emotional conflict or turmoil within you. It may indicate anger or frustration that lacks an outlet.

Mystical Meaning Superstition says that this is an obstacle dream that indicates separation from what you desire. If your house is damaged by a storm, people with evil intention are nearby.

STORY (*see also* Buildings *and* House)

Psychological Meaning The stories of a building represent levels of consciousness. The top floor may represent your spirituality, and the basement represents the unconscious. The floors in between represent the many states of mind that you experience.

Mystical Meaning If you dream of being at the top of a big building, you will achieve success.

STRANGER (*see also* Shadow)

Psychological Meaning A stranger represents those aspects of yourself that you either reject or are unfamiliar with. Are there aspects of your personality that you deny? If the stranger is frightening, he may symbolize things you have repressed.

Mystical Meaning Superstition claims that to dream of talking to a stranger means you will hear news from afar. Some oracles claim that this is a dream of contrary meaning that indicates that friends will help you.

STRANGULATION

Psychological Meaning If you dream of being strangled, it may represent something in your life that you feel is emotionally restrictive. To dream of strangling someone may express your frustrations with that person in real life. Alternatively, the person being strangled may represent an aspect of yourself that you are not allowing to be expressed.

Mystical Meaning The dream seers claim that if you make a wish after waking from a dream about strangling someone, the wish will come true.

STREET (SEE ROADS)

STRUGGLE

Psychological Meaning This dream may represent the frustration you feel about your circumstances or an inner conflict of some kind.

Mystical Meaning Your dream may be expressing something about the nature of struggle. Sathya Sai Baba explains: "There is no struggle; only the karmic pattern of the past, which has created apparent problems for the present and future..... Let the love flow and surrender everything to God. Then all your worries, fears, frustrations, doubts, and struggles will fade away. They are all aspects of illusion."

SUFFOCATION (SEE ALSO DROWNING)

Psychological Meaning This dream may indicate that you feel emotionally overwhelmed by a situation that causes you anxiety. You may feel unable to cope. Similarly, you may feel that an emotionally overbearing partner or parent is stifling your psychological growth. It is important that you re-establish your sense of self-identity.

Mystical Meaning Dream superstition says that this dream is a warning about sorrow and ill health.

SUICIDE

Psychological Meaning You are turning your feelings of aggression against yourself. Perhaps you are unable to overcome feelings of guilt or feel degraded and helpless. You may feel unable to cope with a problem that has troubled you for some time. Part of you is crying out for help. I suggest that you talk over your problems with someone you can trust. A problem shared is a problem halved.

Mystical Meaning A dream of disappointment, say the dream oracles.

SUIT (SEE ALSO CLOTHES)

Psychological Meaning A suit may represent your desire to impress someone. It may represent the confident side of your personality or the aspect of your self that you display at work. Perhaps the suit is a pun for "following suit" or being "well suited" to someone.

Mystical Meaning The Gypsies say that to dream of wearing a suit foretells success.

SUMMER (SEE SEASONS)

SUN (SEE ALSO MOON)

Psychological Meaning The sun is a masculine symbol. It is the conscious mind and the intellect. It can be a symbol of the true self and may represent intelligence, as distinct from intuition. A sunrise may indicate a new beginning, whereas a sunset may show the end of a phase. If the sun in your dream is scorching hot, it may indicate that your intellectual powers are dominating the psyche and are in danger of destroying your emotional life.

Mystical Meaning Mankind's first god was the Sun. It drove away the darkness and with it the perils of the night. Invariably it has been considered a symbol of blessing. In the Tarot cards, the sun card represents joy and exuberance. Dream lore generally says the same: to dream of the sun promises happy times ahead.

SWAN

Psychological Meaning A swan is a beautiful, elegant, and calm bird. Your dream may be saying that the right way to behave is with dignity and grace.

Mystical Meaning A swan, with its long neck, may also be a phallic symbol. In the Greek myths, Zeus loved Leda, wife of Tyndareus, King of Sparta, and seduced her by transforming into a swan.

SWEEPING

Psychological Meaning You are getting rid of old ideas and attitudes. Sweep away the junk from the past and open a new and better phase for the future.

Mystical Meaning Superstition says that it is unlucky to sweep waste out of the house, as you may sweep your good luck with it. Dreams of sweeping can have similar negative connotations.

SWIMMING

Psychological Meaning Expanses of water usually symbolize the unconscious. To dream of swimming shows that you trust the unconscious and are supported by it. You have confidence and are receptive to its creative power. If you dream of swimming underwater, it may indicate that you have accepted and are at one with your unconscious. This union is even more apparent if you dream of being able to breathe underwater.

Mystical Meaning Swimming strongly in clear water means you will achieve great success in love and business. The opposite applies if you struggle or the water is dirty.

SWORD

Psychological Meaning A sword can represent aggression, but also discrimination, truth, and justice. Attacking someone with a sword may indicate hostility toward that person or what he or she represents, and being stabbed represents your feeling that you've been defeated over something. A sword can also be a phallic symbol.

Mystical Meaning As a symbol of truth, the sword is your consciousness that frees itself from the "devouring mother" aspect of the unconscious. This symbol for the process of individuation often occurs in myths and stories in which the hero slays the dragon or demon with his sword.

SYRUP

Psychological Meaning Are you exhibiting sickly sweet emotions? Syrup may represent excessive sentimentality or nostalgia.

Mystical Meaning Some superstitions associate dreaming of sweet things as sexy. It is now known that the human brain produces a chemical called phenylethylamine when lovers are in a state of excitement. It is also found in chocolate.

TABLE

Psychological Meaning At home and at work people meet and discuss plans over a table. In your dream, it represents your relationships with other people. Items put onto the table represent something about your life that is being brought into the open. Perhaps the dream is saying that you should be more open with people. Perhaps you should "put your cards on the table."

Mystical Meaning A table is an omen of domestic comfort and a happy, contented marriage partner.

TAIL

Psychological Meaning If you dream of growing a tail, it may represent your animal nature. Since the tail is behind you, it may refer to a rejection of the sexual side of yourself.

Mystical Meaning To dream of cutting off the tail of an animal foretells that you will be careless, say the oracles.

TAMING

Psychological Meaning If you dream of taming a wild animal, it may show that you are getting your emotions under control.

Mystical Meaning If you dream of taming a lion, you will be successful in everything you do. Some oracles claim it means you will marry a very intelligent person.

TATTOO

Psychological Meaning The dream may be about emotional situations that have affected you. They've left their mark. It may also be referring to a behavior pattern that has become ingrained into your personality.

Mystical Meaning Your dream may be of a sexual nature. "Tattoo" is a Maori word, and until recently tattooing was accepted in most parts of Polynesia as the ultimate beauty treatment. Many Polynesians had every part of the body done, except the eyes. In many cultures, it is seen as a symbol of sexuality and virility. The inhabitants of the Marquesas consider a tattooed tongue supremely erotic.

TEACHER (SEE SCHOOL)

Common Dream

TEETH

I dreamed that my teeth were falling out. In real life, my teeth are perfectly all right even though I'm 39 years old. Why should I have this dream?—Katie P., New Orleans, Louisiana

Psychological Meaning Dreaming of teeth falling out may represent insecurity. These dreams often occur at a time of transition between one phase of life and another. When you lost your milk teeth, you also gradually lost your childhood innocence. Losing your teeth therefore shows that today you have similar feelings of uncertainty and self-consciousness as you did in childhood. The dream could also highlight your worries about getting older or your sexual attractiveness.

Animal teeth may represent aggressiveness, and false teeth may represent concern about your self-image. The dream could also be triggered by subtle toothache that you are not yet consciously aware of.

ASK YOURSELF

1. *Do I feel insecure because I'm starting a new phase of life?* Katie's dream may highlight her worries about soon reaching 40.

2. *Am I facing reality?* Dreams about losing teeth may represent a retreat to the innocent times when you were a toothless baby and dependent for nourishment on your mother's milk.

Mystical Meaning The Nilotes of the Sudan believe that if a woman has a toothy grin it is a bad omen. It symbolizes the mouth of a wild animal, which will frighten the cattle. Superstitious lore insists that maidens with a wide smile be made beautiful by having their front teeth removed. An African witch doctor would therefore interpret dreams about losing teeth as a sign of prosperity.

TELEPHONE

Psychological Meaning To dream of a telephone ringing may be your unconscious trying to get your attention. What you hear through the phone is a message from your unconscious. The content of the message may reveal a great deal about your hopes and fears. You may be facing up to issues you have previously avoided.

Mystical Meaning Many people believe that to dream of receiving a telephone call is lucky, for it brings advantages in business. However, if you dream of making a call, there will be postponement of a date. All long-distance calls are said to bring happiness.

TELEVISION (SEE ALSO FILM)

Psychological Meaning A television may represent your mind with its flow of thoughts. You are objectively viewing yourself. What is it that moves across this screen of your consciousness? Is your head filled with interesting information or just a lot of mindless soap operas? The programs you dream of watching are an intimate yet objective representation of the things that play on your mind.

Mystical Meaning Modern dream superstition say that if you enjoy dreaming about watching

---

FAMOUS DREAMER

Julius Caesar
Roman emperor

Nineteen centuries before Freud, the night before Julius Caesar led his army across the Rubicon River to attack Rome, he dreamed that he slept with his mother. Caesar interpreted this dream to mean that the invasion would succeed.

Unfortunately, he later failed to heed the dream warning of his wife, Calpurnia, who warned him to "beware the Ides of March." On March 15th, in 44 B.C., Caesar was assassinated in the Senate by republicans, including Brutus and Cassius, who feared his monarchical aspirations.

television you will achieve success, but if you are upset by what you see, you will be led astray by others.

TEMPLE (*SEE* CHURCH)

TEST (*SEE* EXAMINATION)

THEATER

Psychological Meaning Dreams are themselves like a theater in which your problems, hopes, and fears are acted out by characters generated by your incredible imagination. To dream of a theater is therefore like a dream within a dream. Consequently, these dreams are often lucid because the dream symbolism helps the dreamer realize that he is dreaming. If you dream of watching or acting in a play, pantomime, or circus, consider what aspect of your personality each character represents. You are seeing your life and the way you behave from a new perspective. The dream performance will give you insight into the way you behave and the way you present yourself to the world.

Mystical Meaning Sages who have reached an exulted level of consciousness often point out that life is like theater. You play a part for a short time in a cosmic game. When you die, you take off the costume and return to your true identity. A curious superstition claims that if you dream you cut new teeth, it is a sign you will hear of the birth of a child who will do great things in the theater.

THREAT

Psychological Meaning If you dream of threatening someone, it may represent your need to assert yourself in real life. However, if you are being threatened, you need to determine the cause of this feeling. Some dreams may have an overall menacing atmosphere, and it is hard to determine the cause of this anxiety. These threatening dreams fascinated the Surrealist painters.

It is most likely that your dream is caused by problems in your relationships. You may feel emotionally threatened by a partner, or perhaps you worry about the threat of redundancy or a management change at the workplace. Similarly, inner emotions can threaten your emotional equilibrium. You may have repressed emotions, such as resentment, anger, eroticism, or fear, that are trying to find a way to be expressed.

Mystical Meaning Some oracles consider this to be a contrary dream. Everyone is going to be sweet and nice to you.

THREE (*SEE* NUMBERS)

THUNDER

Psychological Meaning Thunder may represent your feelings of anger. You may have had or be planning an argument. Your relationships may be stormy.

Mystical Meaning The Ancient Greeks believed that storms were caused when Zeus quarreled with his consort, Hera. In the Sumerian mythology that may date from Neolithic times, the storm was associated with the roar of the bull and fertility rites. Your dream may represent the untamed and hugely powerful forces within the psyche.

TICKET (*SEE ALSO* KEY)

Psychological Meaning A ticket may represent the start of a series of psychological events. You may have given yourself permission to begin your exploration of the unconscious. Similarly, the ticket may symbolize your approval to start a new project. You may have decided the direction in which you would like to take your life. If you dream of losing your ticket, you are uncertain about what direction your life is taking and may feel confused about what to do. You may feel psychologically unprepared to deal with an issue from your waking life.

Mystical Meaning You will receive some news that will clarify your position.

TIGER

Psychological Meaning A tiger may symbolize something that frightens you. It may represent repressed feelings and emotions or a situation in waking life that terrifies you. Courage will see you through this period of adversity.

Mystical Meaning In the children's poem *Tyger Tyger* by the mystical poet William Blake, the tiger represents material existence. His "fearful symmetry" is the suffering that people experience in the world of opposites, as opposed to innocent oneness with God. Humanity's destiny

TIME

is to regain innocence by passing through the world of experience. Your dream may be dealing with these perplexing cosmic issues.

TIME

Psychological Meaning Preoccupation with time in a dream may reflect your anxieties about being unable to cope with the pressure life imposes on you. Certain times may have specific meanings to you. For example, one minute to midnight implies a pensive situation or a situation that is about to change dramatically. You may associate noontime with lunch and nourishment or five o'clock with finishing work. Perhaps the dream is saying that you must set yourself a deadline or, conversely, set yourself fewer deadlines. And while on the subject of time, did you know that by the time you reach 70 you will have spent about six years of your life dreaming and will have slept for about 20?

Mystical Meaning As you come close to spiritual truth, time becomes less important. Sometimes in dreams, past, present, and future become one. "How are we to know that the mind has become concentrated? Because the idea of time will vanish. The more time passes unnoticed, the more concentrated we are.... All time will have the tendency to come and stand in the one present. So the defini-tion is given, when the past and present come and stand in one, the mind is said to be concentrated."—Vivekananda

TOILET

Psychological Meaning The cause of your dream may simply be a need to use the toilet. Your unconscious recognizes your body's need and uses the dream to wake you up. Freud had a field day with this one. He associated dreams of excretion with the anal phase of psychosexual development. A child will experience erogenous satisfaction from excretion. A child reprimanded for wetting the bed, or insensitively treated during potty training, may in adult life experience similar feelings of guilt and shame toward sexual functions.

Surprisingly, Freud also believed that a need to use the toilet in dreams represented creativity. Alternatively, dreaming of using the toilet may be a way to show your desire to rid yourself of something that contributes nothing to your well-being, such as an archaic form of behavior or an obsolete lifestyle. Similarly, your unconscious may be drawing your attention to an illness in which using the toilet symbolizes your body's need to rid itself of toxins.

Mystical Meaning Believe it or not, to dream of a toilet indicates legal trouble connected with property deals.

TOMB

Psychological Meaning A tomb may be the entrance to the unconscious. It may also represent those parts of yourself that have been buried away. You may have qualities and talents you are not using. If you dream of seeing your own name above the entrance to the tomb, this is not an omen of death. The dream is saying that what lies within the tomb are the aspects of yourself that have died. You need to rediscover yourself.

Mystical Meaning Your dream may symbolize spiritual death and rebirth. In Celtic times, burial mound tombs were considered to be the womb of the Earth Mother, from which the new spiritual person was born. Later superstitions claim that to dream of a tomb foretells disappointment. Another curious superstition says it foretells a marriage.

TRAVEL

TONGUE

Psychological Meaning A tongue may represent the things you say. You may need to express yourself or may have already said too much. Perhaps you've been saying something "tongue in cheek"? As the tongue plays a part in sexual relations, your dream may be saying something about this area of your life.

Mystical Meaning If you dream of your own tongue, you will tell lies. If you see another person's tongue, they will lie about you. An infected tongue means careless talk.

TOWER

Psychological Meaning A tower may be a symbol for aloofness. Are you so involved in cerebral activities that you have lost touch with your feelings? A tower can also of course be a phallic symbol.

Mystical Meaning To see a tall tower is a sign of good fortune. Climbing a tower brings success, but descending brings failure.

TOY

Psychological Meaning In part, children use toys to develop their social skills and express their role within the family. Dreaming of playing with toys may therefore be an innocuous way to express your hidden feelings. Consider what each toy represents as part of you or your life. Your dream may also be saying that you are only playing with life and must get down to something realistic and practical. The dream could be a pun for toying with ideas or people's feelings.

Mystical Meaning Generally a fortunate omen that predicts happiness for children and families.

TRAFFIC (SEE ALSO CAR)

Psychological Meaning A traffic jam may express your frustration that life is not proceeding as smoothly as you would like it to. You feel stuck. If you dream of being a traffic cop, it may show your desire to impose your own rules on society. You may believe that your social role makes you uncomfortable and alienated from others. Let's face it, not many people like traffic cops.

Mystical Meaning Family problems will be solved but you'll need a lot of patience if the traffic is in a jam, say the wise sages of superstition.

TRAIN (SEE ALSO JOURNEY)

Psychological Meaning Your future is "on track." As trains follow a fixed route, this dream may suggest that you are being helped with your journey through life. To dream of missing a train or passing your destination may indicate that you feel that you have missed an opportunity. Also, are you a conformist? Jung believed that to dream of taking a public vehicle often means that the dreamer is not finding his own way forward and is behaving like everyone else. (Freud believed that to dream of missing a train meant missing death. He also was convinced that all dreams involving motion represented disguised wish fulfillment for sexual intercourse. In particular he claimed that a train represented a penis, and when it went into a tunnel this indicated sexual intercourse.)

Mystical Meaning Dreamers of long ago believed that to dream of traveling indicates a change in fortune. It is particularly fortunate if the destination is toward high hills or mountains. And, if the journey is in a straight line, your good fortune comes swiftly.

TRAPPED

Psychological Meaning This dream probably expresses the way you feel about your situation. You may feel trapped in a marriage, by parenthood, or within a dead-end job. Some areas of your life may need reform. On another level, you may be held captive by your own conservatism or stubbornness. If you change the way you do things, you may gain a greater sense of freedom.

Mystical Meaning The Gypsies say that to dream of seeing an animal trapped in a net indicates that you have to proceed with great caution or your plans will fail.

TRAVEL (SEE JOURNEY)

Common Dream

TREASURE (SEE ALSO MONEY)

I am digging in the garden of my childhood home and have uncovered a box of treasures. My life has been pretty bad lately. Does my dream indicate a change for the better?—P.T., Swindon, England

Psychological Meaning Digging up buried treasure or finding money symbolizes rediscovering a part of yourself. Is there something that you have neglected or repressed? It could be that you had an ambition in life and only now have found the opportunity to try again. There may be a wealth of past experience that you can draw on—something from your childhood, perhaps?

The dream may also have a literal interpretation. If you're worried about finances, now may be the time to start a new venture. The dream may symbolize other things too, such as power, independence, or security. Examine your life; there may be unlooked-for opportunities just below the surface.

ASK YOURSELF

1. *What am I searching for?* The treasure of your dream may symbolize the things you've always wanted from life. They may not necessarily be material, but the dream may suggest that now is the time you are searching your heart to discover what you really want from life.

2. *Is the treasure part of me?* The treasure may symbolize you as a complete and whole person. Maybe something that has hitherto been neglected or repressed is surfacing again. An artistic talent, positive attitude, self-respect, or opportunity, perhaps?

Mystical Meaning Old dream superstitions disagree with the modern interpretations for this dream. To dream of digging for treasure indicates that someone you have loved and trusted is not worthy of your love. However, if you dream of finding gold, in any shape or form, then all will be well.

TREE

Psychological Meaning Trees are symbols of the soul and the life principle. The type and condition of the tree tell of your spiritual condition at the moment. For example, a withered tree may show that you lack inspiration and the desire to live life to the fullest. It may also show your concerns about getting older. Damage to any part of a tree represents damage to aspects of yourself. The tree's branches represent your higher functions; the trunk, your social role; and the roots, the foundations of your personality and unconscious.

Mystical Meaning A tree can also be a symbol of time. The root represent the past; the trunk, the present; and the branches, the future. Perhaps your dream contains a prophecy or says something about your hopes and fears for the future? It is said to be lucky if you dream of climbing a tree.

TRIAL

Psychological Meaning This dream may be your conscience at work. The judge may represent your innermost self. If you are the accused, you may be feeling guilty about something or may be punishing yourself in some way. Who is your accuser? This person may represent an aspect of yourself. Perhaps you are being too hard on yourself?

Mystical Meaning Most dream oracles say that this dream foretells legal disputes.

TRUMPET

Psychological Meaning A loud trumpet may be your unconscious attempting to draw your attention to an issue that you have ignored or are unaware of. The dream may indicate that you should draw attention to yourself or the ideas you have. It may be a pun for "blowing your own horn" or suggesting that you should jazz up your life.

Mystical Meaning To dream of playing a trumpet or hearing one being played is an omen of disappointment, say the oracles.

TWIN

Psychological Meaning Twins represent polarities within the psyche. Examples are introversion and extroversion, ego and shadow, and masculine and feminine. Perhaps the dream is simply saying that you are of two minds about an issue or that you have to duplicate everything you do.

Mystical Meaning Many ancient cultures considered twins to be divine. A very widespread and ancient belief, found among many peoples, says that twins always have different fathers. One of these fathers is supernatural, a god or spirit of some kind. Your dream may be showing you the spiritual side of yourself.

TWO (SEE NUMBERS)

TYRANT (SEE ALSO FATHER)

Psychological Meaning This may be a negative aspect of the father archetype. You may fear being yourself. The dream may also be saying that you are being forced to do something against your will. The tyrant may therefore represent the person or situation that is restricting your personal freedom.

Mystical Meaning Dream oracles interpret this as a contrary dream. You will meet someone nice.

FAMOUS DREAMER

Kirk Douglas
Actor

In 1991, film star Kirk Douglas suffered serious injuries in a helicopter accident after it collided with a light aircraft at Santa Paula, California. He received serious back and head injuries and was fighting for his life. What happened next was more than a dream of flying; Douglas may have really left his body. "It was like I was suspended in space," he said. "There was no concept of time. I saw the most vivid colored lights. It was like a most glorious tunnel of life.

"There was never a moment I was as close to God as I was then. I will never take life, things, or people for granted again. I'm more appreciative of being able to open my eyes in the morning and see those I love close by."(See also Flying.)

UFO

Psychological Meaning Carl Jung believed that UFOs are a symbol, akin to the reappearance of Christ, representing hope in an age of technology. They take on an almost religious dimension as circular mandala symbols representing the higher self. Jung wrote that the worldwide stories of the UFOs are "a symptom of a universally present psychic disposition." The unconscious can manifest itself everywhere and crosses social divides. In dreams, UFOs may represent your desire to find the true spiritual purpose of life and the wholeness of self.

Mystical Meaning Why did the ancient dream seers give no interpretation for this dream? Perhaps the knowledge is hidden away somewhere in the ancient X Files?

UGLY

Psychological Meaning An ugly person appearing in a dream may represent an aspect of yourself that frightens or repulses you. You may have repressed or rejected feelings that may be beneficial to your psychological wholeness.

Mystical Meaning The fairy tale *The Beauty and the Beast* illustrates that you should not judge things by their appearance. Similarly, what may at first appear to be a frightening aspect of your self may in reality mask the true self and its inner beauty.

UMBRELLA

Psychological Meaning An umbrella may be a symbol of protection. As rain can represent the release of emotional tension, an umbrella may illustrate that you are prepared for this outpouring of emotion. It could also represent financial protection and security. In the United Kingdom there's a saying about bank loans: "The manager will only lend you an umbrella when the sun shines." Perhaps your dream contains similar puns.

Mystical Meaning To dream that you have lost an umbrella is fortunate. It predicts a valuable present from a relation. However, if you dream of finding one, you will experience a severe loss in business.

UNDERCLOTHES

Psychological Meaning Underclothes may represent your hidden attitudes and prejudices. If you dream of feeling ashamed at being seen in your underwear, it may indicate an unwillingness to reveal your feelings or to have your attitudes made public. What color is your dream underwear? Red may reveal hidden passions; black, dark thoughts; and yellow, a secret cowardice. If your underwear is dirty or torn it may show that you are not at ease with yourself or feel uncomfortable about your sexuality.

Mystical Meaning Some wise dream oracles say that to dream of being in your underclothes is an omen of stolen pleasures that will rebound with grief.

UNDERGROUND

Psychological Meaning The underground usually symbolizes the unconscious. Things that are uncovered, dug up, or that emerge from the ground represent qualities that are coming from the unconscious. If it is repressed material, these images may be frightening and may appear as zombies, rats, or monsters. If you dream of exploring caves or mines, it may show that you are discovering the innermost recesses of the unconscious.

Mystical Meaning To dream of being in the subway predicts a loss of money.

UNDERWORLD

Psychological Meaning Descent into the underworld may represent death and rebirth. If you dream of an underworld like Hell or Hades, it may symbolize your despair. You may need some help in dealing with your emotional problems.

Mystical Meaning Superstition says that this dream predicts a loss of reputation.

UNDRESSED IN PUBLIC

I dreamed of forgetting to wear my clothes to work. It was highly embarrassing—everybody laughed at me!—T.H., Glasgow, Scotland

Psychological Meaning This is a well-known anxiety dream. Dreams like this are sometimes interpreted as a fear of sexual relationships. Alternatively, they can signify the "naked truth" about yourself. Perhaps, you fear failure or that you will make mistakes and be ridiculed? In your waking life, you need to overcome feelings of vulnerability and need to learn self-confidence. Being partly dressed may symbolize that you are not prepared for what lies ahead. Thoroughly examine your plans and perfect them.

Freud believed that to dream of being naked was an unconscious wish for the free, unclothed periods of early life. Most psychologists consider that dreams of nudity highlight feelings of vulnerability. The dreamer may be conscious of faults and failings.

ASK YOURSELF

1. *How do I feel about my nudity?* Anxiety may symbolize the vulnerability mentioned above, but a feeling of approval may symbolize your pleasure at being free of inhibitions. You may be expressing your openness and honesty.

2. *How do people in my dream react to my nudity?* If they mock you, you may be harboring feelings of guilt and a fear of revealing your feelings. You could have a fear of sexual relationships. Indifference may suggest that something you are concerned about revealing is not really very important. Approval suggests a shedding of inhibitions.

Mystical Meaning Dream oracles say that to dream of undressing means that you will make a grave mistake in your business affairs unless you listen to advice.

UNICORN

Psychological Meaning In mythology, unicorns are either white or multi-colored. They unite the spectrum, showing that the one is the essence of the many. They are the mythical embodiment of the inner realm of the imagination. They may also represent power, gentility, and purity. Your dream may be an expression of inspiration and wonder at the marvels of the inner world.

Mystical Meaning Dream oracles say that this dream means you will have some correspondence in connection with official affairs.

UNIFORM

Psychological Meaning Your dream may be commenting on your conservatism. Are you living your life in an overly regimented manner? Perhaps you are conforming too much. Alternatively, you may feel a need to fit in and be less individualistic.

Mystical Meaning Superstition says that this dream indicates that you will make a journey full of adventure and of special interest to you regarding matrimonial matters.

URINE

Psychological Meaning Urine may represent the feelings you reject. You are trying to cleanse yourself of the things that you consider unworthy. However, dreams of urinating are usually caused by a full bladder and have little symbolic significance

Mystical Meaning Urine has for centuries been regarded as a protection against ghosts and evil spirits. Also it was believed that if a girl urinates in a man's shoes he will fall madly in love with her. Clearly, these concepts are of great significance when interpreting your dream.

FAMOUS DREAMER

Charles Dickens
Novelist

One night, Charles Dickens dreamed he saw a woman in a red shawl with her back toward him. "I am Miss Napier," she said as she spun around. The dream seemed to be nonsense but the next night, after giving a literary reading, some friends came backstage and introduced him to a woman they wanted him to meet. Her name was Miss Napier.

VACATION

Psychological Meaning Your dream may be showing you that you need to take a break. Often these dreams feature anxieties. You may dream of missing your plane, a disaster while on vacation, or a problem such as carrying too much luggage. Listen to what your dream is telling you and take it easy for a while.

Mystical Meaning If a jilted young woman dreams of being on vacation, she will win back the affections of her sweetheart, say the oracles.

VALLEY

Psychological Meaning The mountains on either side of you set limitations on the direction you can go. Your dream may show that the choices you have are limited. You are forced to move forward. A journey through a valley sometimes symbolizes the transition from one set of circumstances to another (i.e., through the valley of death to a new life). You may be going through difficult but ultimately beneficial spiritual changes.

Mystical Meaning As a spiritual dream symbol, a valley may represent judgment and the importance of modesty: "Every valley shall be exalted, and every mountain and hill shall be made low; and the crooked shall be made straight, and the rough places plain" (Isaiah 40:4). Similarly, in the *I Ching* it says: "High mountains are worn down by the waters, and the valleys are filled up. It is the law of fate to undermine what is full and prosper the modest. And men also hate fullness and love the modest."

VAMPIRE (*see* Bat)

VAULT

Psychological Meaning A vault may represent the unconscious. What you find inside may be of significance. For example, if the vault is a crypt, the corpses may represent parts of yourself that are no longer an active part of your personality. They may represent problems and issues that have been laid to rest. If you find yourself in a bank vault, it may symbolize opportunities for happiness and spiritual unfolding. The treasures are your rich psychological potential, which you have found by exploring the unconscious.

Mystical Meaning A very old dream book says: "If a man dreams he is wandering in black vaults or cellars it is a sign he will marry an artful widow and shall be her drudge, never fathoming her wickedness and craft." You can't get more specific than that!

VEGETABLES (SEE ALSO FOOD)

Psychological Meaning These may be a symbol for psychological growth. Your dream may also be telling you that you need to improve your diet.

Mystical Meaning Freud says that dreaming of eating is symbolic of the sexual act and that most vegetables are phallic symbols. He is not alone. Some superstitions claim that vegetables shaped like a man are aphrodisiacs.

VEHICLE (SEE CAR)

VEIL

Psychological Meaning A veil conceals. Are you trying to hide something? Perhaps you are afraid to express part of your personality? Try to decide what is being hidden. A Freudian psychologist interprets a veil as a symbol for a woman's hymen. The dream may show a fear of sexual intercourse.

Mystical Meaning Nuns sometimes wear veils. As a spiritual symbol, this dream could represent a rejection of worldly things. Dream superstition says that to dream of a black veil is a sign of parting from one you love. A white veil indicates a wedding.

VENTRILOQUISM

Psychological Meaning Perhaps you are putting words into people's mouths in waking life. Or maybe you only hear what you want to hear. Projecting your voice may symbolize your desire to influence what people say. Furthermore, ventriloquism can represent a lack of correspondence between your true self and the image you present to the world.

Mystical Meaning Treason is afoot! Be careful in all your dealings, warn the soothsayers.

VICTIM

Psychological Meaning Does your dream amplify feelings that you already have in waking life? You may feel victimized by the people around you. Alternatively, you may have been punishing others, and your dream has turned the tables on

you. Your dream may be an expression of your feeling of guilt.

Mystical Meaning According to most dream oracles, this is a dream that should be reversed. You will be victimized if you dream of hurting others, and vice versa if you are the one who is the victim.

VILLAIN

Psychological Meaning A villain may represent part of your personality that needs reform. He may represent the rebellious side of yourself and your secret desire to break the rules of society. Perhaps he represents feelings you have for revenge or your wish to undermine someone's plans. He may represent a vice such as smoking, excessive drinking, or overindulgence.

Mystical Meaning To dream of a ruffian or villain denotes a letter or gift from your sweetheart.

VINE

Psychological Meaning A symbol of plenty. The vine may represent your sensuality and indulgence. Similarly, it may represent the harvest and a time of material prosperity. If your dream deals with health issues, the form of the vine may be suggestive of the nervous system.

Mystical Meaning Any dream connected with vines and grapes is said to be good so long as the vine flourishes. A green vine with green grapes will make your dearest wishes come true.

VIOLENCE

Psychological Meaning If you dream of behaving violently, you may harbor hidden feelings of resentment toward someone who is preventing you from progressing. Alternatively, you may be denying something within yourself. This dream can show the need to assert yourself when dealing with people and to be more accepting of your own failings. You have too much repressed emotion. If the violence in the dream is directed toward you, you may be punishing yourself and you may feel guilty about an issue. Does the outside world make you feel vulnerable at this time? You may feel that everything is against you now, but you should remain hopeful, knowing that a change for the better will inevitably come in time.

Mystical Meaning Another dream that should be reversed, says superstition. If you are violently attacked, it means better times for you.

WATER

VIRGIN

Psychological Meaning Your dream may be nostalgic. Are you looking back to the innocent days before you experienced the pain and complexities of human relationships? A virgin may represent something in your life that is pure and unsullied.

Mystical Meaning The Virgin Mary may represent the anima in a man's dreams. She is a spiritual guide that leads the man to personal wholeness.

VOICES (*SEE* SOUNDS)

VOLCANO

Psychological Meaning An erupting volcano may be the awakening of negative feelings that have been pushed underground into the unconscious. You may have been holding back your true feelings for so long, you feel that you want to explode.

Mystical Meaning To dream of a volcano is the prelude to a period of peace and happiness. Superstition also says that the happiness is increased if you are nearly enveloped in flames.

VOMIT

Psychological Meaning This dream may be an expression of your desire to be rid of feelings that cause you upset. It may be that you "can't stomach" a situation or feel sick and tired about the way someone has been behaving. In some cases, this dream may represent feelings of self-disgust. For example, you may be so repulsed by something, it makes you want to vomit. You need to quickly get to the heart of these extreme feelings.

Mystical Meaning To dream of vomiting, say the ancient lost texts, shows that the poor shall profit from the rich man's loss.

VULTURE

Psychological Meaning Vultures are horrible creatures who live off the misfortune of other animals. Some people are like this. Are you? Or perhaps someone is taking advantage of you?

Mystical Meaning The Gypsies believe that to dream of vultures indicates that you are surrounded by corrupt people.

WAGON

Psychological Meaning A wagon may represent slow but sure progress. If you dream of being on a wagon train of pioneers, it may show your desire to explore the unconscious or your hope for a more exciting lifestyle. The dream may be a pun for temperance, "on the wagon."

Mystical Meaning If you ride someone else's wagon you will be poor, but if you dream it is your own you will be rich, says ancient folklore.

WAITER

Psychological Meaning A waiter may represent a helpful influence or a person in your life who is being of service to you. It may also be a pun for "waiting"; your dream may be telling you not to act yet. A waiter does the bidding of others. Perhaps you feel that people treat you like their personal servant?

Mystical Meaning The most reliable superstitions say that if you dream of being served by a waiter at a hotel there will be good luck, but the dream spells trouble if you're served in your own home.

WALL

Psychological Meaning A wall may represent an obstacle that prevents you from attaining what you want. This may be an obstruction from real life or something within yourself. Perhaps you are being like a brick wall by refusing to show your feelings, or perhaps someone you know is. Alternatively, it may represent a problem you cannot solve yet. You've come up against "a brick wall."

Mystical Meaning Walls spell difficulty and obstacles relating to money. But all bodes well if you dream of finding a gateway through.

WAR

Psychological Meaning A war is being waged within yourself. Is it necessary, or would a reconciliation be better than victory? You may feel a conflict between what you want to do and what you think you ought to do. Perhaps you are being too hard on yourself? Carl Jung considered dreams of war to be between the dreamer's conscious and unconscious minds. They may represent the struggle between the deep instinctive forces and the rules of con-

WEDDING

scious conduct. However, sometimes this inner turmoil is necessary in order to allow the wisdom of the conscience to activate. Accept that part of yourself that is trying to find expression. Through acceptance comes peace.

Mystical Meaning A warning of difficulties and danger.

WASHING

Psychological Meaning Washing may represent inner cleansing. You are getting rid of old attitudes, habits, and emotional reactions. If you wash clothes, it may symbolize an improvement in the way you present yourself to the world. Washing plates may indicate purity of psychological nourishment. Washing underwear may indicate the resolution of feelings of sexual uncertainty. Washing another person may show your desire to make that person better.

Mystical Meaning It is auspicious to dream of washing clothes or white linen, but stained clothes predict misfortune. It is also fortunate to dream of washing yourself. However, beware if you dream of taking a bath fully clothed, for this means disappointment.

WATCH (SEE CLOCK)

WATER

Psychological Meaning Water usually represents feelings and emotions. Like the waters of the womb, it can also represent security, life, and birth. The nature of the water can reveal your emotional state. For example, if you dream of crashing waves or rocky seas, it may show that your emotions are out of control. A fast-flowing river may show emotions that are rushing ahead too fast, but if the waters are peaceful, then so are you.

Mystical Meaning Deep pools and lakes of water can represent the unconscious. Like the lake in the King Arthur legends, magical gifts may appear to change your life.

WATERFALL

Psychological Meaning A waterfall may represent exuberance and an uninhibited outpouring of creative energy. You are celebrating life. However, if you dream of being pulled over a waterfall in a boat, your feelings and excitement are out of control and may be getting the better of you. You've gone over the top.

Mystical Meaning There are two traditional interpretations of this dream. You will either be invited to a place of amusement or you will be gossiped about. I suggest you book tickets to Las Vegas.

WEAPONS

Psychological Meaning Weapons can represent anger, resentment, or conflict in your life. If you dream of using weapons against a person you know, it may indicate that you harbor hidden anger or resentment. Perhaps you have not expressed this in waking life. If you do not know the person, then he or she may represent aspects of yourself that you don't like. You may have inner conflicts that need to be resolved. Swords, arrows, knives, guns, and daggers are also phallic symbols showing aggressive male sexuality.

Mystical Meaning The books of dream fortune say that this dream means that you have enemies who pose as friends. Be careful, or they will betray your confidence.

WEATHER

Psychological Meaning The weather in a dream may represent your state of mind. Stormy skies may show arguments and anger; sunshine may show happiness; rain may show release from tension; and snow may indicate that your emotions are frozen.

Mystical Meaning Dreaming of fine weather predicts happy events, but if the weather is bad so are your fortunes.

WEDDING (SEE ALSO RITUALS)

Psychological Meaning A wedding is a union of opposites. To dream of a wedding is most likely to represent the coming together of the opposite aspects of your personality. For example, the couple may represent the fundamental creative forces of life—male and female, matter and spirit, conscious and unconscious, rationality and imagination. This union of diverse forces in your psyche suggests that you will achieve inner wholeness.

Mystical Meaning There are mixed interpretations for this dream in the old dream books.
Generally it is seen as a good omen and a possible
prophecy for marriage. And here's a horrible
superstition that will keep you awake: In many
parts of Europe it is believed that whoever falls
asleep first on their wedding night will be the first
to die.

WEEDS

Psychological Meaning Weeds represent the
habits and attitudes that disrupt your inner harmony. Weed out bad habits and you'll be a much
better person and feel greater happiness. Your
dream is showing you ways to improve yourself.
On another level, weeds may represent people in
your life who are not contributing to the good of
the whole. They may be selfish, stingy, or have
a corrupting influence. Root out these bad
"friends."
Mystical Meaning To dream of gathering weeds
is a good sign. Some sources say that it brings
tremendous good luck, but not if the weeds are
nettles or thistles, for these predict misfortune.

WEEPING

Psychological Meaning Dreams confront you
with emotional issues that you would usually
rather avoid in waking life. Clearly, something is
upsetting you deeply. The other symbols in the
dream may help you identify the cause of your
unhappiness.
Mystical Meaning The oracles say that this is a
contrary dream denoting festivity, joy, and
laughter.

WELL

Psychological Meaning The earth symbolizes
the unconscious, and the feelings are symbolized
by water. A well is therefore a symbol to show
that you can access the deepest recesses of the
unconscious. From this source you may draw up
into your consciousness emotions, knowledge,
happiness, and wisdom. It is the foundation of
life, the divine nature.
Mystical Meaning Psychologist Carl Jung was
inspired by the imagery of the 5,000-year-old
Chinese oracle, the *I Ching*. In the hexagram of *The
Well*, it augurs supreme good fortune for this
symbol: "It has a spring and never runs dry.
Therefore it is a great blessing to the whole land.

The same is true of the really great man, whose
inner wealth is inexhaustible; the more that people draw from him, the greater his wealth
becomes."

WHEEL (*SEE ALSO* CIRCLE)

Psychological Meaning The turning of a wheel
may represent the progress of your life. If it is
broken or there are obstructions, it may symbolize that you feel that things are not working out
as you would like. If you dream of being at the
wheel of a car, it may show that you have taken
control of your progress.
Mystical Meaning Your dream may be an
insight into the nature of reality. The Buddha
said: "As long as one feels that he is the doer, he
cannot escape from the wheel of births."

WHIP

Psychological Meaning Your dream may have
sexual undertones in which the whip is a nega-
tively charged symbol of sexual submission. Also,
it can represent your awareness of power, domi-
nation, and obedience in relationships. The whip
may be a symbol of authority or simply may be
telling you that you need to whip up your enthusiasm for something.
Mystical Meaning The dream oracles say that if
you dream of whipping someone you will soon
experience trouble. However, if you dream of
being whipped, you will "render a good service to
someone."

WHITE (*SEE* COLORS)

WIFE

Psychological Meaning This dream may be
about your real wife or may represent feminine
qualities. A Freudian analysis may propose that
the way you relate to her may contain elements
reminiscent of your relation with your mother.
Mystical Meaning To dream of an unmarried
man walking with a woman who claims to be his
wife indicates unexpected news.

WIG (*SEE ALSO* BALDNESS)

Psychological Meaning For a man, this dream
may be revealing your feelings of insecurity and
a desire to hide your feelings of insufficiency. Are
you trying to disguise an aspect of your personality you feel ashamed about? For a woman,

dreaming of wigs may symbolize her desire to change the way she presents herself to the world. Are you pretending to be someone you're not?

Mystical Meaning Surprisingly, there are many dream interpretations about wigs. A blond wig means you will have many admirers, a dark wig brings loyalty, a white wig predicts riches, and a brunette wig predicts that the person you marry will be poor.

WILDERNESS

Psychological Meaning This dream may represent a time of self-assessment and a spiritual beginning. Great men like Jesus, the Tibetan lamas, or Hindu sages spent time in the solitary wastelands in order to come closer to their spiritual nature. Away from the distractions of the world, they can recognize the divine within. Your dream expresses the same sentiments.

Mystical Meaning If you dream of walking through a wilderness, this signifies difficulties concerning a cherished plan. If the sun is shining, the final outcome will be successful.

WIND

Psychological Meaning Dreams about wind can symbolize unsettled emotions. You may feel that there's a need for a change in your life.

Mystical Meaning Dreaming of wind predicts troubles ahead. However, it may be comforting to know that this dream predicts that someone else will be made happy by your loss.

WINDOW

Psychological Meaning A window may represent the way you view your circumstances. If you look out a window it may represent your view of the world, but if you are on the outside looking in, then the window represents your view of yourself. Freud considered windows to be feminine sexual symbols.

Mystical Meaning A joyful scene viewed from a window bodes happiness ahead. But if you witness a dreadful event, trouble will affect you. A broken window means disappointment.

WINE

Psychological Meaning Red wine may symbolize blood and therefore the life force. To dream of drinking wine may augur well for health and show that you are starting a more satisfying phase of life. Red wine could also symbolize the passions. Old bottled wine may symbolize maturity.

Mystical Meaning In France, and now in California, it is believed to be bad luck to pass wine around a table in a counterclockwise direction. To dream of drinking wine is a sign of a comfortable home. If wine is spilled, someone will be injured. If you dream of making wine, you will have success. And if you dream about being drunk on wine, you will soon have a big success.

WINNING

Psychological Meaning If you dream of winning a prize or contest, this illustrates your feeling of confidence. It may be a reassurance from your unconscious that you have what it takes to gain success.

Mystical Meaning The dream oracles suggest that this dream means the opposite.

WISE PERSON

Psychological Meaning Listen to the advice given to you by a wise person in your dreams. It is likely to be exactly the guidance you need. It is the unconscious guiding you.

Mystical Meaning Some oracles claim that this dream means you will soon receive a message.

WITCH

Psychological Meaning Since the advent of Christianity, witches have been given bad press. Their original role was as priestesses of the Earth Mother and as bringers of divine wisdom and healing. A witch may represent these qualities in you. In most dreams, witches represent the destructive aspect of the unconscious. This may be the result of repression of a part of yourself that is trying to gain recognition. She may encapsulate negative qualities such as moodiness, dislike of women, deceit, or jealousy. You will need to consider your personal associations with this image and notice the feelings that the dream triggers to fully understand its exact meaning.

Mystical Meaning The fear of the devil and his witches lies at the heart of many omens and superstitions. Since the Middle Ages, it has been believed that dreams of witches are an ill omen.

WOLF

Psychological Meaning Wolves are usually seen as something threatening that attacks during the night, when you are most vulnerable. In dreams they can represent everything you are afraid of in yourself, including self-destructive tendencies, aggression, or uncontrolled sexual desire. They could also represent a worldly trouble, such as a financial problem, i.e., "keeping the wolf from the door." Celtic revivalists give the wolf better press. It is your instinctive nature, your familiar that guides you through the forests of the night

Mystical Meaning The wolf in the story of *Little Red Riding Hood* represents the frightening aspect of the male and the fear of sexual contact. Told at bedtime, the fairy tale warned girls of the dangers of sex before marriage.

WOMAN

Psychological Meaning If you are a woman, a female figure may be a symbol for yourself. She may also symbolize your mother. How you react to her and what she says may reveal a great deal about the way you deal with people in waking life. If you are a man, a woman may represent the other half of your personality—the side of you that is intuitive, sensitive, and nurturing. She may appear in a helpful or fearful guise depending on the degree of acceptance you have for your anima.

Mystical Meaning It is deemed fortunate by superstition to see many women in your dream, for this brings wealth and fame. There are also specifics. An ugly woman means worry, but a beautiful one means happiness; a woman dreaming of being pregnant will have happy news; and if a woman dreams of being a man, she will one day give birth to a son.

WOMB

Psychological Meaning Psychiatrists have suggested that a dream of returning to the womb may represent a deep need for security. It is the ultimate protective love of the mother. Womb symbols may occur in dreams as caves, rooms, or confined yet protected spaces. They are a retreat from life's problems.

Mystical Meaning In the mystical teachings of Kundalini yoga, the "green womb" is a name for Ishvara (Shiva) emerging from his latent condition. This dream may therefore be deeply spiritual, showing awakening higher consciousness.

WORKSHOP

Psychological Meaning You may be undertaking work on yourself. Your dream may give you methods to start this self-improvement. Perhaps the thing being fixed or made gives you a clue about what aspect of yourself needs attention. Your dream may also give solutions to practical problems and show latent skills that you may want to develop.

Mystical Meaning To dream of workers or a workshop is an excellent sign, for according to superstition, this means happiness in both love and business.

WORMS

Psychological Meaning These may be phallic symbols. Associated with dirt and decay, worms may indicate that you have a negative attitude toward sex. Alternatively, they may symbolize helplessness. If you feel downtrodden and oppressed, perhaps its time for the "worm to turn." If you are a gardener, worms may represent something positive. Worms are great in the compost heap and in the garden. They aerate the soil, eat predatory bugs, and just generally do wonderful things. As a dream symbol they may show that you are transforming a bad situation into a good one. For an angler worms may represent bait. Are you "baiting an argument" or perhaps preparing to "fish for compliments"?

Mystical Meaning Dream books claim that worms indicate a danger of infectious diseases. If you dream of destroying worms, you will receive money.

WRAPPING

Psychological Meaning Are you trying to hide something about yourself? Dreaming of wrapping something may be a symbol to show that you conceal your feelings. Unwrapping something may show the opposite—you are beginning to open up. The dream may also be a play on words, to say that you have concluded something—you've "wrapped it up."

Mystical Meaning To dream of receiving a parcel is considered fortunate, but to unwrap it spells bad luck.

WRITING

Psychological Meaning Your dream may be revealing your thoughts and true feelings. The person the writing is addressed to may represent the nature of the issues that you are trying to express. If you dream of someone else writing, it may show an aspect of yourself that is seeking to express itself. The contents of the document may include useful messages from your unconscious.

Mystical Meaning Mystical traditions emphasize the importance of wordless inner silence. "To reconnect consciousness with the unconscious, to make consciousness symbolical is to reconnect words with silence; to let the silence in. If consciousness is all words and no silence, the unconscious remains unconscious."—*N. O. Brown*

 X RAY

Psychological Meaning An X ray may show that you've seen through a problem or issue that has been troubling you. It may refer to the fact that you are perceptive about what motivates people. Perhaps your dream may have identified a health problem of which you are unaware.

Mystical Meaning Sadly, no mystical traditions are associated with X rays, but it is interesting to note that Marie Curie, the discoverer of radium, is said to have been very interested in Spiritualism, mysticism, and dreams.

 YELLOW (SEE COLORS)

YOUNG MAN/YOUNG WOMAN (SEE ANIMA/ANIMUS AND HERO/HEROINE)

YOUTH

Psychological Meaning A youth may represent psychological qualities within yourself that have not as yet grown to maturity. This dream may also be about vitality and sexual desire. Or the dream may simply highlight your concerns about getting older.

Mystical Meaning There will be a reconciliation of family arguments if you dream of seeing a young person. If a mother dreams that her child is young again, she will experience a period of renewed hope and vigor.

 ZERO

Psychological Meaning Zero is represented by a circle, which is a symbol for the wholeness of the self. Alternatively, you may feel it expresses your lot in life. You feel you have nothing.

Mystical Meaning Dream lore says that to dream of naught indicates wasted energy. A change of direction is necessary.

ZIPPER

Psychological Meaning This dream may be a sexual innuendo. A broken zipper may symbolize your frustration at not being able to resolve a problem.

Mystical Meaning Yes, there is a mystical meaning to zippers. If you dream of a broken zipper, it means others will dominate you.

ZODIAC

Psychological Meaning If you dream of your own zodiacal sign, it may represent you. However, other signs represent traits and characteristics associated with the given sign. For example, you may be acting like a determined Aries, a stubborn Taurus, or an eccentric Aquarius. If the whole zodiac wheel is represented, it is a mandala that represents the wholeness of the self, the cosmic you.

Mystical Meaning Some dream oraculums claim that you will emigrate if you dream about the signs of the zodiac.

ZOO

Psychological Meaning A zoo is the place where animals are caged and bred. Has your heart become like a zoo? Do you breed animal-like qualities such as anger, jealousy, and hatred? Alternatively, your dream may represent your good psychological qualities that need to be released. You must decide.

Mystical Meaning Zoos predict lots of travel and an enjoyable sojourn in a foreign country. If you dream that a child is with you, there will be great good fortune.

Index

SCARECROW *See:* MASK.
SCHOOL *See also:* EXAMINATIONS.
SCHOOLTEACHER *See:* SCHOOL.
SCISSORS *See also:* CUTTING.
SCOLDING *See:* SCHOOL.
SCULPTOR *See:* STATUE.
SEA *See also:* DIVING; DOLPHIN; FISH;
    ISLAND; RESCUE; SHIP; WATER.
SEVEN *See:* NUMBERS.
SEWING *See:* NEEDLE; REPAIRING.
SHADOW SELF *See:* FRIEND.
SHAPES *See:* MANDALA; NUMBERS.
SHARK *See:* BITE.
SHEEP *See also:* LAMB.
SHEPHERD *See:* SHEEP.
SHIP *See also:* SAILOR.
SHIPWRECK *See:* SHIP.
SHOT *See:* GUN.
SHRIVELED *See:* ABDOMEN; BREASTS.
SIGNPOST *See also:* CITY; CROSSROADS.
SILVER *See also:* MELTING.
SINKING *See also:* DROWNING.
SISTER *See also:* ANIMA/ANIMUS;
    SHADOW.
SIX *See:* NUMBERS.
SKELETON *See:* BONES.
SKULL *See also:* BONES.
SKY *See also:* FLYING.
SLEEP PARALYSIS *See:* DUMB.
SNAKES *See also:* ANIMALS; EAGLE.
SNOW *See also:* ICE; WEATHER.
SOIL *See:* DIRT.
SOLID *See:* ELEMENTS.
SONG *See:* MUSIC.
SOUNDS *See also:* FLYING; MUSIC.
SOUTH *See:* COMPASS.
SOUTHEAST *See:* COMPASS.
SOUTHWEST *See:* COMPASS.
SPADES *See:* CARDS.
SPIRITS *See:* GHOST.
SPRING *See:* SEASONS.
SQUARE *See:* MANDALA; NUMBERS.
STAGE *See:* AUDITION; BACK;
    THEATER.
STARVATION *See:* EATING.
STATION *See also:* JOURNEY; TRAIN.
STORK *See:* BIRD.
STORM *See also:* SHIP; THUNDER;
    WEATHER.
STORY *See also:* BUILDINGS; HOUSE.
STRANGER *See also:* ANGER; SHADOW.
STRAW HAT *See:* HAT.
STREET *See:* ROADS.
SUBMARINE *See:* SHIP.
SUBWAY *See:* UNDERGROUND.
SUFFOCATION *See also:* DROWNING.
SUGAR *See:* FOOD.
SUIT *See also:* CLOTHES.

SUMMER *See:* SEASONS.
SUN *See also:* DAWN; FATHER; LIGHT;
    MANDALA; MOON;
    RAINBOW; WILDERNESS.
SUNRISE *See:* SUN.
SUNSET *See:* SUN.
SUNSHINE *See:* WEATHER.
SWEEPING *See:* BRUSH.
SWOLLEN *See:* ABDOMEN; FACE.
SWORD *See also:* WEAPONS.

T

TEACHER *See:* SCHOOL.
TEACHING *See:* SCHOOL.
TELEVISION *See also:* FILM.
TEMPLE *See:* CHURCH.
TEN *See:* NUMBERS.
TEST *See:* EXAMINATION; FAILURE.
THEATER *See also:* CURTAIN.
THISTLES *See:* WEEDS.
THREE *See:* NUMBERS.
TICKET *See also:* KEY.
TIGER *See also:* ANIMALS.
TOMB *See also:* DESCENT.
TOP FLOOR *See:* STORY.
TOP HAT *See:* HAT.
TORTOISE SHELL *See:* SHELL.
TOWN *See:* CITY; JOURNEY.
TRAFFIC *See also:* CARS.
TRAIN *See also:* FAILURE;
    FRUSTRATION; JOURNEY.
TRAPDOOR *See:* DOOR.
TRAVEL *See:* JOURNEY; TRAIN.
TREASURE *See also:* ANIMALS; DIVING;
    DRAGON; MONEY.
TREE *See also:* AXE; ROAD.
TRIANGLE *See:* MANDALA; NUMBERS.
TRUNK *See:* TREE.
TURKEY *See:* BIRD.
TWO *See:* NUMBERS.

U

UGLINESS *See:* MAN.
UGLY *See also:* WOMAN.
UNDERCLOTHES *See also:* WASHING.
UNDERWEAR *See:* NUDITY.
UNPREPARED *See:* EXAMINATION.
UPSTAIRS *See:* BUILDINGS.

V

VAMPIRE *See:* BAT.
VAPOR *See:* ELEMENTS.
VAULT *See also:* BANK.
VEGETABLES *See also:* FOOD; MARKET.
VEHICLE *See:* CAR.

VESSEL *See:* EMPTY.
VOICES *See:* SOUNDS.

W

WAGON TRAIN *See:* WAGON.
WALKING *See:* WILDERNESS.
WALL *See also:* CITY; CLIMBING.
WARSHIP *See:* SHIP.
WASHING *See also:* BATH; FOOT.
WASP *See:* INSECTS.
WATCH *See:* CLOCK.
WATER *See also:* ANCHOR; BAPTISM;
    BATH; BOAT; DIVING; DROWNING;
    ELEMENTS; FLOATING; FLOOD;
    GARDEN; LAKE; MOON; SWIMMING;
    WELL.
WAVES *See:* WATER.
WEAPON *See also:* FATHER.
WEDDING *See also:* RITUALS.
WEEDS *See:* FIELDS.
WELL *See:* DESCENT.
WEST *See:* COMPASS; JOURNEY.
WHEEL *See also:* CIRCLE.
WHISTLE *See:* STORY.
WHITE *See:* CLOUDS; COLORS; VEIL.
WIG *See also:* BALDNESS.
WIND *See:* AIR.
WINDOWS *See:* HOUSE.
WINE *See also:* BOTTLE; CELLAR; CUP.
WINGS *See:* ANGEL.
WINTER *See:* SEASONS.
WISE OLD MAN *See:* FATHER.
WOMAN WEARING MAN'S HAT *See:* HAT.
WOMB *See also:* BATH; CAVE.
WORKER *See:* WORKSHOP.

Y

YELLOW *See:* COLORS; DAFFODIL;
    UNDERCLOTHES.
YOUNG MAN/YOUNG WOMAN *See:*
    ANIMA/ANIMUS; HERO/HEROINE.
YOUTH *See also:* SEASONS.

Z

ZERO *See also:* NUMBERS.
ZODIAC *See also:* SKY.
ZOMBIES *See:* UNDERGROUND.